Norfolk Record Society
Volume LXXI for 2007

POVERTY AND WEALTH

SHEEP, TAXATION AND CHARITY IN LATE MEDIEVAL NORFOLK

*The Sheep Accounts of Norwich Cathedral Priory
1484 to 1534*

MARK BAILEY

*Income Tax Assessments of Norwich,
1472 and 1489*

MAUREEN JURKOWSKI

The Cartulary of St Mary's Hospital, Great Yarmouth

CAROLE RAWCLIFFE

Norfolk Record Society
Volume LXXI for 2007

© The Norfolk Record Society, 2007

First published in 2007
by the Norfolk Record Society

ISBN 978-0-9556357-0-0

Produced by John Saunders Design & Production
Printed by Biddles Ltd. King's Lynn

Contents

MAPS

TABLES

General Introduction

This volume illustrates differing aspects of life in Norfolk towards the end of the medieval period. The coverage is both rural and urban. On the one hand, the Norwich Cathedral Priory sheep accounts record in detail the vicissitudes of an increasingly important branch of Norfolk agriculture as operated by one of the major flock owners in the county. On the other, the Norwich income tax assessments and the cartulary of St Mary's Hospital at Great Yarmouth provide evidence on wealth and attitudes to poverty within two of the three principal urban centres in Norfolk. Moreover, both these urban sources have a value that transcends property-holding and charity within their two communities. Thus the Norwich returns of 1472 and 1489 provide rare evidence for the workings of two national taxes whose records do not generally survive. In the case of St Mary's cartulary, its importance extends beyond the medieval period, as the version edited here is in large part the translation made by the early 17th century antiquary and urban historian, Henry Manship, and throws light on early modern attitudes to borough history and to borough records.

Editorial practice

To make them more accessible, the Latin portions of the manuscripts edited here have been translated into English. Where this has happened, Christian names have been translated from the Latin, but surnames are given as in the original documents. Place-names have been modernised in the Norwich Cathedral Priory sheep accounts but ward names occurring in the Norwich tax assessments are given as written. This edition of the cartulary of St Mary's Hospital, Great Yarmouth, retains Henry Manship's 1614 spelling for documents 1–9 and the original 15th century English spelling for document 11.

Throughout the text asterisks, *....*, indicate insertions, angle brackets, <....>, show deletions, and oblique strokes, /..../, are used for marginalia. Editorial comments and additions are given in italic between square brackets. Certain deletions in the sheep accounts repeated elsewhere in the text are omitted without comment.

Abbreviations

BL	British Library
CCR	Calendar of Close Rolls
CFR	Calendar of Fine Rolls
CPR	Calendar of Patent Rolls
DNB	Dictionary of National Biography
EHR	English Historical Review
HMC	Historical Manuscripts Commission
NA	Norfolk Archaeology
NRO	Norfolk Record Office
NRS	Norfolk Record Society
TNA	The National Archives

Acknowledgements

The Norwich Cathedral Priory Sheep Accounts (from NRO DCN 62 and 64) and the 1472 Norwich Tax Assessment rolls (NRO NCR case 7 shelf i) are published by kind permission of the Norfolk County Archivist, Dr John Alban, in whose custody they are. The Dean of Norwich, the Very Reverend Graham Smith, gave his consent, on behalf of the Chapter of Norwich Cathedral, to the publication of the Cathedral Priory Sheep Accounts. The Norfolk Record Society would also like to thank The Bodleian Library, University of Oxford, for permission to publish the Cartulary of St Mary's Hospital, Great Yarmouth, (MS. Gough Norfolk 20, ff.27-72^v), and The National Archives for agreeing to the publication of the 1489 Norwich Tax Assessment (TNA PRO E 179/149/187).

The Society is grateful to Phillip Judge for producing all four maps at short notice.

The Sheep Accounts of Norwich Cathedral Priory, 1484 to 1534

EDITED BY MARK BAILEY

Introduction

Norwich Cathedral Priory was comfortably the wealthiest monastic house in medieval Norfolk, a county which in the early fourteenth century was the wealthiest and most densely populated in England. At this time, the Priory could justly claim to be one of the most enterprising landlords in England, as well as one of the richest. Grain production on its demesne manors in east Norfolk was among the most progressive and intensive in the country, and by the 1340s it was pioneering new forms of accountancy in its estate administration. On the eve of the Black Death the Priory exemplified prosperous and enterprising monastic lordship.[1]

The Accounts

The Priory had a well established cycle of annual accounting and internal auditing for most of its economic and financial activities. The accounting year was usually Michaelmas (29 September) to Michaelmas, the key date of the medieval agrarian calendar. Most of its accounts are manorial, in the sense that they document activity on individual manors belonging to the Priory, although some are centralized estate accounts summarizing information about particular activities or relating to particular monastic offices.[2] When these written manorial and estate accounts first evolved during the thirteenth century, their primary purpose was to ensure that local officials and employees were not defrauding the landlord. However, during the early fourteenth century some English landlords began to require more

---

[1] B.M.S. Campbell, 'Agricultural Progress in Medieval England: Some Evidence from Eastern Norfolk', *Economic History Review* 36 (1983), pp. 26-46; B.M.S. Campbell and K. Bartley, *England on the Eve of the Black Death. An Atlas of Lay Lordship, Land and Wealth 1300-49* (Manchester, 2006), table 18.2 and p. 343; E. Stone, 'Profit and Loss Accountancy at Norwich Cathedral Priory', *Transactions of the Royal Historical Society*, 5th series, 12 (1962), pp. 25-48.

[2] A general background to the Priory can be found in H.W. Saunders, *An Introduction to the Obedientary and Manor Rolls of Norwich Cathedral Priory* (Norwich, 1930); and I. Atherton, E. Fernie, C. Harper-Bill and H. Smith, eds, *Norwich Cathedral Priory: Church, City and Diocese, 1096-1996* (London, 1996). For manorial accounts, see M. Bailey, ed., *The English Manor c.1200 to c.1500* (Manchester, 2002), pp. 97-166.

from their methods of accounting, and to develop more sophisticated forms of profit and loss accountancy, which could then inform future management policies or could be used to calculate the profitability of particular manors or activities. Indeed, Norwich Cathedral Priory was one of the earliest to develop such practices in England.[3]

By the late fifteenth century accounting practices and techniques within the Priory were very well established, so that the sheep accounts edited and translated in this volume comprised just one part of a wider system. However, they were a relatively new addition to that system; in the thirteenth and fourteenth centuries the Priory had enumerated its sheep through the accounts of individual manors, and only introduced a centralized system in 1392.[4] All of the Priory's accounts were themselves subject to an annual audit, a process undertaken during the course of each Lent by an audit committee of senior monks. The committee then presented its findings to the community of monks on the Sunday after Pentecost (mid May to mid June). That evening, an audit feast completed the cycle and closed the accounting year.[5]

The sheep accounts dating from the fifty years between 1484 and 1534 can be grouped into three categories. The first, and most basic, account related to the shepherd of each individual flock (Category One). This was principally a detailed stock account, designed to establish the number and type of sheep in each flock under the care of the shepherd, and to ensure that he (there were no female shepherds) was not defrauding the landlord. Detailed accounts in this category are usually restricted to around half a dozen manors each year, such as Eaton, Fring, Hindringham, Lathes (close to the monastery towards the north of the city), Lomnours (near Great Plumstead), Newton (near Norwich) and Sedgeford. The second type of sheep account was a centralized stock account, which summarised the total number of sheep across the whole of the monastic estate on a single day in a given year (Category Two). This provided officials with a simple, at-a-glance, statement of the location of, and the number of sheep within, every flock. The third was a revenue account, summarising all of the cash receipts and expenditure associated with sheep farming across the whole estate (Category Three). Hence the first category was a variation on the manorial account, while the latter two were central accounts providing essential summaries to facilitate the management of the Priory's entire sheep operation and to determine its profitability.

The sheep accounts are deposited in the Norfolk Record Office and they

[3] Stone, 'Profit and Loss Accountancy', pp. 25-48; R. Virgoe, 'The Estates of Norwich Cathedral Priory 1101-1538', in Atherton, et al., *Norwich Cathedral Priory*, p. 351.

[4] B.M.S. Campbell, *English Seigneurial Agriculture 1250-1450*, (Cambridge, 2000), p. 104.

[5] C. Noble, ed., 'Norwich Cathedral Priory Gardeners' Accounts, 1329-1530', in *Farming and Gardening in Late Medieval Norfolk* (NRS lxi, 1997), pp. 17-22.

are contained among the rolls catalogued as DCN 62 and DCN 64. The DCN 62 rolls are voluminous, each containing a large number of different manorial accounts, but unfortunately the individual membranes are not numbered.[6] Each membrane of parchment varies in width and length, and the accounts were written by various scribes. All three categories of account are usually enrolled along with other local accounts of the Priory dating from the same year. The majority of these are collectors' or messors' accounts for individual manors, so that, say, a shepherd's stock account for Hindringham is enrolled within a large bundle of accounts including a separate collector's account for the manor of Hindringham. The vast majority of the sheep accounts are recorded on separate membranes of parchment, although sometimes the Category One accounts for different flocks are written on the same membrane. Very occasionally, a sheep account is written onto the same sheet as a manorial account; for example, the centralised stock account for 1 December 1488 is written on the same piece of parchment as the collector's account for Pockthorpe.[7] An appendix provides a full list of the sheep accounts used in this volume, and, in this regard, is more precise than the catalogues kept at the Norfolk Record Office. However, this edition does not present the accounts in the order in which they are enrolled, or in their correct catalogue sequence. Instead, they are organized in chronological order and grouped according to each of the three categories of account. Hence fifty-one Category One stock accounts of individual shepherds, dating from 1484 to 1531, are presented first; these are followed by twenty Category Two centralized stock accounts dating from 1488 to 1524; and, finally, come five Category Three revenue accounts, dating from 1525 to 1534.

The relationship between the three categories of account is best understood within the wider context of the organization of the Priory's estate. The landed estates of most Benedictine monasteries were internally divided among their main obedientiaries. The largest allocation of demesne manors was usually made to the Cellarer, who carried the major responsibility for feeding and clothing the community of monks and their multitude of servants, and for maintaining the conventual buildings. However, Norwich Cathedral Priory possessed both a Master Cellarer and a Cellarer. The Master Cellarer was the senior officer, second only to the Prior in the monastery's hierarchy, who was responsible for provisioning and maintaining the Prior's household, and for providing all the monks' bread and

[6] D.M. Welch, 'The Sheep Accounts of Norwich Cathedral Priory' (University of East Anglia, MA thesis, 1996), pp. 5-8. The absence of numbered membranes greatly exacerbates the problem of referencing and locating the individual accounts among the voluminous and varied accounts contained within the DCN 62 rolls: none of the individual rotulets are numbered, and some are not bound and therefore are prone to fall out of sequence.
[7] NRO DCN 62/16.

ale. The Cellarer was charged with supplying the rest of the monks' needs. The creation of a post of Master Cellarer to complement the work of the Cellarer is unusual in English monasteries, and there is some vagueness about the exact division of responsibilities between these two officers at Norwich. Nor is it entirely certain exactly which manors were allocated to which obedientary; neither Saunders nor Virgoe, two fine historians of the Priory's estates, provide a definitive statement of such allocations. However, it is clear that the bulk of the Priory's demesne manors were assigned to either the Master Cellarer or the Cellarer, whose offices together received just under one half of the Priory's annual income of £1,000 to £1,500. Hence, at the beginning of the sixteenth century, the Master Cellarer received gross income of approximately £500 per annum, compared with the Cellarer's of about £250.[8] These were substantial sums of money.

The usual practice on large monastic estates was for each of the senior obedientaries to run their allocated manors and lands as separate agrarian and financial operations. For example, in the fifteenth century the Abbot of Bury St Edmunds ran his own sheep flocks on the abbatial manors of Culford and Fornham All Saints, while the Cellarer of Bury ran a completely independent operation on his manors of Elveden, Fornham St Martin, Ingham and Risby; the sheep of each obedientary, and therefore the income from them, were entirely separate.[9] In contrast, there was no rigid internal separation of sheep rearing between the different obedientaries of Norwich Cathedral Priory, where the sheep flocks were basically regarded as a single enterprise cast across a number of manors. The standard heading used for Category Two accounts states unequivocally that they were listing 'the general sheep...of the flocks and folds of the *monastery* of Norwich' (my italics). However, the accounts also identify a small number of sheep within these flocks belonging exclusively to the offices of Prior and (occasionally) Cellarer. For example, in 1509 the monastery had 7,588 sheep across eight manorial flocks, together with sixty-one sheep of the Prior in one of those and 240 belonging to the Cellarer within two flocks.[10] The sheep assigned to the Cellarer were being fattened for the monastic kitchens.

It is not clear from the accounts which obedientary had ultimate responsibility for the monastery's flocks; indeed, the evidence is contradictory. Some references indicate that the office of Prior carried overall responsi-

---

[8] Saunders, *Norwich Cathedral Priory*, map 1 and pp. 76-7; Virgoe, 'Estates', pp. 342, 348, 357; C. Harper-Bill and C. Rawcliffe, 'The Religious Houses', in C. Rawcliffe and R.G. Wilson, eds., *Medieval Norwich* (London, 2004), p. 85.

[9] M. Bailey, *A Marginal Economy? East Anglian Breckland in the Later Middle Ages* (Cambridge, 1989), pp. 291-2.

[10] NRO DCN 62/23.

bility. For example, the preamble to some Category One accounts states that the shepherds are answerable to the Prior, and it was the Prior who drew up the summary (Category Three) revenue accounts covering all sheep farming on the estate.[11] However, it is obvious from the internal evidence of many of the accounts that the Master Cellarer had a significant, day-to-day, interest in the management of the flocks, and it was the Master Cellarer — not the Prior — who received the income from the manure and cullet rights of the flocks, implying that the *land* was assigned to his office. Yet more confusion is created by the double entry of all the income from the sale of the wool from the flocks in both the accounts of the Master Cellarer and the Category Three accounts drawn up by the Prior himself. Furthermore, the latter accounts state explicitly that the sheep belonged to the Master Cellarer, but the standard heading on Category Two accounts states that they belonged to the monastery. This overlapping responsibility is a confusing and ambiguous set of affairs. It may simply reflect duplicate accounting, but it is also indicative of a tangling of, and an old-fashioned vagueness about, the lines of accountability within the Priory. The latter suggestion is strengthened by the findings of successive Episcopal visitations in the early sixteenth century, which identified a somewhat lax regime at the Priory and a disconcerting ignorance about its overall financial situation. The visitations of 1514 and 1520 even noted disapprovingly that sheep were grazing within the cloister. Modern management consultants might have earned hefty fees from Norwich Cathedral Priory.[12]

Stock Accounts of Individual Shepherds (Category One)

These constitute the basic building blocks of the annual system of accounting for sheep, and their format was simple and standardized across the whole estate. They were drawn up only for the Priory's actively managed flocks, and in their layout and content they closely resemble the stock sections of earlier manorial accounts. They begin by identifying the name of the shepherd, the location of the flock, and the period covered by the account. The shepherd was accountable for an exact number of sheep 'remaining' (i.e. carried forward) from the previous account, usually represented by a written or scored 'tally', and then had to provide accurate details of the movement of sheep during the course of the accounting year: deaths through disease, transfers to other manors, sales, births of lambs, intransfers from other manors, purchases, and so on. These details were

[11] NRO DCN 64/10, 16 and 18.
[12] NRO DCN 64/6. *Victoria County History of Norfolk*, volume ii, (London, 1906), pp. 326-7; Noble, 'Gardeners' Accounts', pp. 18-19; A. Jessopp, ed., *Visitations of the Diocese of Norwich 1492-1532* (Camden Society, new series xliii, 1888), pp. 75-6.

provided for each category of sheep, such as ewes, wethers, rams, yearlings, and lambs (see Glossary for each category). Unusually, Norwich Cathedral Priory was inconsistent in identifying yearlings (also called hoggs and gerks) in many of its accounts; a few are careful to distinguish them from mature sheep, but most are not. For example, the shepherd's account for Gnatingdon (in Sedgeford, see Fig. 1) in 1504–5 is explicit that yearlings were categorised as ewes or wethers, rather than as hoggs or gerks.[13] The stock account closed with a summary of the total stock remaining at the end of the account, which would then become the opening position of the next year's account.

The final two sections of the account detailed any sheep belonging to local people grazing with the flock (known as cullet), followed by the record of any manure from the flock used to benefit the arable land of other people. The manure of sheep was a major source of nutrients for replenishing the arable land in a period when inorganic fertilizers did not exist, and so local communities carefully regulated the grazing of sheep to ensure that their manure was effectively targeted and deployed. In East Anglia these arrangements were complex and all-embracing, and known as the 'foldcourse system'. The number of sheep folds within each community was restricted by custom, and all sheep were compelled to lie within one of these folds at most times. The owners of these foldcourses (or liberties of fold), and those with the largest folds, were mainly manorial lords, although local tenants enjoyed the customary right to place a limited number of their own sheep within them. These arrangements minimized the chances of individual sheep wandering into sown crops, while enabling them to be penned on small areas of arable each night in a systematic manner. Those tenants who placed more than their allotted number of sheep in a fold, or non-tenants who wished to use this facility, had to pay for the privilege; these 'cullet' payments are recorded in the sheep accounts. The monastery's flocks were usually penned on its own demesne arable land, but locals could pay (at a going rate of about 12d. per acre) for the fold to be penned on their own fallow land. Hence these 'manure' payments are also recorded in the sheep accounts.[14]

Category One accounts covered a whole year. The seven accounts from 1484 to 1493 all ran from 30 November (St Andrew's day) to 30

[13] NRO DCN 62/22.

[14] K.J. Allison , 'The Sheep-Corn Husbandry of Norfolk in the Sixteenth and Seventeenth Centuries', *Agricultural History Review*, 5 (1957), pp. 12-30; B.M.S. Campbell, 'The Regional Uniqueness of English Field Systems? Some Evidence from Eastern Norfolk', *Agricultural History Review*, 36 (1983), pp. 26-46; B.M.S. Campbell, 'Commonfield Origins: the Regional Dimension', in T. Rowley, ed., *The Origins of Open-Field Agriculture* (London, 1981), pp. 112-29; Bailey, *Marginal Economy?*, pp. 54-85; M. Bailey, 'Sand into Gold: the Evolution of the Foldcourse System in West Suffolk, 1200-1600', *Agricultural History Review*, 38 (1990), pp. 40-57.

November, while those dating from 1499–1500 ran from 25 November to 25 November.[15] Yet the accounts for 1496, and most of the later ones, ran from 25 December for a whole year. The only exception to the principle of an annual account was when the shepherd resigned during the course of the year, at which point the account was formally closed and a new one opened for the incoming shepherd.[16] If we assume that every one of the monastery's shepherds drew up an account each year, then the accounts extant in DCN 62 and 64 represent only a small proportion of the original coverage. The best coverage for a single year is 25 December 1495 to 25 December 1496, for which the individual accounts of twelve shepherds survive.[17]

The shepherds did not write their account themselves, but compiled it with the help and direction of a trained scribe soon after the end of the accounting year. During the course of the year they would have kept their own scored tallies, scribbled notes and perhaps even letters of authorization from monastic officials as a source of reference for this purpose; the scribe would have had access to similar sources of information to verify the shepherds' testimony. The flocks were not wholly self-contained, but were run as part of an integrated estate unit; transfers were carefully coordinated between individual flocks, and most sales and purchases were organised centrally. Detailing the exact numbers of sheep moving to and from a single flock during the course of the year was an important component of the shepherd's account, although the decision to transfer, to buy or to sell stock was not usually his responsibility, because he simply responded to instructions issued by a more senior estate official (the person responsible for authorizing sales or purchases is sometimes identified explicitly). It follows that the shepherds handled little cash and were unlikely to be directly involved in negotiations with potential buyers of livestock or wool. It also follows that the reasons for sales, purchases and transfers are not given in these local accounts. However, the buyer is usually named, together with his place of residence, which is most unusual in medieval stock accounts.

Although each shepherd was required to follow any instructions from estate officials, his main responsibility was the day-to-day care of his flock. Nothing is recorded in the stock accounts about the daily routine of flock management, such as the use of sheepcotes, the arrangements for pasturing or the living arrangements of the shepherd. The accounts contain precise information about the number of deaths, although the exact cause is never given; all are attributed to the generic killer, 'murrain', which could refer

[15] NRO DCN 64/1 and 4.
[16] See NRO DCN 62/22 for an example of a shepherd leaving his post during the course of the year and the account terminating with his departure.
[17] NRO DCN 62/18.

to anything from old age to the various epidemic diseases which commonly afflicted sheep, such as scab, foot rot and liverfluke. Murrain was especially severe in 1496, resulting in the loss of twelve per cent of the sheep on the monastery's estate; it took more than ten years to make good the losses.[18] The scribe exercised some auditing powers by questioning and scrutinizing the shepherd's verbal explanations for the death of sheep in his care, because a dishonest shepherd might, for example, claim that some of his sheep had died when in fact he had sold them and pocketed the proceeds. The glare of the scribe's scrutiny is evident in 1492–3 when the shepherd of Lomnours was pressed to swear on oath that foxes had indeed killed three sheep, because this was such an unusual claim.[19] An unsatisfactory explanation for the disappearance of sheep, or their death through negligence, resulted in the loss being charged against the shepherd personally, described in the account as 'deficient sheep'. The reasons for charging a 'deficiency' are seldom given, although in 1496 Thomas Baxter was charged for one ewe, after it had fallen into a ditch and was subsequently seized and sold by the sheriff of Norwich.[20]

The shepherd's accounts do not usually contain any specific record of the dates when sheep died or were transferred. Very occasionally, an account might state the precise date when a consignment of sheep were sent to the monastic kitchens.[21] The majority of the entries simply indicate whether such movements occurred before or after shearing, which enabled the auditors to calculate the exact number of fleeces due from a particular flock. This reflects the continued importance of wool to the profitability of sheep rearing. The number of fleeces shorn from each flock is not recorded in the shepherd's accounts, although it was normally recorded in manorial accounts, indicating that the Priory collected the wool from all of its flocks immediately after shearing and stored it in a central place. This practice is also suggested by the Priory's preference for selling all of its wool in a single batch to an individual merchant each year.[22] The accounts also provide a systematic record of births among the breeding flocks, whereby the numbers of barren, as well as the number of fecund, ewes are explicitly recorded. The use to which this information was put is not clear from the accounts themselves. At the most basic level it provided officials with a

[18] See the individual shepherd's accounts contained in NRO DCN 62/18, but also compare the centralized stock account of Christmas 1495 (7,163 sheep, NRO DCN 64/2) with that of Christmas 1496 (6,325, NRO DCN 62/18). The numbers on the estate in 1495 were not again surpassed until 1509, NRO DCN 62/23. For other discussions of sheep mortality, see D. Stone, 'The Productivity and Management of Sheep in Late Medieval England', *Agricultural History Review*, 51 (2003), pp. 12-14 and Bailey, *Marginal Economy*, pp. 123-6.

[19] NRO DCN 64/1.

[20] NRO DCN 62/18, shepherd's account of Eaton.

[21] See, for example, the account of Eaton in 1504-5, NRO DCN 62/22.

[22] NRO DCN 64/9.

crude assessment of the shepherd's performance by establishing a lambing rate that could then be checked to ensure that it fell within acceptable margins, but it also provided central officials with an evidentiary base from which to assess the productivity and profitability of their flocks.

The majority of these accounts record little in the way of cash transfers, mainly because most of the activities which generated revenue (such as sales of wool and sheep) were handled centrally. However, the shepherds were required to account for the occasional sale, and for miscellaneous wool pelts which remained in their custody. They also collected small amounts of cash from those local residents who owed for cullet or manure. Such transactions amounted to little more than a few shillings in a single year. However, after 1504 the accounts usually conclude with the explicit detail of a financial reckoning between the individual shepherd and monastic officials. This involved the identification of the petty cash collected by him, offset against salary instalments already paid by the monastery and other petty charges.[23] This represents an attempt to develop the format and contents of the stock account in the early sixteenth century, which is consistent with the evolution of other aspects of the Priory's accounting procedures around this time (p. 17).

Each of the Priory's shepherds was paid around 60s. per annum, together with an allowance of around 5s. for working clothes in the Priory's livery and miscellaneous tips and perks.[24] Their main perk was the right to run their own sheep with the lord's flock free of charge; for example, in 1490 Roger Wrask had 120 ewes in the Priory's fold at Sedgeford.[25] This represented a solid and dependable salary in an era when an unskilled labourer could earn up to 3d. for a day's work. Yet the shepherds worked long hours, supervising the flocks, moving them from pasture to pasture, and penning them on the fallow arable each night. David Stone has argued that the job was not especially attractive in the fifteenth century, judging by the difficulties experienced by many landlords in recruiting and retaining good shepherds.[26] The high turnover of shepherds on the Priory's manors, and the infrequency with which shepherds moved about the estate, would seem to support Stone's point. For example, between 1491 and 1503 at least seven shepherds worked at Sedgeford and at least four at Fring between 1497 and 1503. Thomas Baxter was one of the longest-serving shepherds, serving at Heigham in 1489 and then completing eight consecutive years at Eaton between 1491 and 1499, but he was succeeded by two others in the next four years.[27]

23 NRO DCN 62/22.
24 See, for example, NRO DCN 64/7.
25 NRO DCN 62/17.
26 Stone, 'Productivity and Management', pp. 19-20.
27 NRO DCN 62/16 and 17.

Centralised Stock Accounts (Category Two)

The second type of account was a centralized stock account, which summarized the total number of sheep in each of the flocks and therefore provided officials with a simple, at-a-glance, statement of the number and location of all the sheep on the estate. The total number of sheep on each manor is given according to age and gender, and the person responsible for them is named. The preamble to these accounts is usually explicit that they relate to all the sheep of the monastery, most of which were kept in half a dozen core flocks which were actively and directly managed; these flocks featured in Category One accounts, and they also included some sheep specifically allocated to the Prior and the Cellarer. Finally, these listings also include details of the Priory's sheep which were kept in the folds of other lords, or which had been included in the lease of a manor as part of its stock. Hence the account for 1491 describes the age and gender of the 5,144 sheep of the monastery kept in six large flocks at Eaton, Lomnours, Lathes, Newton, Sedgeford and Hindringham, 226 sheep kept in the folds of two other lords at Little Ryburgh and Sparham, and 315 sheep of the Prior scattered among the monastery's flocks at Eaton, Lathes, Newton, Sedgeford and Hindringham.[28]

The information contained therein was largely copied from the accounts of individual shepherds, as the heading to the account for 25 December 1491 states explicitly.[29] The gathering of this information therefore postdated the compilation of the accounts of individual shepherds, and was drawn up centrally by a monastic official. For example, the centralized account for 1496 is written on the same membrane underneath the individual shepherds' accounts for Intwood and Stoke Holy Cross, confirming the obvious point that the former was drawn up once the latter had all been collected to a single place. However, unlike the individual shepherds' accounts, which provided a dynamic record of sheep movement and flows throughout the year, the centralized stock accounts provided a snapshot of the number of sheep on the estate on a single day of the year. This was always in December, although the exact date varied until about 1500, after which Christmas Day became the standard date on which the Priory counted its sheep.

The earliest extant Category Two accounts are short and sparse, simply providing a basic summary of all sheep in each flock. However, the account of 1509 is significantly longer, because it includes more detail about those sheep which belonged to the particular offices of the Prior and the Cellarer. It also details the transfer of sheep pelts to the monastery itself.[30] This represents an attempt to develop the format and content of the centralized account, and thereafter the sheep of the Prior and Cellarer are usually identified separately.

[28] NRO DCN 62/16.   [29] NRO DCN 62/16.   [30] NRO DCN 62/23.

Centralised Revenue Accounts (Category Three)

These recorded in summary form the annual receipts from, and expenditure upon, sheep farming across the estate, and were drawn up by the office of Prior. The earliest surviving example dates from 1524, much later than the earliest Category One and Two accounts.[31] It may simply be a matter of chance that no earlier Category Three accounts have survived. However, it is likely that these centralized revenue accounts were in fact a later creation, perhaps drawn up for the first time in the 1520s in response to concerns that the Priory needed to take a firmer grip upon its finances (pp. 5, 15–16).

The centralized revenue accounts followed a simple and consistent format, beginning with summary receipts under a series of basic headings: sales of wool, pelts and livestock, and then cash income from manure and cullet rights. The receipt sections reveal that sales of wool were the major source of income from sheep rearing, usually constituting more than half of annual receipts, and that the Priory preferred to sell all its wool in a single lot to one merchant. However, the sale of stock also generated a substantial income each year, indicating that the Priory's flocks served as an important local reservoir of livestock from which other farmers replenished their stock, and that it was also supplying butchers with fattened stock.

The record of expenditure in these accounts is not detailed, but comprises outline summaries under standard headings. The first item was the rent paid by the Priory to hire additional pasture from other landholders for grazing its own flocks. The costs of washing and shearing the sheep were usually a rounded sum, 66s. 8d. (or five marks), which is strongly suggestive of a contracted rate to un-named outsiders. The remaining expenditure was divided between the wages and liveries of shepherds and a single stockman (the latter looked after the small flock at the Priory itself, which comprised livestock awaiting slaughter in the monastery's kitchen); and then the purchase of pitch and grease (which was applied to the sheep to prevent the spread of mites), hurdles (for penning the flocks in small areas), and ruddle and bole (for marking the sheep). The balance of income and expenditure produced a sizeable profit of between c. £60 and £90 each year, which was allocated to the office of Master Cellarer.[32]

These revenue accounts were constructed by the Priory's central administration and they all ran from Michaelmas to Michaelmas, with the exception of one half-year account for March to September 1531.[33] They drew heavily upon a variety of other documents and subsidiary accounts, including invoices and memoranda, and they also contain specific references to information recorded in an auditor's book and the accounts of the

[31] NRO DCN 64/6.   [32] NRO DCN 64/6 to 9, 12.   [33] NRO DCN 64/9.

office of Master Cellarer. By this time the Priory was employing professional auditors to supplement the work of the audit committee, which
reflects the scale and complexity of its organization and, perhaps, a lack of
specialist expertise or even interest among the monks.[34]

Sheep Rearing

The accounts reveal and reflect the importance of sheep rearing to the
economy of Norwich Cathedral Priory in particular, and of East Anglia in
general. Sheep were especially prominent on the lighter soils of the region,
such as the Breckland area of north-west Suffolk and south-west Norfolk,
and the Norfolk Goodsands and Greensands. Yet they were also an important feature of the agrarian economy of the marshlands of eastern Norfolk
and on the heaths around Norwich. Norwich Cathedral Priory had probably first adopted sheep rearing on a large scale in the early thirteenth
century, when, in common with most aristocratic landlords, it had swung
decisively to the direct exploitation of many of its manors and demesnes.
Prior to this date, its manors had been leased to various farmers for a fixed
annual rent. The shift to direct exploitation entailed the employment of
local agents to exploit each of the manorial demesnes and other resources
on the Priory's behalf. Thus it enjoyed the direct profits and windfalls of
arable and pastoral husbandry, but it also had to absorb the risks and any
shortfalls. The Priory consumed large quantities of the produce from its
manorial demesnes, thus obviating the need to buy much of the basic foodstuffs needed to feed the community of monks and servants, but it also sold
large quantities of produce for cash. Sheep production was geared to the
market rather than to consumption, principally through the sale of wool.
Some meat was also fattened for either sale to outsiders or for consumption
by the monks; older sheep were usually selected for fattening, because few
medieval sheep were culled before their wool yielding days were finished.[35]

By about 1400 market conditions were less favourable to aristocratic landlords. The demographic decline triggered by the Black Death of 1349 had
helped to reduce the profitability of agriculture by creating conditions of
over-supply for foodstuffs and raising the costs of labour, which was now in
relatively short supply. Consequently, many aristocratic and ecclesiastical
landlords withdrew from the direct exploitation of their demesnes, preferring
to lease them instead to local tenants. This policy was essentially defensive
and risk-averse, providing the comfort of a fixed rent and none of the hassle
of running a sizeable agrarian operation during an era of reduced agrarian
profits. Between 1380 and 1420 the Priory swung in and out of direct

[34] Noble, 'Gardeners' Accounts', pp. 18-19; Virgoe, 'Estates', pp. 354-6.
[35] Stone, 'Productivity and Management', pp. 1-2; Virgoe, 'Estates', pp. 352-3.

demesne cultivation on its manors, until in 1422 only the arable demesne at Sedgeford was still exploited directly. By 1431 Sedgeford, too, had been leased, marking the final abandonment of direct arable cultivation on the Priory's estates.[36] However, the Priory continued to retain direct control over some of its sheep flocks and pastures, even on manors where the arable and other components of the demesne — such as meadows, mills, wood-lands and warrens — were leased. By the late fifteenth century sheepfolds were the only major demesne asset to be exploited directly on the estate.

The Priory maintained between five and eight thousand sheep during the period covered by the accounts, all of them assumed to be the Norfolk breed, a hardy animal with a fleece of medium weight.[37] Most sheep were concentrated in half a dozen actively managed flocks, which divided into two distinct groups: one group on the light soils of north-west Norfolk, based on the manors of Fring, Gnatingdon, Hindringham and Sedgeford, and the other around Norwich, notably Catton, Eaton, Lathes, Lomnours, Newton and Thorpe Episcopi. The Priory made occasional adjustments to the location of its active flocks. For example, Thorpe Market was an important centre in the 1480s, but was closed down in 1491 and the sheep transferred elsewhere, and Lomnours was actively used until it was finally leased in 1500.[38] In contrast, in 1497 an active flock was opened up at Fring for the first time.[39]

The flocks of the Priory were generally organised into those containing ewes and those of wethers. The ewe flocks were essentially breeding units, and included a few rams and the new born lambs. After a year, the lambs were re-categorised as hoggs and gerks, and transferred out to other ewe or wether flocks. Wethers produced the heaviest fleeces, and so these flocks were geared towards wool production. Sheep were routinely transferred from one flock to another over the whole estate, so that, for example, in 1485 sixty-six lambs were driven from Easton to Hindringham (sixteen miles) and 200 ewes from Thorpe Market to Sedgeford (thirty-four miles). The costs of such long drives are recorded in the revenue accounts.[40] Some of the flocks close to Norwich contained older sheep being fattened at the end of their working lives for consumption within the monastery, or for sale within the city itself.

The average flock size on the Priory's estate tended to be larger than

---

[36] Virgoe, 'Estates', pp. 354-6; Campbell, *English Seigneurial Agriculture*, pp. 235-6.

[37] K.J. Allison, 'Flock Management in the Sixteenth and Seventeenth Centuries', *Economic History Review*, second series, xl (1958), p. 106; Welch, 'Sheep Accounts', p. 16; P. Wade-Martins, *Black faces. A History of East Anglian Sheep Breeds* (Norfolk Museums Service, 1993), pp. 10-24.

[38] NRO DCN 62/16 and 17.

[39] NRO DCN 62/19.

[40] See, for example, the 22s. spent in 1525-6, NRO DCN 64/6.

those of other contemporary flockmasters. Flocks owned by the Townshends and Fermours contained on average just under 800 sheep each, compared with over one thousand on the Priory's estate.[41] The overall composition of the flocks was skewed towards ewes, which usually comprised just under one half of all sheep on the Priory's estate, while wethers made up around one third. These proportions are broadly similar to those on the Townshend flocks, and reflect the persistent need to replenish the flocks through breeding. It is likely that the proportion of ewes had increased during the fifteenth century, because flock owners could reduce their costs by replacing most of their losses from their own stock rather than having to buy from the market.[42] The lambing rates on the estate were usually between 0.6 and 0.8 lambs per ewe, which was about standard for East Anglian flocks of this period.[43]

Hence during the fifteenth century sheep rearing was the only sector of agriculture in which Norwich Cathedral Priory maintained an active and substantial interest. By 1500 it maintained up to ten sizeable flocks on as many manors, containing in excess of six thousand sheep. In all other areas of agriculture the Priory had become a landlord who simply collected rents for the farm of its landed resources. Why did it adopt a different policy with its sheep? The answer lies in the economics of fifteenth-century sheep rearing and the effectiveness with which the Priory could manage this particular activity. Sheep rearing was not labour intensive compared with grain farming, requiring merely the supervision of a shepherd aided by some seasonal labour during the annual washing and shearing. The ability to minimize costs was particularly important to protecting profits when labour was scarce, and therefore expensive, and when the price of wool was relatively low. Other cost-saving tactics included reducing the amount of additional feed given to the sheep, diminishing expenditure on the grease and unction used to treat disease, and making less use of winter shelters such as sheepcotes, which otherwise required maintenance. Finally, costs could also be reduced by consolidating or increasing the size of individual flocks supervised by a single shepherd. In general, landlords were better placed than peasants to obtain such economies of scale, because they had the financial resources and the land to construct larger flocks. Furthermore, such activity was also relatively simple for landlords to supervise and to audit without the need for manifold local agents.[44]

[41] Allison, 'Flock Management', p. 100.

[42] C. E. Moreton, *The Townshends and their World: Gentry, Law and Land in Norfolk, 1450-1551* (Oxford, 1992), p. 171; Stone, 'Productivity and Management' , pp. 14-16.

[43] Welch, 'Sheep Accounts', pp. 20, 23; Moreton, *Townshends*, pp. 167-71; Allison, 'Flock Management', p. 103; Bailey, *Marginal Economy?*, pp. 122-8.

[44] See a more detailed discussion of this point in M. Bailey, *Medieval Suffolk. An Economic and Social History 1200 to 1500* (Woodbridge, 2007), pp. 214-19; Stone, 'Productivity and Management', pp. 18-20.

The importance of sheep-rearing to the financial strength of the Priory is clearly apparent from these accounts. By the end of the fifteenth century the market for wool was booming once again, after a lengthy period of recession which had lasted since the beginning of the century. A conscious decision was made within the Priory to exploit this expanding market, because the increase in the number of its sheep was both dramatic and sustained. In 1475 the Priory recorded 1,225 sheep on its estate, 4,925 in 1488 and 8,377 in 1524.[45] Hence in the 1470s the Priory probably received around £12 per annum from sales of wool, but by the 1520s and 1530s this had risen to at least £75 per annum. By the latter date the Priory had settled upon a policy of selling all of its wool output to a single merchant, the purchaser in 1531 being a member of the famous Spring dynasty of Lavenham. Wool sales usually dominated the revenue obtained from sheep farming, because sheep were only sold for meat at the end of their lives in order to maximize their yield of wool. However, by the 1520s a striking feature of the Priory's management of its sheep is the importance of sales of stock in raising revenue. Around one third of its income from sheep came from such sales, which reached a peak of £73 in 1530.[46] Much of this livestock was sold as stock to supplement the folds of other flockmasters, as indicated in 1497 by the sale of 240 sheep from Lathes and Newton to Lady Eleanor Townshend.[47] Yet some of the Priory's sheep were destined for local meat markets. For example, in 1505 a total of 424 wethers from Eaton and Newton were sold to Robert Brown, described as a butcher of Norwich, for £26 10s., and in 1509 £10 was raised by the sale of 240 sheep to two other city butchers.[48] These are significant transactions, reflecting the importance of the urban market for meat in late medieval England, even though some historians have argued that a substantial trade in mutton did not develop until the mid sixteenth century.[49]

The compilation of centralized revenue accounts for sheep in the 1520s and 1530s provides a clear statement of the profits made by the Priory from its entire sheep operations. The gross income from this source varied between £116 in 1533–4 and £154 in 1529–30, which converted into a net surplus of between £58 (1533–4) and £91 (1529–30) once expenses and costs had been deducted. This was equivalent to around one third of the total net revenue of the Master Cellarer.[50] The expansion of the Priory's flocks in the last two decades of the fifteenth century made a significant impact on its finances.

[45] Allison, 'Flock Management', p.100; NRO DCN 62/16 and 64/2.
[46] NRO DCN 64/8.
[47] NRO DCN 62/19.
[48] NRO DCN 62/22 and 23.
[49] See, for example, Moreton, *Townshends*, pp. 170-1, and Wade-Martins, *Black Faces*, p. 9. Yet see Bailey, *Medieval Suffolk*, pp. 267-8.
[50] NRO DCN 64/8 and 12; Virgoe, 'Estates', p. 357.

These hard figures underline why the sheep accounts were so important to Norwich Cathedral Priory, but what makes them interesting to a wider audience and thus worthy of translation and publication? The first reason is that sheep in general, and wool in particular, occupied an important place in the English economy, to a degree that was unusual elsewhere in Europe. It is instructive that in the early sixteenth century a visiting Venetian merchant was greatly impressed by the enormous number of sheep in England, and the high quality of their wool.[51] A significant proportion, perhaps more than half, of this wool was exported to the Continent. Richard Britnell has estimated that in the early fourteenth century more than 5,000 tonnes of English wool were exported in either raw or finished form each year, representing the fleeces of perhaps 10 million sheep, although this had declined to under 3,000 tonnes between the 1430s and 1460s. Yet the volume of exports picked up again after the 1480s, and by the early sixteenth century annual exports were comfortably exceeding 4,000 tonnes. Between the 1460s and 1520s sheep were 'undoubtedly the most dynamic sector of the agrarian economy'.[52] Hence these accounts provide detailed information about the activities of a major landlord at a time when sheep constituted one of the most important and vibrant sectors of the English economy.

The second reason is that detailed accounts of sheep rearing are rare from the fifteenth and early sixteenth centuries, for all its wider importance. In contrast, manorial accounts dating from the thirteenth and fourteenth centuries are relatively common, and provide detailed statistical information about sheep rearing on individual demesnes, but the withdrawal of many of the great landlords from this activity in the fifteenth century resulted in a significant contraction in the volume of documentation. Britnell argues that a small number of enterprising peasant farmers built up their flocks to fill the gap created by the withdrawal of landlords from sheep rearing, although such people did not keep written records of their activities (or, if they did, the sources have not survived).[53] However, the organization of sheep rearing was somewhat different in fifteenth-century East Anglia, where it continued to be dominated by seigneurial, not peasant, flocks. The peculiar East Anglian institution of the foldcourse restricted peasant involvement in sheep rearing and presented lords with extensive control over folds. Hence in the early sixteenth century some of the region's aristocratic landlords were still actively managing substantial flocks of sheep: Norwich Cathedral Priory ran over 8,000 sheep, the abbey

[51] B.M.S. Campbell, 'The Land', in R.E. Horrox and W.M. Ormrod, eds, *A Social History of England 1200-1500* (Cambridge, 2006), p. 187.
[52] R.H. Britnell, *Britain and Ireland 1050-1530. Economy and Society* (Oxford, 2004), pp. 417–19.
[53] Britnell, *Britain and Ireland*, pp. 414-5.

of Bury St Edmunds had around 4,000, and the foldcourses of Thetford Priory had a capacity for nearly 7,000.[54] A few gentry lords were also aggressively acquiring their own, or leasing other, foldcourses, and constructing even bigger enterprises. The Townshend family expanded their operations in west Norfolk from ten flocks containing 6,477 sheep in 1475 to twenty-six flocks and 18,468 sheep in 1516, while in 1521 the Fermours of East Barsham owned 15,568 sheep in twenty flocks.[55] The continuing importance of landlords in sheep rearing in East Anglia explains why a good number of the few English sheep accounts to survive from this period emanate from this region.[56]

The final reason is that these accounts reveal something important about the evolution of centralized accounting systems in the late Middle Ages. English estate management in the thirteenth and fourteenth centuries was based substantially upon a system of local accounts drawn up by manorial officials. However, after the late fourteenth century this system came under increasing pressure. First, the swing from direct to rentier farming on the estates of the great landlords resulted in a shift from amateur local officials towards professional officials with responsibility for groups of manors rather than for a single manor. Second, the unfavourable economic conditions of the fifteenth century squeezed agrarian profits, as yields from land fell and costs escalated, which forced many lords to manage their economic affairs more carefully and prudently. These pressures forced subtle changes to the ways in which landlords managed their estates. For example, methods of rent management became more sophisticated on many estates, through the development of highly detailed lease agreements, the evolution of arrears management, the use of petitions by individual officials, and the allocation of debts to individual officers.[57] Furthermore, the emphasis of estate management shifted from the locality back towards the centre, which encouraged the development of more comprehensive systems of centralized accounting. The centralized accounts of Norwich Cathedral Priory drew upon a wealth of information contained in other, often local, accounts, in order to inform its administrators more accurately about their most important agrarian activity, during an era of challenging economic conditions. It is clear that Norwich Cathedral Priory was developing and improving the content and format of its centralized accounting of sheep during the period

[54] Bailey, 'Sand into Gold', pp. 40-57; A. Simpson, *The Wealth of the Gentry 1540-1660* (Cambridge, 1961), p. 184; Bailey, *Marginal Economy?*, pp. 247, 292-3.

[55] Britnell, *Britain and Ireland*, p. 419; Allison, 'Flock Management', p. 100; C.E. Moreton and P. Rutledge, eds, 'Skayman's Book, 1516-18', in *Farming and Gardening in Late Medieval Norfolk* (NRS lxi, 1997), pp. 96-8.

[56] Such as those for the Townshend estate, Moreton and Rutledge, 'Skayman's Book', p. 102, fn. 14. See also Simpson, *Wealth of the Gentry*, pp. 181-96.

[57] See, for example, D. Stone, *Decision-Making in Medieval Agriculture* (Oxford, 2005), pp. 216-30, and Bailey, *The English Manor*, pp. 108-10.

covered by these accounts, as evidenced by the subtle changes in the content of Category One and Two accounts, and the likely creation in the 1520s of the Category Three account. Such broad developments in accounting technique and method have attracted limited attention from historians, but they might reasonably be regarded as a managerial innovation of the fifteenth and early sixteenth centuries.[58]

Editorial Method and Acknowledgements

The original documents are written in Latin, which—despite some technical words and phrases associated with either accounting methods or sheep farming—is relatively simple and straightforward. The Latin has therefore been translated into English to increase its accessibility. Any difficult, uncertain or unusual words are included alongside the translation in [*italics*], in exactly the form they appear in the manuscript. An insertion of words by the editor, usually as a brief note of explanation or clarification, is treated in the same manner. Place names have been modernized, but surnames are transcribed as they appear in the original text. Additional notes made in the margin of the original manuscript are placed in the footnotes.

The original documents enumerate in Roman numerals, and make extensive use of the long hundred (120): the latter has been accommodated in converting to Arabic numerals. It was common for medieval accountants to count sheep, rabbits and doves using the long hundred, although, unhelpfully for the reader, this was not an invariable rule. The use of the long hundred is usually evident by the presence of a superscript^{ma} (shorthand for *centum major*) after the Roman numeral, and is distinguished from a superscript^{mi} (for *centum minor*) for the short hundred (100). Hence CCC^{ma} is $3 \times 120 = 360$, while $CC^{ma}C^{mi}$ is $(2 \times 120) + 100 = 340$. Similarly, M^{ma} is $10 \times 120 = 1,200$.

The Norfolk Record Society and I are grateful to Doug Welch, whose MA dissertation on the DCN 64 accounts provided the inspiration for this edition, and who kindly placed his translations at our disposal. The Master and Fellows of Corpus Christi College, Cambridge, funded the microfilming of all of the accounts, enabling me to work on this edition while resident first in Cambridge and then in Leeds. Professor Carole Rawcliffe kindly and readily answered a number of queries about medieval Norfolk and the Priory itself, while David Dymond, Peter Northeast and David Pritchard helped address some troublesome Latin. Elizabeth Rutledge was a supportive and able editor.

[58] Bailey, *The English Manor*, p. 111.

Norwich Cathedral Priory Sheep Accounts, 1484–1534[1]

1. STOCK ACCOUNTS OF INDIVIDUAL SHEPHERDS[2]

DCN 64/1: 30 November 1484 to 30 November 1485.

[*Lathes*]. Account of Robert Rudkyn, shepherd there, from the feast of St Andrew the Apostle in the 2nd year of King Richard III until the same feast following in the 1st year of King Henry VII.

Ewes. The same shepherd received from remainder[3] those [*sheep*] given at the beginning of the account, by the tally, 978.

Of which, sold to Fraunceys of Pulham *before shearing*, 20 *25s.* And in murrain before lambing and shearing *23* and after shearing *9*, 32. And sent to the lord's fold in Eaton before shearing, 200. And sent to Richard Salthous, Cellarer of the monastery, after shearing, 135. And received from the lord's fold at Heigham [*next to Norwich*] after shearing, 201. And remaining for the monastery within the time of the account, because they were given to John Maykyn,[4] 792.

And minus the deficient[5] [*sheep*], 1, paid for *12d.* And remaining, 791.

Wethers. From remainder of the last account, 1, which was sent to Plumstead after shearing to the fold of Lomnours, and it remains there. And this equals [*i.e. adds up to the first figure given*].

Lambs. From 735 ewes were born 527 lambs. Thereafter, in murrain, 9. And remaining, 518. And barren ewes, [*total*] 208.

Of which, sold to John Dussing, 33 *14s. 8d.*, at 5½d. each. And given to the shepherd for the annual marking[6] [*signato a(nnu)o*], 1. And remaining there, 484. All sent to Lomnours under the custody of the said Robert Rudkyn. And equals.

---

[1] All the accounts printed here are held at the Norfolk Record Office.

[2] For discussion of the different accounts, see Introduction, pp. 5-12.

[3] The total 'from remainder' refers to the sheep remaining at the end of the previous account, which therefore becomes the opening charge upon the shepherd at the beginning of this account.

[4] John Maykin was an employee of the Priory, probably a shepherd on another manor, see below p. 22.

[5] A deficient sheep is an accounting device, rather than a sheep with a particular weakness or inadequacy. See Introduction, p. 8.

[6] Lambs were daubed with dye to identify them as the property of the Priory.

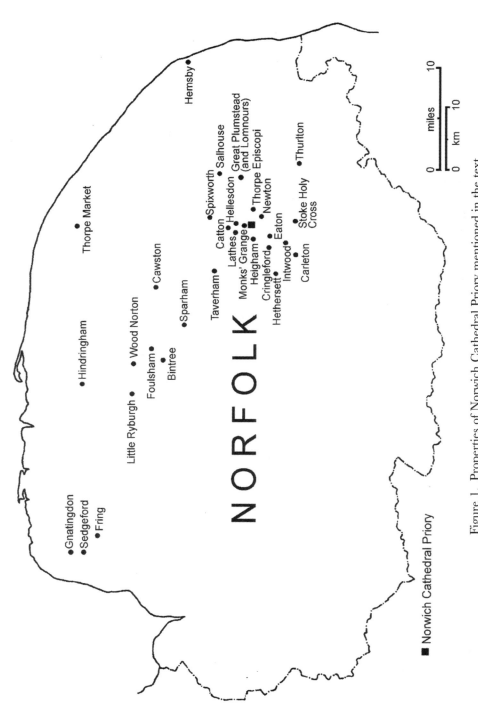

Figure 1. Properties of Norwich Cathedral Priory mentioned in the text.

[*Cullet*][7] No cash received before shearing for cullet from the farmer.[8] Nor for 80 ewes in his contract.[9] But he is charged for 30 hoggs before shearing within the time of the account until the next shearing, which now remain.

[*Manure*][10] Nothing from anyone for the 15 acres of land leased by the Hospital of St Mary Magdalene.[11] Nor from 1 acre which the same shepherd manured with the lord's fold, because as contracted. Nor from anyone for the manure of the lessees of Catton, just as they can if they wish.[12]

Ewes remaining, as above, 791.

DCN 64/1: 30 November 1489 to 30 November 1490. [*The manuscript is badly torn and in very poor condition.*]

Eaton. Account of Thomas Baxter, shepherd there, for the aforesaid time.

Tally. The same received by his tally from last year, 719 [*sic*]. Of which:

Wethers. From remainder, 1. And [*ms torn*].

Ewes. From remainder, 715. And bought [*ms torn*] 76. And received from the fold of Thorpe Market after [*ms torn*], 101.

Of which, sold by John Russell [*sum missing*]. Sold to Henry Grey, knight, 81. And to the aforesaid Henry from the stock belonging to the lord prior, after shearing [*sum missing*] sold to Thomas Bay, 10. And in murrain before shearing, 6, and after shearing, 11. [*ms torn*] the stock belonging to the lord prior, before shearing, 3, and after shearing, 2. Total expended, 174. And remaining [*sum missing*].

Lambs. From remainder, nothing. But received from births of the ewes, 451. And sterile [*ewes*], 264.

And, of which, in murrain at the time of the castration,[13] 12. And sold to

---

[7] For cullet, see Glossary.

[8] See Glossary for the medieval meaning of farmer.

[9] The farmer — the lessee — of the arable demesne of the manor is permitted by the terms of his lease to have 80 ewes in the sheep fold of the Priory. It is noted here, but no charge is levied.

[10] The fold is penned on areas of fallow arable on many nights of the year, in order that the manure and urine of the sheep can replenish nutrients in the soil. Usually, this penning was confined to the demesne land of the Priory, but other local people may pay the Priory to pen the fold on their land.

[11] The leper Hospital of St Mary Magdalene in Sprowston, a mile or so to the northeast of the city. See *Victoria County History*, ii, pp. 448-9, and C. Rawcliffe, *The Hospitals of Medieval Norwich* (Norwich, 1995), chapter one.

[12] A rather odd phrase, but it simply reiterates that anyone can pay to have the manure from the demesne animals (which in this case are included as part of the lease of the manor) deposited on their arable land, see Introduction, p. 6.

[13] The castration of the young male lambs.

Lady Grey...[*rest of name and the number missing*]. [*Given*] to the stockman and shepherd, as contracted [*ex cons'*], 3. And sent onto the fold of Hindringham [*ms torn*] after shearing with 66 lambs born to some of these aforesaid sheep, that is to say from 87. And of which barren, 21. Thereof in murrain, 2. And given [*ms torn*] by the shepherd, 4, for 2s. paid to the lord prior [*ms torn*].

Manure. Nothing from [*ms torn*] there, because to the farmer as contracted.

Cullet. From Robert Grene, farmer, for his ewes and hoggs, that is for 90 in his contract [*nothing*] and 27 *4s. 6d.* at 2d. per head.[14] John Russell, ewes, nothing, because as contracted. <Ewes> hoggs of the light of St John[15] 10 *20d.*. From Thomas Sculyerd, ewes, 39 *6s. 6d.* From the cowherd, ewes, 80 *nothing, because out of custom*. But [*ms torn*] 23 sheep. Total head [*of sheep*] 269. Total money, beyond contracted, 14s. 10d. Total head of sheep remaining, 720 [*ms torn*].

Thorpe Market. Account of the said Thomas Baxter, shepherd there, for the aforesaid time.

Tally. The same received by his tally given to him at the last account, 729. Of which:

Ewes. From remainder, 40, and received from hoggs and gerks from the last account, 689.

Of which, sent to the fold of Sedgeford before shearing *wrongly named, because hoggs to wethers*[16] 200, and to the fold of Heigham after shearing, 91. And sent to the fold of Lomnours after shearing, 106. And to the fold of Lathes after shearing, 140. And sent to the fold of Eaton after shearing, 100. And remain, 92.

Thereof, in murrain before shearing, *May*[17] 24. And in murrain after shearing, [*the pelts sent to John*] Maykyn, 11. And in murrain before shearing, [*the pelts*] given to John Russell, 18. And in murrain before shearing, the pelts produced at the account, 2.[18] And in the murrain after

[14] Grene's contract for leasing the demesne arable allows him to fold 90 sheep with the Priory's fold, but he has to pay the going rate for any number beyond that total.

[15] Literally 'the light of St John'. A light, presumably a candle, was maintained at an altar dedicated to this saint in the parish church of Eaton, and this entry implies that stock had been donated to yield a modest income for this purpose. This could conceivably refer to a gild dedicated to this saint, although the only documented gild in Eaton was dedicated to St Andrew, K. Farnhill, *Gilds and the Parish Community in Late Medieval East Anglia, c.1470-1550* (Woodbridge, 2001), p. 183.

[16] This inserted comment reveals that hoggs had been erroneously categorised as ewes, and were now being recategorised properly. See Introduction, p. 6, for the Priory's inconsistent approach to identifying yearlings separately.

[17] John Maykyn was the shepherd at Lathes this year, a manor close to the monastery itself. The carcasses of the dead sheep, or their pelts (see n. 18 below), were clearly sent to him.

[18] A sheep which died before shearing was skinned for its pelt, which could fetch as much as

shearing, 18. And remaining, <20> [*sum missing, the total should be 19*].

Lambs. From remainder, nil. But received from the fold of Lathes after shearing, 497. And received from the fold of Lomnours, 240. And received from Lathes from the pure[19] [*de meris*] lambs of the lord, 13. And remaining, <740> 750.[20]

Manure. Nothing received from 15 acres, nor from 12 acres, nor from anyone, but from the profits of the vill, the total for manure, 13s. 4d.

Cullet. From local stock for one year ending at Michaelmas in the sixth year of King Henry VII [*29 September 1490*], namely each category [*of sheep folded*] with another, namely Thomas Crabbe 22 *22d.*, Simon Saund[e]rs 8 *8d.*, Adam Hanworth 46 *3s. 10d.*, Robert Hanworth 12 *12d.*, William Tungate 44 *3s. 8d.*, Nicholas Gene 24 *2s.*. From stock for half of one year ending at the Annunciation of St Mary in the 5th year of Henry VII [*25 March, 1490*], at ½d. per head, namely Henry Reppes 80 *3s. 4d.*, Robert Crabbe 20 *10d.*. Total, 17s. 2d.

Total head [*of sheep*] remaining, 769. Of which, [*sum missing*] are ewes, [*sum missing*] lambs for hoggs.

Lathes. Account of John Maykyn for the aforesaid time. And received by the tally from last year, 786.

Ewes. From remainder, 786. Of which, received from Thorpe Market after shearing, … [*number and around two words missing*] of the lord from Newton Flotman, 30. Total, 956.

Of which, [*ms torn*] but of which he says himself to have been ignorant up to the present time. But by the grace of the Lord he has a day [*to respond*] in person, before the morrow of the [*feast of*] the Purification of St Mary the Virgin [*3 February*] [*ms torn*] at 16d. per head, 40 *53s. 4d.* And if he does not prove the purchase then they shall be charged [*ms torn*] by the aforesaid John Russell before lambing and shearing, 18 *31*. But similarly until the said morrow of the Purification, just as advised, they shall be regarded as deficient ewes *24*.[21] And in murrain after shearing, 6, of which the pelts given to Henry Porter. And sold to the same after shearing, 40. And remaining, 852. And in murrain afterwards, 4. And remaining, 848. And

fleece on its own. Pelts are therefore identified explicitly in the accounts, to flag to the auditors that a financial charge should be levied on an official for the pelt. The skin of a sheep which had died after shearing was much less valuable, and does not feature as consistently in these accounts.

[19] Pure, meaning personal to the Prior.

[20] The account continues on the dorse of the roll, which is therefore headed 'Thorpe Market, continued'.

[21] An interesting dialogue between the scribe and the shepherd, setting out the terms and timeframe by which the shepherd must verify the loss/disappearance of 24 ewes. It is clear that they will be charged against him personally if he fails to persuade the Prior's officials on 3 February but they are not charged in this account.

in murrain among the pure [*personal*] ewes of the lord, 5. And remaining, and given to John Bronde, 843.[22]

Lambs. From remainder, nothing. But from births, and born to the ewes mentioned above, 816. And thus 264 [*ewes were*] barren. Of which, sent to the fold of Thorpe Market, [*sum missing*]. And given by the auditor to the stockman and shepherd of the ewes, 3. And [*ms torn*]. Of which, sold at Wroxham, 1 *3½d.* [*number and grand total missing*].

Manure. And manure for the bailiff of Magdalene as contracted for the time of this account, given as right. And sold for cash, nothing. Total, nothing.

Cullet. The first half of the year.
From the stock of Robert Bataly, 7 ewes *14d.*, 4 hoggs *8d.* … [*torn Ms*] Thomas Cook 10 *20d.* 6 hoggs *12d.* [*ms torn*]. From the aforesaid shepherd, 50. Item, 30 [*ms torn*] Total, [*sum missing*]

Cullet for the second half of the year, paying for that term.
Item, for the second half of the year paying at the next shearing from Robert [*ms torn*], Thomas Cook 16, Henry [*?*]Porter 2, the Prior of St Leonards[23] by the above John Russell 20, John Maykyn 50, lord William Calthorpe 40. The aforesaid shepherd as contracted, 80. Total, paying at 1d. per head, together the total is 227, thus 18s. 11d. [*ms torn*]

DCN 62/17: 30 November 1489 to 30 November 1490

Newton. Account of William Staunford, shepherd there, as for one year ending at the feast of St Andrew in the 6th year of King Henry VII.

Tally. Item, the same shepherd receives by the tally from remainder under the charge of John Russell in the body of this account, 679. Of which:

Rams. From remainder, 112. Of which, sold to John Fissher, 40. And expended in hospitality[24] as on previous occasions, 3. And in murrain before shearing, 6. And remaining, 63.

Wethers. From remainder, 483. Of which, sold to Ed. Methillar and Robert Browne, 63. And in murrain before shearing, 10. And in murrain after shearing, 4, given for hospitality of the Prior. And remaining, 406.

Total remaining, 482 [*because*] 13 [*sheep were*] re-categorised as hoggs from gerks this year. Of which, 63 rams, <406> 419 wethers.[25]

---

[22] Marginal note: 'Remain on the tally'.

[23] The priory of St Leonards, a cell of Norwich Cathedral Priory, located in Thorpe by Norwich: *Victoria County History*, ii, pp. 329-30.

[24] These rams are slaughtered and used to feed people for a special occasion.

[25] These yearlings had been wrongly categorised as females, and are now being properly categorised as hoggs, which are castrated yearlings. Yet this account follows the Priory's (unusual) policy of not recording hoggs separately from wethers, or distinguishing gerks from

Ewes. From remainder, 35. And he responds for 36 [*sheep*] moved up from gerks and hoggs this year, total 71.

Of which, expended in hospitality, 5. And in murrain, 3. And given to John Cade, 1. Total, 9. And remain, 62.

Hoggs. From remainder, 49. Of which, 36 moved up to ewes, as above. And moved up to wethers, as above, 13. Total, equals.

Lambs. From births of the ewes above, 6. Of which, 2 in murrain. And remaining, 4.

Total of all heads, 548. Of which, 63 rams, 419 wethers, 62 ewes, 4 lambs. <63 rams, 419 wethers, kept with the stock of the lord Prior 3 ewes with gerks, 4 lambs> The stockman certifies that they remain in the fold there to the end of this account.

Heigham [next to Norwich]. Account of Thomas Baxter, shepherd there, for the period aforesaid.

Tally. The same shepherd is charged by his tally from last year, 747. Of which:

Wethers. From remainder, 707. And bought from John Fissher by the Master [*Cellarer*], <102> *34*. And received from the fold of the lord in Thorpe Market *after shearing*, 80. Total, 821.

Of which, in murrain before shearing, 11. And in murrain after shearing, 10. And sold to Ed. Mechiller, 63. And sold by John Russell to John Plumpstede, 21. And remaining, 716. Of which, sold to John Fissher before shearing, 122. And deficient upon John Mayken, because not given to the shepherd, 1. And remaining, <713> 593.

Rams. From remainder, 40. And bought by the Master [*Cellarer*] from John Fissher, 21. And received from the fold of Thorpe Market after [*shearing*], 11. And in murrain after shearing, 3. And sold to Thomas Toly after shearing, 21. And remaining, 48.

Ewes. From remainder, nothing. But bought from John Fissher after shearing, 47. And sent to the fold of Eaton. And equals.

Manure. Nothing from anyone for manuring 30 acres of demesne land of the Abbey of St Benedict because by indenture and contract.[26] Nor from anyone for 20 acres of land manured on the demesne land of John Appilyerd, esquire, because in his contract and indenture. Nor from anyone or any other farmers, because nothing.

Cullet. From the stock of John Maykyn 42 wethers *3s. 6d.* 1 hogg *2d.*; John <Mathewe> *Sawer* 8 ewes *16d.* 2 rams *2d.* 4 hoggs *8d.*; Robert Colles, Walter Colles, Matilda Colles 40 wethers; Thomas Sturmyn

---

ewes. The following entry under ewes implies another error of categorisation, by recording more hoggs among ewes. See Introduction, p. 6.

[26] The Abbey of St Benet at Holm held land throughout Norfolk, *Victoria County History*, ii, pp. 330-36.

20 ewes *20d.* The said shepherd accounts for 50 wethers. Total 167. Of which, deducted because by contract, 80. And to account for cash, 87. Total money, beyond 3d. deducted by the auditor, 6s. 7d.
Total head remaining, 641. Of which, <713> 593 wethers, 48 rams.

Sedgeford. Account of Roger Wrask shepherd there for the year ending as above.
Tally. The same shepherd responds by the tally for last year's account, 632. Of which, remaining with the same shepherd, and also 60 ewes with the farmer. Of which:
Wethers. From remainder, 542. And received from Thorpe Market before shearing, 200. And received from Hindringham from lambs of the previous year moved up to wethers *before shearing*, 40. And received from Hindringham after shearing, 41. Total 823. Of which, in murrain before shearing, 43. And sold from old stock by the lord Prior to William Peresson of Holme, 10 at 12d. each *10s.* Total, 53. And remaining, 770. Of which, 69 [*belong to*] the lord [*Prior*], and 701 of the monastery.
Ewes. From remainder, 90. And remaining, 90. Of which 30 of the lord [*Prior*], 60 with the farmer.
Lambs. From births of the said 30 ewes of the lord Prior, 12, sold *6s* to Thomas Bullok by [?*John*] Maykyn for 6d. each. And equals.
Total head remaining, 860. Of which, 770 wethers, of which 69 of the lord Prior and 701 of the monastery. 90 ewes, of which 30 of the lord Prior, 60 with the farmer, now on the tally of the shepherd as within the ewes. Total stock remaining with the shepherd, beyond [*those with*] the farmer, 800. Of which, 701 of the monastery, 99 of the lord Prior.
Cullet. The same shepherd is charged for 360 wethers *30s.* at 1d. each; John Boteler 35 wethers *2s. 11d.*; John Maykyn 49 wethers *4s. 1d.*; John Russell 40 wethers *nothing*, because as contracted; John Russell 16 ewes *nothing*, 5 hoggs *nothing as contracted*; the said shepherd as contracted 120 ewes nothing; Thomas Falyate 40 wethers *3s. 4d.*; John Smyth 24 wethers *2s.*; Nicholas Rust 10 wethers *10d.*; Christine Sherman 7 wethers *7d.*; John Alman 13 wethers *13d.* [*Total*] 708, of which 44s. 9d. in money.
Manure. Nothing received from anyone in money for manuring with the lord's fold, beyond 85 acres assessed at 2s. per acre and thus valued at £8 10s., nothing because on the land from which the lord has taken the third sheaf of corn [*super terram unde dominus procepit [sic] terciam garbam*].
Allowance. For one barrel of bitumen, 4s. 4d.

DCN 64/1: 30 November 1492 to 30 November 1493. [*The membrane is torn down its left hand side*]

Newton. Account of Robert Howlyns, farmer there, from the feast of St Andrew the Apostle in the 8th year of King Henry VII [*30 November 1492*] through to the same feast thereafter, in the following year, the 9th year of the same reign of the King.

Wethers. From remainder, 429.

Of which, in murrain before shearing, 26, the pelts given to the stockman. And in murrain after shearing, 6. And given to the kitchen steward of the lord Prior before shearing, 1, the pelt remaining with the steward. And remaining, 396.

[*Ewes*]. Nothing to account, because with the lease. Memorandum, 32 belong to the lord.

[*Wethers of the lord Prior*]. From remainder, 174.

Of which, in murrain before shearing, 3, the pelts given to the Prior. And sold to Thomas Dey before shearing, 20 at 20d. per head *33s. 4d.*. And remaining, 151.

[*Ewes of the lord Prior*]. Nothing to account, because part of the same at lease. Total, nothing.

Stock. Thereof nothing, because the same exist as the stock of the lord pertaining to the farmer. Total, none.

Total head, 579.

Of which, 396 [*are*] wethers of the monastery, 151 ewes of the Prior, 32 ewes in the lease.

Sold thence by the monastery, nothing; 33s. 4d. the lord Prior.

[**Lathes**]. Account of Thomas Beny, shepherd there, for the aforesaid time.

Ewes [*from remainder*], 792.

Of which, in murrain before shearing, 20. In murrain after shearing, 9. And sold to William Giles of Stoke, 20, at 16d. each *26s. 8d.* And sent to the fold of Hindringham after shearing, 20. And remaining, 723. Thereafter, received from Lomnours after shearing, 180. And remaining, 903.

Wethers of the lord Prior. From remainder in the last account, 2. And remaining, 2.

Ewes of the lord Prior. From last year, 37. Of which, in murrain after shearing, 1. And remaining, 36.

[*Ms torn, but this is a new category of sheep*]. From remainder in the last account, 7, and in murrain after shearing, 3. And deficient sheep, 3 And remaining 1.

[*Ms torn*] From the flock of sheep charged upon Thomas Baxter at Eaton last year without tally, but afterwards [*ms torn*] deducted from the same shepherd, 3. And remaining, 3. Total, 4.

Total head, 945.

Of which, 2 [*are*] wethers of the lord Prior, 36 ewes of the lord Prior, 907 ewes of the monastery.

Cullet [*the manuscript is badly torn down both the left and right margins*]. Sheep for agistment. The contract of the shepherd accounts for 20, *[*for which*] nothing*. From the same for 2 ewes over and above [*the terms of the contract*] 2 *4d.*, Robert Narburgh, 5 ewes *10d.*, 4 lambs for the aforesaid current year *4d.* Robert Cook 9 ewes *18d.*, 4 lambs for half the year *4d.* Thomas Cook 8 ewes *16d.*, 3 lambs for half the year *3d.* David Martyne 4 ewes *8d.*, 2 lambs for half the year *2d.* [*forename missing*] Roper of Fibridge Street 5 ewes *10d.*, 2 lambs for half the year *2d.* Peter Tylney of Trowse ewes of [*Robert*] Bataly 6 *12d.*, 3 lambs for half the year *3d.* Walter Fere, farmer of the land of the lord Prior at [*place missing*] 2 *2d.* Master Bagot 31 ewes *6s. 2d.*, 6 lambs for half the year *6d.* [*ms torn*] 6 *12d.*, 3 lambs for half the year *3d.* William Calthorpe, knight, [*number and also forename missing*] Clere, squire, 11 ewes *22d.* Lady Joanne Blakeney by the tenure of John [*surname and short entry missing*] 44 ewes for the half year, nothing, because in the contract of the stockman, 3s. 8d. The Master Cellarer 10, for which *nothing*. Total 27s. 5d. Total head, 241.

Manure. Nothing for the 15 acres manured for the bailiff of Magdalene, because as of the contract for the land with this lease. Nothing for the 12 acres of manure for the farmers of Catton, because included within the contract. Beyond this, nothing received in cash for manure. There, and in respect of the hurdles, their use and times kept, nothing. Total, nothing.

Sale of sheep. For those of the monastery, 26s. 8d. For deficient sheep, 12d. For cullet, 27s.5d. For 8 deficient lambs, 5s. 4d.

[*Lambs*]. Born from all ewes, namely from 754 ewes of which 160 were barren, 594. Total clear, [*number missing*] and sent to Hethersett, 121. And sent to the fold at Hindringham, 458. [*an entry is missing*], 3. And in murrain, 3. And deficient by his own admission, 8. [*number and further details are missing*] sent to Hindringham. And thus equals.

Total head of sheep at Lathes, 946. Of which, 2 wethers of the lord prior, 36 ewes of the lord prior, total 38. Ewes of the monastery, 907, 1 small lamb of the monastery, total 908.

[**Lomnours**]. Account of Robert Rudkyn, shepherd there, for the afore-said time.

Ewes. From the remainder, 766. From the lambs elevated to gerks, 7. Total, 773.

Of which, in murrain before shearing, 16, and after shearing, 8. And sold to John Gosselyne before shearing, 31, at 11d. each *30s. 1d.*. [*one entry missing*] And remaining, 718. Sent to Lathes after shearing, 180. And remain, 538. And sent to the fold of Sedgeford *after shearing*, 240. And to the fold of Eaton *after shearing*, 160. And remain, 138. And sold after shearing to William Goodwyne, *medio*[27] of Bintree, 40 at 12d. each *40s.* And sold to William Roper, 20 at 11d. *18s. 4d.* And given to the wethers, because misallocated, 14. And remaining, 64. And deficient, 4. And remaining, 60.

Wethers. From those misallocated as ewes, 14 as above. And received from Sedgeford, 722. Of which, in murrain after shearing, 3. And remaining, 733.

Lambs. From remainder, nil. [*From the issue of 704 ewes*], of which 131 were barren, 573 lambs. Of which, paid as tithe, 49. Of the lord, remain 524. Of which allowed to the stockman by the auditor, and to the shepherd in the preceding, 3. [*one entry missing*]. And remain, 511 [*sic*]. Of which sent to the fold of Hindringham, [*sum missing*]. And sold to Rust of Mulbarton, 80 at 6d. each *40s.* And devoured by foxes, by the oath of the stockman, 3. And deficient, 3, each at 6d. And equals.

Manure. Thereof, nothing, because of the transfer of the flocks and remaining pasture from Postwick. Total, nothing.

Cullet. Thereof nothing beyond the contract of the shepherd. Total, nothing.

Thus the charge [*onus*] on the said Robert Rudkyn is placed upon [*transferred to*] William Albon by the tally.

Total head remaining, 793. Of which, 60 [*are*] ewes, 733 wethers.

The sale of sheep and lambs, £6 8s. 5d. for the lord. [*Robert*] Rudkyn [*for*] deficient lambs 18d., deficient sheep, 3s. 6d. Total, £6 13s. 5d.

DCN 62/18: 25th December 1495 to 25th December 1496.

Catton. Account of John Barsham, shepherd of the lord Prior, for the year ending at the feast of the Nativity of the Lord, in the 12th year of King Henry VII.

He responds for the tally. The same shepherd responds for receipts from Richard Isbelles, lately shepherd there, because remaining at the last account, 577. Of which:

Wethers and Ewes. From remainder, nothing. But received 60 *wethers* from the fold of Lomnours. And received from lambs of last year, of which wethers and ewes, 577. And received from the fold of Crouchstoke [*Stoke Holy Cross*], 239 *wethers*. Total head now, 876. Of which, sent to the fold of Cawston to agist there, 120 wethers. And sold to John Boteler of Caister next to Yarmouth, 50 *wethers* each 14d. *58s. 4d.* And in murrain, the

---

[27] *Medio*, perhaps meaning the middling sort or, more likely, the middle one of three with the same name, i.e. between senior and junior.

pelts thereof sent [*to a monastic official*], both wethers and ewes, 245. And sent to the ewe fold of Lathes, 140. Total given, 575. And remain, *of which 250 wethers, 71 ewes* 231.

Lambs. From remainder, none. But received from the fold of Lathes, 255. Of which, sold to Robert Stile of Bintree, 20 at 3½d. each *5s. 10d.* And remain, 235.

Total of all heads remaining there, 556. Of which, 250 wethers, 71 ewes, 235 lambs.

Memo for 3 wethers and 2 ewes, because they were taken and seized as stray [*extrahur'*] and given to the said shepherd by the stockman of the lord at the feast of the Annunciation of the Blessed Virgin Mary in the 11th year of the said King [*25 March 1496*] until the year and day aforesaid.

Stock of the lord Prior for himself.

Wethers. From remainder, 40. And received from last year's hoggs, 10. And remaining 50.

Ewes. From remainder, none. But received from last year's hoggs [*sic*], 10. And remaining, 10.

Lambs. From remainder, nothing. Nor anything received from births of the said ewes this year. But received from the fold of Lathes from stock of the lord, 10. And remaining, 10.

Issued as stray. To this account comes Catherine Robynson, widow, and by the testimony[28] *of Laurence Erle* she claims deprivation of five riggs coloured black, which were deemed stray and remained in the fold of Catton for 5 years. And because she claimed within the requisite timeframe, the same riggs are released to the same Catherine, [*who*] pays for pasture and agistment for the same time.[29]

Manure. But *through John Barsham* responds for 2s. received from John Keton senior for manuring of 1 acre of land manured twice [*duplicit'*]. And for 18d. received from Henry Isbelles for manuring 3 roods of land also manured twice. And for 6s. received from William Dyngle for manuring 3 acres of land also manured twice. And for 2s. received from Robert Heylesden for manuring 1 acre of land also manured twice. Total, 11s. 6d.

Memo for the preceding year. And through Richard Isbelles manuring 1 acre for John Keton senior at Catton, manured the Deles[30] once simply [*simplicit'*], 12d.

---

[28] The latin word is *testimon'*, translated here as testimony but it could also mean will.

[29] The lord enjoyed the privilege of claiming stray animals for himself. Marginal note: 'Agistment 2d. paid to the stockman who paid the lord'.

[30] 'Deles' is probably a local name for part of the open fields. It might possibly mean 'dole', a strip of land in the open fields, but this is not a very common East Anglian term.

Cullet. And for 5d. received from the agistment of 5 wethers of Henry Isbelles agisting there from the feast of the Nativity of St John the Baptist in the 11ᵗʰ year of King Henry VII to the end of this account [*24 June to 25 December 1496*], each 1d. And for 9d. received from the agistment of 9 lambs and ewes for the same term aforesaid, 9d. Total, 14d. Beyond this, the said shepherd has 20 as in his contract.

Cullet remaining in the fold there charged for the following year [anno futuro onerand'].
That is to say, lord Simon Lynne *4* lambs, Richard Fox *14* lambs, Simon Barker *2* lambs, paying for each head as aforesaid, 2d., 19.

Eaton. Account of Thomas Baxter, shepherd, for the term written within.
He responds for the tally. The same shepherd responds for the remainder from the preceding account, 1,056.
Ewes. From remainder, 1,056. And received from the fold of Hindringham, 120.
And received from the fold of Wood Norton, 105. Total head of sheep, 1,281. Of which, sent to the fold of Hindringham, 20. And sent to John Botolf of Hemsby, farmer there, 60. And sold to the Prior of Lynn, 200, 12d. each *£10*. And sold to Edward Magnes, 13 each 16d. *16s. 4d.* And through the lord given to Thomas Aleyn of Earlham, 12. And in murrain, the pelts thereof have been sent, 84. And deficient upon the said accountant because they were killed in the wood of the lord, 10 *8s. 4d. price per head [blank]*, as the accountant says. And remaining, 882.
Rams. From remainder, none. But received from the fold of Newton, 17. *And received from Thomas Sprotte, 6. Total, 23.* And remaining, 23.
Wethers. From remainder, none. But received from Thomas Sprotte, 59. Of which, sent to the fold of Wood Norton, 39. And in murrain, the pelts thereof sent, 18. And deficient upon the said accountant, 1, because as he says it strayed into the ditch of the castle of Norwich, whereupon Richard Brasier, sheriff of Norwich, seized and sold it. And remaining, 1.[31]
Lambs of this year. From births of the said ewes issued this year, 319. Of which, sent to the fold of Hindringham, 250. And sold to Robert Colles of Stibbard [?]Araughtes, 20 at 3½d. each *5s. 10d.* And sold to John Hille and Edmund Colles of Stibbard [?]Arahighte[32], 46 at 3½d. each *13s. 5d.* And given with the authority of the auditor to the stockman and the shepherd, 3. And equals.
Total of all head remaining there, 906. Of which, 23 rams, 1 wether, 882 ewes.
Memo, 60 with the farmer of Hemsby.

---

[31] Marginal note: 'Deficient, 1'.
[32] These probably refer to a manor within Stibbard.

Stock of the lord Prior for himself.
Ewes. From remainder, 94. And received from Hindringham after
shearing, 20. Total head, 114. Of which, in murrain, the pelts thereof sent,
6. And remaining, 108.
Lambs of this year. From births of the said ewes issued this year, 30, which
sent to the fold of Hindringham, and equals.

Manure. And manured for cash for Walter Colles, 2 acres *2s.*, for Robert
Steliard, 3 acres *3s. 2d.*, for Robert Long, 2 acres *2s. 4d.*. Total 7s. 6d.
Cullet given. And for 10d. received from William Grene for pasture of 20
ewes for the quarter ending at the feast of the Purification of the Blessed
Virgin Mary within the time of this account [*2 February 1496*] *½d. each*
And for 2s. 6d. received for agistment of ewes agisting there for one year
ending at the end of this account, for 2d. each, that is to say lord John
Felmyngham *10* for the light of St John, [*and*] William Halle *4*. Beyond
60 as contracted with the said shepherd. Total, 3s. 4d.

Hindringham. Account of John Dowdy, shepherd of the lord, for the year
ending at the Nativity of the Lord in the 12th year of King Henry VII [*25
December 1496*].
He responds for the tally. The same shepherd responds for the remainder from
the account of the preceding year, 831. Of which:
Ewes. From remainder, 40. And received from the fold of Eaton, 20. Total,
60. Of which, sold to Edmund Rust of Bintree, 16 each 10d. *13s. 4d.*,
which are stock of the lord. And in murrain, the pelts thereof sent, 19. And
remaining, 25.
Lambs of the preceding year. From remainder of lambs of the preceding year,
791.
Of which, sent to the fold of Cawston to agist there as wethers, 252. And
sent to the fold of Sedgeford as ewes, 100. And sent to the fold of Eaton as
ewes, 120. And sent to the fold of Sedgeford as rams, 13. And in murrain,
the pelts thereof sent, 306. And equals.
Lambs of this year. From remainder, none. But received from the fold of
Sedgeford, 429. And received from the fold of Eaton, 250. Total head
now, 679. And remaining, 679.
Total of all head there remaining, 704. Of which, 25 ewes, 679 lambs.
Manure. And for manure for Adam Mason, 1 acre *12d.*, John Meye 2
acres *2s.*, within the period of this account. Total, 3s.
Cullet given. And for 3s. 3½d. received from diverse [*people*] for agistment
which was between the term and Michaelmas last past, ½d. each, that is to
say, William Kyng *34*, Edward Aleyns *20*, Thomas Gregory *20*,
Thomas Lopham *3*, Richard Chapman *2*, beyond 50 as in the contract
of the said shepherd. 79, total money, 3s. 3½d.

Stock of the lord Prior for himself.
Ewes. From remainder, 10. And remaining, 10.
Wethers from lambs of the preceding year. From remainder of lambs from the preceding year, 40. Of which, in murrain, the pelts thereof sent, 4. And sent to the fold of Eaton after the shearing of the ewes, 20. And remaining wethers, 16.
Lambs of this year. From remainder, none. But from the fold of Eaton, 30. And remaining, 30.
Total head, 56, of which 16 wethers, 10 ewes, 30 lambs.

Between the Master [Cellarer] and the accountant. The same accountant is charged with his arrears from the last account, 30s. 10d. And for manure as above, 3s. And for cullet, as above, 3s. 3½d. Total, 37s. 1½d.
Of which, allowed to him for his stipend for one year finishing at the Nativity of the Lord next [*25 December*], except 8d. of which [*already*] received by him from the lord Prior, 10s. from the same through John Clerk, and 5s. through William Kerre for the sale of furze [*firres*]33, 36s. Also allowed to him for grease bought with bitumen, 16d. Total, 37s. 4d. And he owes. Item the same shepherd receives from the lord Prior beyond the account, 5s. 2½d. And thus *the shepherd* owes clear, 10s. [*sic*]

Newton. Account of Robert Howlynes, keeper of the sheep there [*custodis bercarii*] for the year ending at the Nativity of the Lord in the 12th year of King Henry VII [*25 December 1496*].
He responds for the tally. The same responds for the remainder of the preceding account, 453 wethers. And received from the fold of Intwood, 100. Total head now, 553. Of which, sold to the Cellarer, 40 at 16d. each *53s. 4d.* And given to the kitchen of the lord Prior, 7. And sent to the fold of Wood Norton, 19. And sent to the stockman, which remain in the close of the lord called Buttes in Newton, 3. And in murrain, the pelts thereof sent, 33. And in murrain in the close aforesaid, the pelts thereof are of no value because it is not possible to treat [*excoriar'*] them, 10. And sent to the fold of Eaton, because wrongly categorized as wethers and they are rams, 17. And remaining, 424.34
Total of all head remaining there, 424 wethers, beyond those remaining in the Buttes close, 3.

Stock of the lord Prior for himself.
Wethers. From remainder 181. And remaining, 181.

---

33 The furze would have been cut and sold from the heathland pastures on which the sheep grazed by day. Heath was a common feature of the medieval East Anglian landscape, and furze was sold as a hot, fast-burning, fuel, see Bailey, *Medieval Suffolk*, pp. 96–8.
34 Marginal note: 'Remain in the close'.

Manure and Cullet. Of which, nothing, because with the lease of the manor.

Plumstead. From remainder with Thomas Sprotte, 70 wethers. And received from stray, 1. Total 71. Of which, sent to Thomas Baxter at Eaton with six categorised as wethers and they are rams, 65. And in murrain, the pelts thereof sent, 2. And deficient upon the said Thomas Sprotte, 4, at 16d. each *5s. 4d.* And equals.[35]

Lathes. Account of Robert Long, shepherd of the lord there, for the year ending at the Nativity of the Lord in the 12th year of King Henry VII [*25 December 1496*].
He responds for the tally. Ewes. The same shepherd responds for the remainder from the account of the preceding *year*, 788. And received from the fold of Catton, 140. And received from the fold of Wood Norton, 60. Total head there, 988. Of which, sold to the Cellarer, *after shearing* 20 price of each 12d. *20s.* And sold to lord Geoffrey [*blank*] of Great Ryburgh, 40 each 10d. *33s. 4d.* And in murrain, the pelts thereof sent, 166. And deficient upon Thomas Beny, shepherd there in the preceding year through the reckoning [*per numeracionem*] of the stockman at the time when the flock was given to the said Robert Long, now the shepherd there, as testified by the stockman, 9, each 10d. *7s. 6d.*[36] And by the reckoning of the said stockman deficient upon the said Robert Long, now the shepherd, 5 each 10d. *4s. 6d.*[37] And remaining, 748.
Lambs. From births issuing from the said 748 ewes, beyond 480 barren, 268. Of which, given with the consent of the auditor to the stockman and shepherd as *Markynglambes*, 3. And sent to the fold of Catton, 265. And equals.
Total of all head there remaining, 748 ewes.

Stock of the lord Prior for himself.
Wethers. From remainder, 1. And remaining, 1.
Ewes. From remainder, 36. Of which, *after shearing* sold to Robert Stile of Bintree, 10, price of each 10d. *8s. 4d.* And remaining, 26.
Lambs. From births issued from the said ewes, beyond 26 barren, 10, which were sent to the fold of Catton. And equals.

Manure. And the same shepherd manured during the term of this account for the farmer of Magdalene, as contracted, 15 acres. And manured for others sold for money, nothing during the term of this account. Total in money, nothing.

---

[35] Marginal note: '4 deficient'.
[36] Marginal note: '9 deficient, 7s. 6d.'
[37] Marginal note: '5 deficient, 4s. 2d.'

Cullet. And for 7s. 4d. received for agistment of sheep by the said shepherd, beyond 50 in his contract, William Halle *2*, lord Simon Lynne *8*, Simon Barker *10*, Thomas Beny *6*, lord John Felmyngham for the light of St John *3 and 1 beast* agisting there for the whole year, price 2d. each. 7s. 4d.

Lomnours. Account of William Allon, shepherd of the lord Prior there, for the year ending at the Nativity of the Lord in the 12th year of King Henry VII [*25 December 1496*].
He responds for the tally. The same shepherd responds for the remainder from the preceding account, 860.
Wethers. And received from the fold of Intwood, 102. Total head now, 962. Of which, sent to the fold of Wood Norton under the custody of Thomas Martyns, 40. And sent to the fold of Catton, 60. And in murrain, the pelts thereof sent, 61, of which 10 in deficiency of the said shepherd, because he negligently drove them out of the close of Lomnours *into the ditch of the said close* and killed them, of which priced 16d. each.[38] And remaining, 801.
Total of all head remaining there, 801 wethers.

Stock of the lord Prior for himself.
Wethers. From remainder, none, but received from the fold of Intwood, 10. And remaining, 10.

Manure. Nothing charged for any manure in the term of the account in Freethorpe, because manured there through the shack[39] [*shaka*] *with the sheep aforesaid*. He is exonerated.
Cullet. Nor charged for anyone for cash, because no cullet there this year, beyond 40 as contracted with him [*i.e. the shepherd*].

Sedgeford. Account of Robert Mayne, shepherd there *for the last half of the year and Roger Wrask for the first half of the year, thus* responding through the stockman of the lord there, for the term aforesaid.
He responds for the tally. The same shepherd responds for the remainder from the account of Roger Wrask, lately shepherd there in the preceding year, 1,370. Of which:
Wethers. From remainder, 1. And remaining, 1.
Rams. From remainder, 43. And received from *the fold* of Hindringham, 13. Total head now, 56. Of which in murrain, the pelts thereof sent, 14. And remaining, 42.

[38] Marginal note: '10, 13s. 4d.'
[39] Shack is the period immediately after the harvest when the grain stubble on the open fields is made available for communal grazing.

Ewes. From remainder, 1,326. And *after shearing* received from the fold of Hindringham, 100. Total head now, 1,426. Of which, in murrain, the pelts thereof sent, 130. And deficient upon Roger Wrask, shepherd there for the first half of the year through the reckoning of the stockman at the time when the flock was given to the said Robert Mayne, 16 each 12d. *16s.*[40] And remaining, 1,280.

Lambs of this year. From births issuing from the said ewes this year, 484. Of which, given to the fold of Hindringham, 429. And sold to the said Robert Mayne, shepherd, 40 *draughtes*,[41] each 3½d. [*sic*] *11s. 8d.* And given as contracted [*as*] *Markynglambes*, 3. And in murrain, the pelts thereof sent, 8. And remaining, 4.

Total of all head there remaining, 1,327. Of which, 1 wether, 42 rams, 1,280 ewes, 4 lambs.

Manure. And manured for Richard Crispe for money in Chapelcroft in Sedgeford, 2 acres. Total, 2s.

Cullet. Thereof, nothing, beyond 80 in his contract there.

Cawston. *Wethers.* From remainder in the fold of Thomas Woodhous, esquire, none. But received from the fold of Hindringham, 252. And received from the fold of Catton, 120. And received from the fold of Intwood, 120. Total head, 492. And remaining, 492.

Intwood.

Wethers. From remainder, 363. Of which, sent to the fold of Cawston to agist there, 120. And sent to the fold of Newton, 100. And sent to the fold of Lomnours, 102. And in murrain, the pelts thereof sent, 41. And thus equals.

Stock of the Prior for himself.

Wethers. From remainder, categorized as ewes, 10, which wrongly categorized and they are wethers, and were sent to the fold of Lomnours. And equals.

Wood Norton. From remainder with Thomas Martynes, 364 called lambs. Of which, sent to the fold of Lathes after shearing, 60 ewes. And to the fold of Eaton, 105 ewes. And in murrain, the pelts thereof sent, 135. And deficient upon the said Thomas Martynes, 64 each 6d. *32s.*[42] And equals.

Wethers. From remainder, none. But received from the fold of Lomnours, 40. And received from the fold of Newton, 19. And received from the fold of Eaton, 39. Total head now, 98. And remaining, 98.

---

[40] Marginal note: 'deficient, 16'.
[41] Meaning unknown, but clearly lambs with particular characteristics.
[42] Marginal note: 'deficient, 64'.

Crouchstoke [*Stoke Holy Cross*].
Wethers. From remainder with William Giles there, 431. Of which, sent *after shearing* to the fold of Catton, 239. And in murrain, the pelts thereof sent, 46. And remaining 146.

DCN 62/19: 29 September 1496 to 29 September 1497.

Sedgeford. Account of John Carman, shepherd there, in the year ending at the feast of Michael the Archangel in the 13ᵗʰ year of King Henry VII [*29 September 1497*].
Wethers. From remainder, 1 *the account of Robert Mayne*. And remaining, 1.
Rams. From remainder 42, of which in murrain before shearing, 8. And sent to the fold of the lord in Fring, 34. And equals.⁴³
Ewes. From remainder, 1,280. Of which, in murrain before shearing, 37. And sold before shearing to John Pully of Foxley, 38 at 10d. each *23s. 4d.* And deficient upon Robert Mayne, 14 at 10d. each *11s. 8d.* Afterwards, he is charged with 4 gerks moved up from lambs of last year. <And received from Fring after shearing, because they were from Hindringham, 154>. And sent to the fold of Hindringham after shearing, 10. And remaining, 1,359.
Lambs. From remainder, nothing, because moved up. But from the issue of 1,211 ewes, 917. And barren, 294. Of which, in murrain, 42. And given to officials as contracted, 3. And sold to Richard Crispe of Fring, 62 at 4d. each, 20s., beyond 2 given [*as a tip*].⁴⁴ And sent to Fring, 480. And to Hindringham, 325. And deficient, 5. And equals.
Total head remaining, 1,360. Of which, 1 wether and 1,359 ewes.
Cullet. And 80 [*sheep*] of the said shepherd, nothing, because contracted. Total, nothing.
Manure. And manured with the flocks and folds aforesaid, 25 acres of Richard Crispe before the harvest and 15 acres afterwards, 12d. per acre before the harvest *10s.* and 16d. per acre afterwards *20s.* And for ½ acre of Robert Tyler manured, 8d. Total, 30s. 8d.
Total 30s. 8d, of which allowed for grease, *17d.*, for carriage of hurdles, *4d.*, [*total*] 21d. And he owes 28s. 11d. Of which, allowed to the same shepherd for his stipend for the quarter finishing at the Nativity of the Lord in the 13ᵗʰ year of the said King [*25 December 1497*], 13s. 4d. And he owes 15s. 7d. Of which, allowed for his expenses, 4d. And he owes, 15s. 3d.⁴⁵

⁴³ Marginal note: 'Fring'.
⁴⁴ Bulk purchases usually attracted a small discount from the vendor, who would provide some stock free of charge as a form of inducement: this was known as *advantagium*.
⁴⁵ Marginal note: 'Memorandum he owes for 5 deficient lambs, which the lord orders to be respited without charge [*dominus respectuari precipit sine onere*].

Lomnours. Account of Robert Hekelton, after the departure [*post recessum*] of William Albon, shepherd there, for the aforesaid time.

Wethers. From the remainder of the last account, 801. And received from Catton after shearing, 60. And received from Cawston after shearing, 470. Total, 1,331.

Of which, in murrain before shearing, 42. In murrain after shearing, 10. And sold to John Cob of Pulham before shearing, 130 at 16d. each *£8 13s.*, of which 6 given [*as a tip*]. And sold before shearing to John Medelton, 80, at 14d. each *£4 13s. 4d.* And sent to the fold of Fring after shearing, 120. And sold to William Thakker and Edward Maging before shearing, 122 at 16d. each and 2 given [*as a tip*] *£8*. And deficient, 9 at 16d. each.[46] Total discharged, 513.

And remaining, 818.

Cullet. Beyond 40 in the contract of the shepherd, nothing.

Manure. And manure for 2 acres of William Goodwyne *2s.* charged to William Albon. Total, 2s. And manure in the fields of Catton at the open time,[47] 1 acre of William Dyngle *12d.* And 2½ acres of John Keton senior *2s. 6d.*, and 1 acre of Henry Isbelles *12d.* Total 4s. 6d. charged to Robert Hekelton.

Crouchstoke [Stoke Holy Cross]. *Wethers*. And charged within the custody of William Giles, 146 wethers. Of which, sent to Eaton before shearing, 23. And in murrain before shearing, 92. And deficient, 31 at 16d. each.[48] And equals.

Wood Norton. *Wethers*. From remainder, 98. Of which, sent to the fold of Hindringham, 74. Of which, in murrain before shearing, 21. And deficient upon Thomas Barre, 3 at 16d. each.[49]

Cawston. *Wethers*. From remainder, 492. Of which, in murrain before shearing, 12. And to the fold of Lomnours, 470. And deficient upon the account of Richard shepherd of Thomas Wodehous esquire, 10. And equals.[50]

Hemsby. As in the preceding [*account*], 60 ewes.

Hindringham. As in the preceding [*account*], 60 ewes.

---

[46] Marginal note: '12s.'

[47] The open [*aperto*] time was the period of each year when common pasture rights applied to the open fields, usually lasting from the harvest to the late winter or early spring.

[48] Marginal note: '41s. 4d.'.

[49] Marginal note: '4s.'.

[50] Marginal note: '13s. 4d.'.

Sedgeford. With the lease of Richard Crispe and his fellow lessees [*sociis suis firmar'*] there, 60 ewes.

Eaton. Account of Thomas Baxter, shepherd there.
Wethers. From remainder, 1. And remaining, 1. And received from Stoke, 23. And remaining, 24.
Rams. From remainder, 23. And remaining, 23.
Ewes. From remainder, 882. Of which, in murrain before shearing 82. And in murrain after shearing, 19. And sent to the fold of the lord at Hindringham after shearing, 40. And remaining, 741.
Lambs. From remainder, none. But from births issuing this year from 800 ewes, 415 [*lambs*], beyond 385 barren [*ewes*]. Of which, sold to John Dussing of Kirkby, 82 at 4d. each *26s. 8d.* with two given [*as a tip*]. And sent to Hindringham, 266. And allowed to the official as contracted, 3. And remaining, 64.
Total head, 852. Of which, 24 wethers, 23 rams, 741 ewes, 64 lambs.
Cullet. From the custodian of the light of St John, 14 ewes, *2s. 4d.* From William Halle for 6 ewes, 12d. 16 ewes of Thomas Aleyn, nothing as leased. Total, 3s. 4d.
Manure. And manure for 10 acres of the said shepherd *10s.,* 1½ acres of Thomas Stulyerd *18d.* Total, 11s. 6d.
[*Grand*] total, 14s. 10d.

Distinct stock.[51]
Ewes. From remainder, 108. In murrain before shearing, 8. And remaining, 100.
Lambs. From remainder, nothing. But from the births of [*those*] 100 ewes, 60 issues, 40 barren. And remaining, 60.
Total, 160.

Lathes. Account of Robert Long, shepherd there, for the time aforesaid to the year ending at the feast of Michael the Archangel in the 13th year of King Henry VII [*29 September 1497*].
Ewes. From remainder, 748. And received from Catton after shearing, 71. And received from Catton *after shearing* from lambs there, now categorized as ewes, 100. Total, 919. Of which, in murrain before shearing, 34. In murrain after shearing, 60. And sold to John Cobbe of Pulham after shearing, 10, each 10d. *6s. 4d.* And sold to lady Townesend[52] after shearing, 120, each 10d. *100s.* Total discharged, 224. And deficient in

[51] Distinct from the other sheep, i.e. belonging to the Prior.
[52] Eleanor Townshend, widow of Roger, who after his death retained a direct interest in sheep farming. The Townshends occasionally bought stock from the Priory, although these large quantities were highly unusual: see Moreton, *Townshends*, pp. 19-21, 164, 184-5, 237.

his hands 3, each 10d.[53] And driven off [*effugantur*] by John Staunford lately of North Elmham, butcher, with other sheep of his to Hevingham, 2. And remaining, 690, and recompensed because deficient at Catton, 20. And remaining, *he owes 1 at Catton*, 671.

Lambs. From remainder, nothing. But from births of 709 ewes, issuing 469 [*lambs*]. And 240 [*ewes*] barren. And sold to John Cobbe, 122 at 6d. each *60s. with 2 given in the price*. And sold to Ed. Colles, 90 at 4d. each with 1 given [*as a tip*]. And sent to the fold at Hindringham, 144. And to the official as contracted, 3. And remaining, 110. Memo that 1 after shearing charged on Catton.

Total of all head, 781.

Cullet. And from lord Simon Lynne 10 *20d.*, Thomas Bene 7 *14d.*, Roger Porter 4 *8d.*, Walter Fyme 5 *5d.*, William Haugh 3 *6d.*, and 50 of the said shepherd, nothing because as contracted, from John Foxe *marbeler* [54] 12 *2s.*. Total, 91. And the total remaining, 6s. 10d.

Manure. And manured for the farmer of Magdalene, as contracted, 15 acres *nothing*. And 1 acre of the said shepherd *12d.*. Total, 12d.

Stock of the lord Prior for himself. As in the preceding [*account*], 1 wether, 26 ewes, 14 lambs of this year. Total 41.

The lord with his papers [*papiris suis*] and the said Robert Long account for the two years preceding before the end of this account, and on the feast of St Lucy the Virgin in the 13th year of King Henry VII [*13 December 1497*] there, Robert Long is quit and he is paid for his stipend until the feast of the Nativity of the Lord and for the same quarter.

Newton. Account of Robert Hewlynes, keeper of all sheep there, for the aforesaid time.

Wethers. From remainder, with 3 in the close [*called*] Buttes, 427. And received from Catton after shearing, 70. Total, 497.

Of which, in murrain before shearing, 20. And in murrain after shearing, 18. And sold to lady Townesend[55] after shearing, 120, at 14d. each *£7*. And sold to John [?]Tuesdon after shearing, 40 at 16d. each *53s. 4d.* And sent to the kitchen before shearing, 4. Total, 202. And remaining, 295, with 8 in the Buttes close.

Distinct stock of the lord Prior. Wethers. From remainder, 181. And received from the fold of Catton, 50. Total head, 231. Of which, sold to John

---

[53] Marginal note: '2s. 6d.'
[54] Dealer or worker in marble.
[55] Eleanor widow of Roger Townshend.

Medilton among others before shearing, 40 at 14d. each *46s. 8d.* And remaining, 191.

Catton. Account of John Barsham, who is shepherd there for the first half of this year.
Wethers. From remainder, 250. Of which, in murrain before shearing, 120, of which killed by dogs [*blank*]. And sent to the fold of Newton after shearing, 70. And sent to Lomnours, 60. And equals.
Lambs. From remainder, 235. Of which, sent to Lathes, 100 moving up to gerks. And in murrain, 112. And sent to Lomnours after the tally there, 2 *wethers*. And to Lathes after the tally of ewes, 1. And in murrain, because confirmed by the testimony of the stockman, 3. And deficient, 37, with 20 received from the stock of the lord Prior, [*total*] 57, of which sent to Lathes, 20, and thus net deficient, 37. And equals.

Stock of the lord Prior.
Wethers. 50. And sent to Newton. And equals.
Ewes. From remainder, 10. Lambs, now gerks, 10. And sent to Lathes, and equals.

DCN 64/4. 25th November 1499 to 25th November 1500

Hindringham. Account of John Sparhauk, shepherd there, from the feast of St Catherine the Virgin in the 15th year of King Henry VII [*25 November 1499*], through to the same in the next year following, in the 16th of the reign of the same King. And in the 12th year of lord William Spynk, Prior.
Tally. The same received by his tally from last year, 843. Of which:
Wethers. Item, from remainder, 6. And received from hogg lambs of last year after shearing, 114. Total, 120. And sent to the fold of Fring, 120.[56]
Ewes. From remainder, 55. Of which, sold to William Wadker, 41 *26s. 8d.* And in murrain after shearing, 14. Remaining, nothing.[57]
Lambs born last year. From remainder, 782.
Of which, 114 hoggs sent as above to Fring. And of the young gerks sent to Sedgeford after shearing, 80. And of older gerks sent to Newton after shearing, 150. And older gerks from the same sent to Eaton after shearing, 255. And in murrain, both before and after shearing, 116. And remaining, 42 [*sic*]. Of which, [*sum missing*].[58]
Crone Ewes. Afterwards received from Sedgeford after shearing, 80. And

---

56 Marginal note: 'Fring to respond for 120'.
57 Marginal note: 'Sold, 41'.
58 Marginal note: 'Sedgeford to respond 80, Newton to respond 120, Eaton to respond 255'.

received from Lathes after shearing, 45. And remaining, [*sum missing*].
Lambs of this year. From those born this year, 403. Received from Lathes afterwards, 507. And received from Eaton after shearing, 340, both male and female. And remaining, [*sum missing*].
Total, 1,014. Of which, 10 wethers, 32 ewe stock, 125 ewes, 847 lambs for hoggs and gerks.
Cullet. Beyond the shepherd and the stockman, total nothing.
Manure. And for manure for John Clerk, 4 acres *4s.*. William Barsham, 1 acre *12d.*. John Mey, ½ acre *6d.*, Thomas May, 1 acre *12d.*. Total, 6s. 6d.

The shepherd is to be charged. And owed to the said shepherd for his stipend for the quarter ending at the Nativity of the Lord forthcoming [*25 December 1500*], 11s. 8d. Of which, charged against him for the manure, as above, 6s. 6d., and [*thus*] owed for his wages, 5s. 2d. And for [*purchases of*] grease [*pro sepo unction'*] this year, 20d., for which the said John has paid. And thus owed to the shepherd at the said Nativity of the Lord, 6s. 10d., which *lord* Robert Watts, the new Master of the Cellar, paid on the morrow of [*the feast of*] St Catherine [*26 November*].

Fring. Account of Robert Mayne, shepherd there, according to the response by Thomas Mey, the shepherd last year, just as the stockman has accounted with him [*prout staurarius cum computante comput'*].
Tally. The same accountant is charged of the tally of Thomas May this year, 1,227. Of which:
Rams. From remainder, 34. And hitherto remaining, 34.
Wethers. From remainder, 1,193.
Of which, in murrain before shearing during May's time, 8. And received from Hindringham after shearing, 120. And remaining, 1,285 [*sic*].
Total head, 1,319. Of which, 34 rams, 1,285 wethers.
Manure. And 15s. received from Richard Crisp for manuring by the fold, with hurdles included there, earning £2 cash gross, nothing here because in the account of the Master [*Cellarer*]. Total, as appears in the account of the Master Cellarer.
Cullet. For the cullet of wethers there, namely from John Fawkener, 126 wethers *15s.* for the half year ending at the time of this account, 1½d. per head. And the other half to be accounted at the next shearing to the benefit of the new Master Cellarer. Nothing for the 80 sheep for the shepherd's contract, nor for the stock of the stockman, because not charged out of custom, nothing. But for the agistment of Thomas May, 40 *6s. 8d.,* at 2d. each for the whole year to the end of this account. Of which, given [*ms torn*] to the Master [*ms torn*].

Sedgeford. Account of the said Robert Mayne, shepherd, responding with the stockman there for the aforesaid time.

The same responds by the tally of John Browne, the shepherd there from the previous year, 1,396. Of which:

Wethers. From remainder of last year, 1 *12d.*. And sold to Robert Browne, and equals.

Ewes. From remainder, 1,374.

Of which, sold after shearing to the said Robert, 19 at 12d. each *19s.* And in murrain before shearing, 48. And in murrain after shearing, 22. And sent to the fold of Hindringham after shearing, 80 crones. And received from Hindringham from gerks after shearing, 80. And remaining, 1,285. Thereof, deficient upon John Broun above mentioned, given for the work of the present shepherd, 4 at 10d. each *3s. 4d.*.

And allocated from the gerk lambs of last year, 5. And remaining, 1,286.[59]

Lambs from last year. From remainder, 21. Of which, sold to William Elsy after shearing, 16 *5s. 4d.*. And allocated to the ewes, above, 5. And equals.

Lambs. Item, from the issue of ewes, as above, 836.

Of which, sold to Robert Brown, 824 at 4d. each *£13 14s. 8d.*. And given for *merkinglams* as contracted, 3. And remaining, 9.

Cullet. From the stock of the shepherd, 100 as contracted, nothing. But 20 from foreign agistments for the year to the end of this account, 20d., 1d. each. Of which, given [ms torn] Master [ms torn].

Manure. From manure, for 24 acres of land manured for Richard Crispe, 12d. per acre, of which 20 acres *20s.* before Michaelmas [29 September] and 4 acres *4s.* after Michaelmas to the new Master Cellarer, for the acres as above 24s. Of which, given [sum missing].

Total head remaining, 1,295. Of which, 1,286 ewes, 9 lambs.

Lathes. Account of Robert Hekelton for the aforesaid time there.

Tally. The same received by his tally from last year, 781. Of which:

Ewes. From remainder from last year, 769. Of which, sent to Hindringham after shearing, 45. And received from Newton before shearing, 120. And from there after shearing, 31. And in murrain, both before and after shearing, 26. And sold to Ed. Godwyn, 1 *12*. And sold to Robert Hides, 1 *10d.* And deficient, for [? indecipherable word], 20 *20d.* And in murrain after shearing, the pelt lost according to the accountant, 1. And remaining [sum missing].

Hoggs and gerks from the lambs of last year. From remainder, 12. Of which, sent to Newton before shearing, 8. And sold to Thomas Denham, 4 weak sheep *12d.* And equals.

[59] Marginal note: 'Received from Hindringham, sent to Hindringham'.

Lambs. Item, from the issue of the aforesaid ewes, 570.
Of which, sent to Hindringham, 507. And sold to John Stacy, 60 at 4d.
each *20s*. And given for marking annually as contracted, 3. And equals.
Total head remaining, 826.
Manure. Nothing beyond the 15 acres manured for the farmers of St
Magdalene as contracted, nothing.
Cullet. From the agistment of the stock leased, that is to say for the whole
time of this account, 2d. each, above and beyond the 60 contracted with
the shepherd, 34 ewes *5s. 8d.*. Of which, to the lord for 3 quarters, 4s.
3d. To the Master Cellarer for 1 quarter, 17d.

DCN 62/22: 25 December 1504 to 25 December 1505.

Thorpe Episcopi next to Norwich. The account of John Gladon, shepherd there, from the feast of the Nativity of the Lord in the 20th year of
King Henry VII [*25 December 1504*] by John Bronde, stockman, as deputy
[*deputatum*] of the said John Gladon and Walter Ball, shepherd there from
the feast of Epiphany [*6 January 1505*] of the Lord in the year abovesaid
until the feast of the Annunciation of the Blessed Virgin Mary next
following [*25 March 1505*] for a quarter of one year.
He responds for the tally of ewes. The same stockman responds for the
remainder from the preceding account on behalf of the aforenamed John
Gladon, 620. Thereof, in murrain, 6, of which the pelts sent to John
Bronde, stockman. And deficient, 1. And remaining now, as above, 613.
Thereof, sent to the aforesaid Walter Balle as the said stockman is satisfied
he received, as above 613. Of which, deficient, 1. And remaining there
now, 612.

The account of John Sweth, shepherd there, from the feast of the
Annunciation of the Blessed Virgin Mary in the 20th year[60] of King Henry
VII [*25 March 1505*] until the feast of the Nativity of the Lord next
following in the same year of the reign of the said lord King, 21 [*25
December 1505*].
He responds for the tally of ewes. The same shepherd responds for the
remainder as above, 612. And received from the fold of Hindringham at
the feast of Michael the Archangel [*29 September*], 60 ewes. Total head now,
672. Thereof, sent to the kitchen of the convent on the order of the Master
Cellarer at the feast of Peter *ad vincula* [*1 August*], 10. And in murrain before
shearing, 6, the pelts thereof sent. And in murrain after shearing, 19, the
pelts thereof sent to the stockman. And remaining there now, 637. Of

---

[60] The manuscript states the *21st* year, but this is a scribal error.

which, deficient upon the shepherd there, 5 ewes, price per head *12d.* total 5s. And remaining there now, 632.

Lambs of this year. From births of the aforesaid ewes arrived this year, beyond 10 other lambs delivered, 358. Of which, allowed for *Markynglammes*, as contracted as [*noted*] in preceding [*accounts*], 3. And in murrain, 20, the pelts thereof sent to the stockman. And there remaining, 335. And sent to the fold of Hindringham at the feast of Michael the Archangel [*29 September*], 335, and thus equals.

Total head of sheep there now remaining, 632 ewes.

Cullet. Also for agistment of 60 ewes of John Heylesdon of Catton from the Nativity of St John [*24 June*] to the feast of the Nativity of the Lord [*25 December*] for one half year, price per head *1d.* total 5s., beyond 40 ewes as contracted with the shepherd for the aforesaid time. Total 5s.

Manure. And the said shepherd and sheep aforesaid manure 2 acres of land of Nicholas Pampyng *2s.*, and 2 acres of Robert Wryght *2s.* after the feast of St Faith [*6 October*], [*total*] 4s.

Total, of which Nicholas Pampyng paid 12d. to the stockman. And Robert Wryght paid the same shepherd 2s., and the 12d. residue due from Nicholas Pampyng is assigned to the said shepherd.

Between the Master Cellarer and the said shepherd on 26 November in the 21st year of King Henry VII [*1505*]. The said shepherd is charged with 5s. as the price of 5 ewes deficient upon the said shepherd. And he is charged 5s. for cullet. And 4s. for manure, and for 12s. 8d. received from the Master Cellarer for part of his stipend at the feast of Peter in chains [*1 August*] last past. Total charge, 26s. 8d. Of which, he is allowed for [*his stipend*] for two quarters of one year finishing at the feast of All Saints in the 21st year of King Henry VII [*1 November 1505*], 23s. 4d. Total discharged, 12d. And thus the shepherd owes 2s. 4d., which remains in the hands of John Bronde, stockman, and accounted within other accounts between the Master Cellarer and the stockman.

Memo that John Sweth, the aforementioned shepherd, presented himself on 7 February in the 21st year of King Henry VII [*1506*] in the presence of William Elsy, auditor, John Bronde, stockman, and John Jurdon: the said shepherd had 7 deficient ewes [*charged*] upon him from the time of his last account to this day, price per head 12d. *7s.* because the payments are blocked [*obstupantur*] by the hand of the lord on 7 February. And Lord Robert, Prior, paid the said shepherd on the said 7 February the blocked 7s. in full payment of his stipend for one quarter of a year finishing at the feast of the Purification of the Blessed Virgin Mary last past [*2 February 1506*]. And Master George Hyngth, Master Cellarer, paid the said shepherd on the said 7 February 3s. 4d. for his livery for the year ending at the feast of St Michael in the 21st year of King Henry VII [*29 September 1505*].

Thorpe Episcopi. Account of John Hekylton, shepherd there,[61] from the feast of the Nativity of the Lord in the 20th year of King Henry VII to the said feast next following in the 22nd year of the same lord King [*25 December 1504 to 25 December 1505*]. And the first year of lord Robert Catton, Prior.

He responds for the tally. The said shepherd responds for the remainder from the preceding account, 526, of which:

Wethers. From remainder, as above, 526. And received from the fold of Hindringham, 52. Total head now 578. Thereof, given to the kitchen of the monastery on the order of the Master Cellarer, at that time in the office of Cellarer, for the harvest, 20. And in murrain, 17, the pelts thereof sent to the stockman. And deficient upon the shepherd there by the reckoning of the stockman, 1 priced 16d. And given to the Cellarer of the monastery, by order of the Master Cellarer, 120. And there remaining now there, 420.[62]

Wethers. Received from the fold of Sprowston by the gift of John Bronde, stockman, 7. And remain, 7.

Total head of sheep there now remaining, 427. Of which, the stock of the monastery, 420 and 7 of the Master Cellarer.[63]

Cullet. Also for agistment of 60 ewes, as contracted with the shepherd for the time aforesaid nothing in cash. But he responds for the agistment of foreign stock, that is from John Botolf *10s.* for one whole year to the feast of the Nativity of the Lord in the 21st year of King Henry VII [*25 December 1505*] for 120 wethers, price for each for the whole year, 1d. And from Robert Harrydaume *4s.* from the feast of the Nativity of John the Baptist in the 20th year of King Henry VII [*24 June 1505*] to the feast of the Nativity of the Lord in the 21st year of King Henry VII [*25 December 1505*], that is for half one year. Total, 14s.

Manure. And the aforesaid shepherd with the aforesaid sheep manured certain lands of Robert Benet in the vills of Freethorpe, Limpenhoe and Southwood from the feast of St Matthew the Apostle in the 21st year of King Henry VII [*21 September 1505*] to the 10th December following,

---

[61] There are two flocks at Thorpe run independently by two shepherds, hence two separate accounts.

[62] Marginal note: 'Memo that 7 wethers pertaining to the office of Cellarer received from Sprowston.'

[63] The original has 540, which is a scribal error: CCCC^ma has been written rather than CCC^ma.

paying gross for the said lands with all the aforesaid manure, beyond the board [*super mensam*] of the shepherd, 5s.8d. Total, 5s. 8d.

Between the Master Cellarer and the said John Hekylton on 11th December in the 21st year of King Henry VII [*1505*]. The shepherd is charged for the price of 1 wether, deficient on the same as above, 16d. Item, for manure, as above, 5s. 8d. Total charge, 7s.
Item, the shepherd claims for the arrears of his stipend for the half year finishing at the Nativity of the Lord in the 21st year of King Henry VII [*25 December 1505*], 23s. 4d. Total claims of the said shepherd, 23s. 4d. Of which, held back as above for one wether, *16d.* deficient on the same. And for manure *5s. 8d.* paid to the same by the aforesaid Robert Benet. Total paid and allowed, 7s. And thus owed to the said shepherd, 16s. 4d., which is paid to the said shepherd in the presence of John Bronde, stockman, and John Gebon on 11th December in the 21st year of King Henry VII [*1505*].

Hindringham. The account of John Laxe, shepherd there, for one whole year ending at the feast of the Nativity of the Lord in the 21st year of the King Henry VII [*25 December 1504 to 25 December 1505*].
[*A large section is crossed out at the head of this account as follows:*] <He responds for the tally. The same shepherd responds for the remainder of the last account, 762. Of which:
Ewes. From remainder, 36. Of which <<sent to>> in murrain, 2, the pelts thereof sent to the stockman *before shearing*. And sent to the fold of Sedgeford, 6. And in murrain after shearing, the pelts thereof sent to the stockman, 2. And deficient upon the said shepherd, 2. And from lambs of last year, which are now moved up to ewes, 526. And received from the fold of Lathes, 6, called crones, at the feast of St Michael [*29 September*]. And remain there, 24.
Wethers. From remainder, 28. Of which, in murrain, 8, the pelts thereof given to the stockman. And sent to the fold of Thorpe, 20. And equals.
Lambs of last year. From remainder, 698, which were moved up to ewes *526 ewes, 172 wethers.* Of which, sent to the fold of Sedgeford, 121. And to the fold of Gnatingdon, 185. And to the fold of Lathes, 60. And to the fold of Thorpe, 60. And to the fold of Eaton, 120. And to the fold [*blank*].
The same shepherd responds for the remainder of last year's account of ewes, 762. And for lambs of last year moved up to ewes, 526. Total head now [*blank*]>

He responds for the tally. The same shepherd responds for the remainder of the last account, 762. Of which:
Ewes. From remainder, 36. And from lambs of last year which are now moved up to ewes, 526. And received from the fold of Lathes, 6, called

crones, at the feast of St Michael [*29 September*]. Total head now, 568.
Of which, sent to the fold of Thorpe under the custody of John Sweth, 60.
And to the fold of Lathes, 60. And to the fold of Gnatingdon, 121. And to
the fold of Sedgeford, 205. In murrain before shearing *92* the pelts
thereof sent to the stockman. And remaining there, 30.

Wethers. From remainder, 28. And from last year's lambs, 172. Total head
now 200.
Of which, delivered to the fold of Thorpe Episcopi under the custody of
John Hekylton, 52. And to the fold of Eaton, 120. And in murrain, 22, the
pelts thereof sent to the stockman. And deficient upon the shepherd, 6,
each 12d. *6s.* And equals.

Lambs of this year. From births of the said ewes issued this year, 22. And
received from the fold of Thorpe under the custody of John Sweth, 330.
And received from the fold of Lathes, 489. Total head, 841. Of which, sent
to the fold of Sedgeford *at the feast of St Michael* [*29 September*], 187.
And allowed for *Markynglammes*, as contracted as [*noted*] in preceding
[*accounts*], 3. And remaining there, 651, of which stock of the monastery,
41, [*and*] of the lord Prior, 10.
Total head of sheep there now remaining, <681> 700. Of which, 30 ewes,
<651> 670 lambs, of which 660 of the monastery <41>, lord Prior 10.

Cullet. Also for agistment of 24 ewes *2s.*of Simon Mason, price for each
from the shearing to the Nativity of the Lord [*25 December*], 1d. And 60
ewes *5s.* of John Smyth for the same time, beyond 60 as contracted with
the shepherd for the same time. Total 7s.

Manure. And the said shepherd with the said sheep manure 4 acres for
Robert Quarle, farmer of the manor there *4s.*, price per acre 12d. And
Thomas Large 1 acre *12d.* And Adam Mason, 2 acres 2s.
Total, 7s., of which paid by Adam Mason at the Nativity of the Lord [*25
December*] to the same John for manure, 2s. And thus he owes 5s.

Between the Master Cellarer and the said shepherd, 27 November in the 21st
year of King Henry VII.
The same shepherd is charged for 6 hoggs, deficient upon him as above,
4s. And with 5s. for manure, as above. And with 3s. 4d. for part of his
stipend at the court held in Lent. *And with 3s. 4d. received after the court
in Lent*. And with 17d. received from John Wyldegrice for half a bushel of
green peas *priced 5d.* and one bushel of maslin *8d.* and one bushel of
forder[64] *4d.* And with 3s. 7d. received from the stockman at Pentecost [*11
May 1505*]. And with 5s. received from the Master Cellarer at the court of
St John.[65] And with 2s. received from Adam Mason at the feast of the

[64] A fodder crop to feed animals, probably oats or peas.
[65] I.e. the manorial court held around the feast of St John. This is probably the Nativity of
St John the Baptist, 24 June, rather than St John the Apostle, 27 December.

Nativity of St John the Baptist [*24 June*] for manure of 2 acres. And with 8s. 8d. received from the Master Cellarer after the feast of St Michael [*29 September*]. And with 20d. received from William Elsy at the court [*held on the feast of*] St Matthew in the 21ˢᵗ year of King Henry VII [*21 September 1505*].

Total charged 38s. The same shepherd claims allowance for his stipend for one whole year ending next Christmas, 46s. 8d. And he claims for grease called *swine alias gresse* 16½d. Total claimed, 48s. ½d. Of which, charged as above, 38s. And thus it is owed clear to the said shepherd beyond the livery here now allowed, 10s. ½d., which is paid in the account by the hand of William Elsy, in the presence of the Master Cellarer, William Faryby, Nicholas Parker of Pockthorpe, John Dowson of Hemsby and others, the 28ᵗʰ of November in the year above said.

Lathes. The account of John Bronde, shepherd there, from the feast of the Nativity of the Lord in the 20ᵗʰ year of King Henry VII to the feast of the Nativity of St John the Baptist next following [*25 December 1504 to 24 June 1505*].

He responds for the tally. The same shepherd responds for the remainder of the preceding account, 810. Of which:

Ewes. From remainder, 810. Of which, sent to the monastery at the feast of the Annunciation of the Blessed Virgin Mary [*25 March*] to the office of Cellarer of the monastery of Norwich, 15. And sent to the Cellarer at the feast of the Finding of the Holy Cross [*3 May*], 20. And in murrain before shearing, 15. And remain there, 760. And the said shepherd found one ewe, out of three ewes [*charged*] upon him as deficient in the year before. And there remaining there now, 761.[66]

Lambs of this year. From births of the ewes issued this year, 542. Of which, sent to the kitchen of the monastery, 35. And remaining, 507.

Total head of sheep now, 1,268. Of which, 761 ewes, 507 lambs.

The account of Richard Deynes, shepherd there, from the feast of the Nativity of St John the Baptist in the 20ᵗʰ year of King Henry VII to the feast of the Nativity of the Lord in the 21ˢᵗ year of the aforesaid King [*24 June 1505 to 25 December 1505*].

He responds for the tally. The same Richard responds for the tally as above, 1,268. Of which:

Ewes. From remainder, 761. And received from the fold of Hindringham, 60. Total head now 821. Of which, sent to the fold at Hindringham, 6. And in murrain, 30, the pelts thereof sent to the stockman. And deficient upon the shepherd, 4 price per head 12d. *4s.* And there remaining there, 781.

---

[66] Marginal note: 'Now found 1 from deficient in the year before'.

Lambs of this year. From remainder as above, 507. Of which, sent to the fold of Hindringham at the feast of Michael the Archangel [*29 September*], 489. And in murrain, 15. And he is allowed for *Markynglammes*, as contracted, 3. And thus equals.
Total head of sheep of the stock of the monastery there remaining, 781.

Memo of the stock of the lord Prior, ewes. Under the custody of the shepherd there of the stock of the lord Prior, 22.

Total head of sheep now remaining, 803. Of which, stock of the monastery, 781, and of the lord Prior, 22.
Manure. And the aforesaid shepherd with the sheep flock aforesaid for the time of this account manured 15 acres for Edmund Payn, the bailiff of Magdalene, as contracted with the same bailiff for manure. From other manuring sold for money this year, nothing. Total, nothing.
Cullet. Also for agistment of 60 [*sheep*] as contracted with the shepherd in the preceding [*accounts*], nothing in money. But from the cullet of foreign sheep[67] agisting there, that is to say from the stock of Edmund Payn, 35 ewes *2s.11d. paid because as the stockman said* for the half year ending at the Nativity of St John the Baptist in the 20th year of King Henry VII [*24 June 1505*], beyond the account made at the Nativity of the Lord for the preceding account; from lord John Syblye 13 ewes *13d.* 2 lambs *2d.* for half a year from the feast of the Nativity of St John the Baptist last past [*24 June 1505*]. Total, 4s. 2d.

Between the Master Cellarer and the said shepherd, 29 November in the 21st year of King Henry VII [*1505*].
The same shepherd is charged with the price of 4 ewes, on the same shepherd deficient, 4s. And with 20d. received from the Master Cellarer at the feast of St Faith last past [*6 October 1505*]. And for cullet of the stock of lord John Syblye for one whole year [*sic*] ending at the feast of the Nativity of St John the Baptist last past [*24 June 1505*], 2s. 2d.
Total charged, <5s. 8d.> 7s. 10d.
The same shepherd claims for his stipend for one half year ending at the Nativity of the Lord in the 21st year of King Henry VII [*25 December 1505*], 23s. 4d. Total claimed, 23s. 4d.
From which, allowances and payments as above, <5s. 8d.> 7s. 10d. And thus it is owed to the said shepherd, 15s. 6d. Of which, paid to the same shepherd by the hand of William Elsy on the vigil of St Andrew [*29 November*] in full payment of his stipend for the term ended at the feast of St Michael the Archangel in the 21st year of King Henry VII [*29 September*

---

67 Foreign sheep, in the sense of the sheep of outsiders.

1505], 3s. 10d. And paid to the same shepherd by the hand of William Elsy around the feast of the Nativity of the Lord [*25 December*] for the term ending at the Nativity of the Lord, 11s. 8d.

Gnatingdon.[68] The account of Nicholas Rust, shepherd there, from the feast of the Nativity of the Lord in the 20th year of King Henry VII to the feast of the Nativity of the Lord in the 21st year of King Henry VII [*25 December 1504 to 25 December 1505*].
He responds for the tally. The same shepherd responds for the remainder of the preceding account, 1,261. Of which:
Ewes. From remainder, 986. And received from the fold of Hindringham, 121. Total head now, 1,107.
Of which, sent to the fold of Newton, 112 wethers from the above remainder, because wrongly categorised. And sold to Alan Smyth, 20 ewes called crones, priced 8d. each *13s. 4d.* And in murrain before shearing, 24, the pelts thereof sent to the stockman. And in murrain after shearing, 29, the pelts thereof sent to the stockman. And remaining there, 922.
Lambs of last year. From remainder, 240. Because [*these were*] moved up to ewes, therefore there remain now, 1,162.
Rams. From remainder, 35. In murrain, 7, the pelts thereof sent to the stockman. And remaining, 28.
Lambs of this year. From births of the ewes issued this year, 810. Of which, sent to the kitchen there at the court [*held on the*] feast of the Nativity of St John the Baptist [*24 June*], 1. Sent to the fold of Sedgeford under the custody of Robert Loon, 806. And he is allowed for *Markynglammes*, as contracted, 3. And thus equals.
Total head of sheep there now remaining, 1,190. Of which, 1,162 ewes, 28 rams.

Memo of the stock of the lord Prior. Under the custody of the said Nicholas for the stock that was lately of Richard Walsyngham, Master Cellarer, 8. Of which, 1 wether, 5 ewes, 2 lambs one of this year.

Manure. And the said shepherd with the said sheep manured for Richard Crysp for the time written a minimum of 60 acres granted to the said Richard, paying for the same manure as part of the farm of the manor of Gnatingdon, as appears by an indenture made between the lord Prior and the said Richard. Item nothing. Total, nothing.
Cullet. Also for agistment of 100 [*sheep*] as contracted with the shepherd there for the same time, nothing in money. Nor anything for the agistment of 80 as contracted with the stockman this year. Total, nothing.

---

[68] The title 'Sedgeford' is crossed out.

Between the Master Cellarer and the said shepherd, 2 December in the 21st year of King Henry VII [*1505*].
Memo that paid to the said Nicholas Rust, shepherd, there by the hand of Nicholas Hunte of Hindolveston in full settlement of his stipend for the term ending at the Nativity of the Lord coming [*25 December 1505*], 15s. And paid to the same on 2 December in the above written year, 8d.

Sedgeford Westmanor. The account of Richard Julyan, shepherd there, from the feast of the Nativity of St John the Baptist in the 20th year of King Henry VII to the feast of St Michael the Archangel following [*24 June to 29 September 1505*] for one quarter.
Lambs of this year. The same shepherd is charged for stock received from the fold of Gnatingdon at the feast of the Nativity of St John the Baptist in the 20th year of King Henry VII [*24 June 1505*], 806. And received from the fold of Hindringham at the feast of St Michael the Archangel in the 21st year of King Henry VII [*29 September 1505*], 187. Total head now, 993. Item, in murrain after shearing, 30, pelts thereof sent to the monastery. And remaining there now, 963.
Ewes.[69] The same shepherd is charged for stock, because received from the fold of Hindringham, 205. And there remain there at the feast of St Michael the Archangel [*29 September*], 205. Of which, deficient upon Richard Julyan, 1 priced 8d. And remain there now, 204.[70]
Total head of all sheep there remaining at the feast of St Michael the Archangel [*29 September*] under the custody of Richard Julyan, 1,167. Of which, 204 ewes, 963 lambs. Which are given into the hands of Robert Loon, now shepherd there, counted at the feast of St Michael the Archangel in the 21st year of King Henry VII [*29 September 1505*]. And thus equals.

Sedgeford Westmanor. The account of Robert Loon, shepherd there by John Bronde, stockman, and Nicholas Rust, shepherd at Gnatingdon, his deputies [*deputat' suos*], from the feast of St Michael the Archangel in the 21th year of King Henry VII to the feast of the Nativity of the Lord in the 21st year of the aforesaid King [*29 September 1505 to 25 December 1505*].
Ewes. The same shepherd is charged with ewes received from Richard Julyan, the most recent shepherd there, 204. And thus remaining there, 204.
Lambs of this year. The same is charged for lambs received from the afore-said Richard Julyan, 963.[71] And remaining, 963.

---

[69] 'Wethers' crossed out.
[70] Marginal note: '1 deficient'.
[71] 'In murrain, 36, the pelts thereof given to the stockman' is crossed out.

Total head of sheep there now remaining, 1,163. Of which 204 ewes, 963 lambs.[72]

Newton. Account of Robert Howlyns, bailiff there, who is charged for the stock of the monastery for one whole year ending at the feast of the Nativity of the Lord in the 21st year of King Henry VII [*25 December 1504 to 25 December 1505*].
Response from the tally of wethers. The same accountant is charged and responds for the remainder in the account preceding, 428. And received from the fold of Gnatingdon, 112. Total head now, 540. Of which, given to the kitchen of the monastery at the feast of Pentecost [*11 May 1505*], 20. And to the said kitchen of the monastery on the feast of the Nativity of St John the Baptist [*24 June*], 20. And in murrain, 16, the pelts thereof sent to the stockman. And remaining there, 483.
Total head of sheep there now remaining, 484. Of which, sold to Robert Broun of Norwich, butcher, 122 price for each 17d. *£8 10s.* And remaining there now, 362.

Eaton. The account of John Sturmyn, shepherd there, for one whole year ending at the feast of the Nativity of the Lord in the 21st year of the King Henry VII [*25 December 1504 to 25 December 1505*].
He responds for the tally. The same shepherd responds for the remainder of the last account, 813. Of which:
Wethers. From remainder, 810. And received from the fold of Hindringham, 120. Total head now, 930.
Of which, given to the kitchen of the monastery between the feast of the Epiphany of the Lord [*6 January 1505*] and the feast of the Purification of the Blessed Virgin Mary [*2 February 1505*] by order of the Master Cellarer, 20. And given to the said kitchen at the feast of St Margaret [*20 July 1505*], 20. And given to the said kitchen at the feast of St Matthew the apostle in the 21st year of King Henry VII [*21 September 1505*], 20. And given to lord Robert Watfeld, the Cellarer of the monastery of the Holy Trinity, Norwich, at the feast of St Edward, King and Confessor, in the above year [*13 October 1505*], 20. And given to the aforesaid Cellarer after the feast of St Martin in the above year [*11 November 1505*], 20. And in murrain, 32, the pelts thereof sent to the stockman. And remaining 798. And received from the stock lately of Robert Walsyngham 18. And remaining there now, 816.
Of which, sold to Robert Broun of Norwich, butcher, 240 priced 16d. each *£16*, beyond 2 not charged. And sold to the same Robert, 62 wethers priced 12d. each *40s.* And remaining there now, 512.

[72] Marginal note: 'Nothing from Crisp for cullet and manure. Memo that the stockman says that Richard Julyan received 1,233, of which he responds for deficient, 2.

Ewes. From remainder, 3.

Total head of sheep there now remaining, 515. Of which, 512 wethers, 3 ewes.

Cullet. Also for agistment of 80 as contracted with the shepherd as in the preceding [*account*], nothing in money. But from the cullet of foreign stock agisting there, namely the stock of Thomas Parker, 21 *21d.* for half a year ending at the feast of the Nativity of the Lord in the 21st year of King Henry VII [*25 December 1505*]; of Walter Parker, 24 *2s.*; of Nicholas Parker of Pockthorpe 17 *17d.* for one half year finishing at the feast of the Nativity of the Lord, 2. And from agistment of the stock of William Grene, butcher, 6 *3d.* for one quarter year ending at the feast of the Nativity of the Lord in the 21st year of King Henry VII [*25 December 1505*]; and of Nicholas Miller, 6 *12d.* for one whole year ending at the feast of the Nativity of the Lord in the 21st year of King Henry VII. Total 6s 5d. Of which, it is allowed to the shepherd 4s. for 6 acres of the land of the Abbot of St Benedict lying within the pasture there. And it is charged, 2s. 5d.

Manure. And the said shepherd with the aforesaid sheep flock manured before the feast of St Michael 3 acres 3 roods of land of Walter Parker *3s. 9d.* And for 6 acres of land of the said Walter Parker after the feast of St Michael [*29 September*] to the feast of the Nativity of the Lord [*25 December*], 6s. And for 2 acres of the shepherd's own land, as contracted, nothing in money. Total, 9s. 9d.

Between the Master Cellarer and the said shepherd, on the feast of St Agnes, 20 January in the 21st year of King Henry VII.[73]

Item, the same shepherd is charged for his arrears of rent this year, 5s. 6½d. And for cullet as above, 2s. 5d.

Total charged, 7s. 11½d.

And the said shepherd claims allowance for his stipend for one quarter year ending at the Nativity of the Lord in the 21st year of King Henry VII, 13s. 4d. And he claims also allowance for his livery for last year, 5s. Total claims of the said shepherd, 18s. 4d. Of which, William Elsy paid the shepherd for part of his stipend at the feast of the Nativity of the Lord in the 21st year of King Henry VII [*25 December 1505*], 3s. 4d. And deducted for his arrears of pelts this year *5s. 6½d.*, allowed for cullet above *2s. 6d.*, allowed 4s. for the land of the Abbey of St Benedict,[74] as above, 7s. 11½d.

Total payments and allowances, 11s. 3½d. And thus it is owed to the said shepherd, 7s. ½d. Which is paid by the hands of the Master Cellarer on 20 January in the 21st year of the King Henry VII [*1506*].

---

[73] The feast of St Agnes falls on 21 January. This is either scribal error, or the text should read 'on the eve of the feast of St Agnes'. Whichever, the year is 1506.

[74] Abbey of St Benet at Holm.

DCN 62/23: 25 December 1508 to 29 September 1509.

Sedgeford. Account of Robert Pepyr, shepherd there, from the feast of the Nativity of the Lord in the 24th year of King Henry VII to the feast of Michael the Archangel following, in the 1st year of King Henry VIII [*25 December 1508 to 29 September 1509*].
He responds for the tally. The same shepherd responds for the remainder of the account immediately preceding, 1,023. Of which:
Ewes. From remainder, 503. Of which, sent to the sheep fold of Thorpe under the custody of Thomas Newton, shepherd of the flock of ewes there, 240. And sent to the fold of the Grange of the monastery under the custody of Robert Chaumberleyn, shepherd there, 120. And sent to the fold of Newton, under the custody of John Smith, shepherd there, 120. And in murrain, the pelts thereof sent to the stockman, 23. Thus equals.
Lambs of last year. From remainder, 520. Of which, sent to the fold of Eaton under the custody of John Sturmyn, 160. And to the fold of Gnatingdon under the custody of Nicholas Rust, shepherd there, <100> 80. And in murrain, the pelts thereof sent to the stockman, 75. And remaining there, 205.[75]
Lambs from the births of ewes issued this year, 260. And received from the fold of Gnatingdon under the custody of Nicholas Rust, shepherd there, 840. Total head, 1,100. And remaining there, 1,100.[76]
Total head of sheep remaining there, 1,305. Of which, 187 ewes, 18 rams, 1,100 lambs. Item, in murrain 59, the pelts of which remain in the custody of the shepherd. And thus, in respect thereof, he made the tally and given to the shepherd on the 28 November in the 1st year of King Henry VIII [*1509*].
Manure. And the aforesaid shepherd manured 14 acres of John Clerk, farmer there, in the north field of Sedgeford, and 5 acres at farm to the east of the aforesaid 14 acres. And 4 acres at the eastern head of the aforesaid 5 acres. And 1 acre 3 roods lying in Barellwong on the south part of the aforesaid 4 acres. And 2 acres on the south part of the said 7 roods. And 5 acres in Halle Botom in the north field of Sedgeford. Total area manured for John Clerk, farmer there, in the north field of Sedgeford, 31 acres 3 roods. And also manured for the aforesaid John Clerk, farmer there, in the south field of Sedgeford, 15 acres of land, of which the first piece [*pecia*][77] lies [*in*] 10 acres at le Westmere next to Corpenhowe, and the second piece

[75] Marginal note: 'Now in ewes, 187, in rams, 18'.
[76] Marginal note: 'Memo that Robert Peper was made to respond himself on the first day of March in the first year of King Henry VIII [*1510*] for the pelts of 59 deaths at the time of his last account: 98 allowed at the time of the account, as above'.
[77] A *pecia* is a parcel of arable land within the open fields, better known in the Midlands as a selion.

at the west part of the Cross of Fring 5 acres, beyond 2 acres manured in the same piece as contracted with the said shepherd. Total of all acres manured for the aforesaid John Clerk this year, 46 acres 3 roods, simply [*simplic'*] manured. And the aforesaid shepherd manured with the aforesaid sheep 3 roods of land of Robert Loon, simply manured. Total, 9d.
Total, 9d.
Cullet. And from agistment of 120 sheep as contracted with the shepherd for the time aforesaid, and so nothing here in cash. But received from foreign stock, namely 6 ewes of Walter Trywe from the feast of St Peter in Chains in the 1ˢᵗ year of King Henry VIII [*1 August 1509*] to the feast of St Michael the Archangel following [*29 September 1509*], price 1d. each. And 10 ewes of Thomas Mason for the time aforesaid, price 1d. each. And 5 ewes of Simon Blomefeld for the term aforesaid, each 1d. Total, 21d.

Between the Master Cellarer and the above named Robert Pepyr, shepherd there, on 28 November in the 1ˢᵗ year of King Henry VIII [*1509*] for his stipend for three terms finishing at the feast of Michael the Archangel in the 1ˢᵗ year of King Henry VIII, 45s.
Item, he claims for his livery this year, 5s.
Item, he claims for 600 *18d.* *Redingballez*⁷⁸ bought, and for oil to grease the sheep *14d.*, 2s. 8d. Total claim, 52s. 8d.
Of which, paid to the aforesaid shepherd by the hand of John Clerk for the term of the Annunciation of the Blessed Virgin Mary [*25 March*], 15s. And to the same by the hand of William Elsy for the term of the Nativity of St John the Baptist in the 1ˢᵗ year of King Henry VIII [*24 June 1509*], 15s. Total paid, 30s.
And 22s 8d. are owed to the same shepherd. Of which, withheld for manuring 3 roods for Robert Loon, as above, 9d. And also for agistment, as above, 21d.
And thus 20s. 2d. are owed to the above written shepherd. Of which, allowed and withheld for his rent for the year finishing at Michaelmas in the 1ˢᵗ year of King Henry VIII [*29 September 1509*], 12s. 6d. And paid to the said shepherd in full payment of all claims of the said shepherd on the aforesaid 28 November, 7s. 9d [*sic*] and thus equals.

Gnatingdon. Account of Nicholas Rust, shepherd there, from the feast of the Nativity of the Lord in the 24ᵗʰ year of King Henry VII to the feast of Michael the Archangel next following, in the 1ˢᵗ year of King Henry VIII [*25 December 1508 to 29 September 1509*]. And in the 5ᵗʰ year of lord Robert, Prior. *He responds for the tally.* The same shepherd responds for the remainder of the account immediately preceding, 1,198. Of which:
Ewes. From remainder, 1,197. Of which, received from the fold of

⁷⁸ The red dye used to mark the sheep to identify the owner, also known as ruddle.

<Gnatingdon> Sedgeford under the custody of Robert Peper, 80. Total head now, 1,277.

Item, in murrain, the pelts thereof sent to the stockman, 55. And sent to the kitchen of the manor of Sedgeford expended at the court [*held on the feast*] of St John[79] in the 1ˢᵗ year of King Henry VIII [*24 June 1509*], 1. And remaining there, 1,221.

Wethers. From remainder, 1. And remaining there, 1.

Lambs of this year. From the births of the said ewes issuing this year, 1,013. Of which, sent to the fold of < Gnatingdon > Sedgeford under the custody of Robert Peper, 840. And sent to the fold of Hindringham under the custody of John Laxe, 168. And sent to the kitchen of the manor of Sedgeford at the court [*held on the feast*] of St John [*24 June 1509*], 2. And it is allowed for *Markynglammes*, as contracted as in preceding accounts, 3. And equals.

Total head of sheep remaining there, 1,222. Of which, 1 wether, 1,221 ewes. And thus, was made the tally and given to the shepherd on 27 November in the 1ˢᵗ year of King Henry VIII [*1509*].

Manure. And the aforesaid shepherd with the aforesaid sheep manured for Richard Cryspe for the time aforesaid a minimum of 30 acres simply manured, of which in one piece on the east part of the manor of Gnatingdon lie 18 acres. And at the northern end of the said 18 acres of land, 12 acres lying in another piece granted to the same Richard, the payments for which are included with the lease of the said manor of Gnatingdon, as appears fully by an indenture made between the lord Prior and the said Richard. Item, nothing there in money. Item, nothing.

Cullet. And from agistment of 120 sheep as contracted with the shepherd for the time aforesaid, nothing. In money nothing also for the agistment of 80 sheep as contracted with the stockman this year. Total, nothing.

Between the Master Cellarer and the aforesaid shepherd on 27 November in the 1ˢᵗ year of King Henry VIII [*1509*].

First, the same shepherd claims for his stipend for three terms finishing at the feast of Michael the Archangel in the 1st year of King Henry VIII [*29 September 1509*], 45s.

Item, he claims for his livery this year, 5s.

And for oil to grease the sheep 12d. Total claim, 51s.

Of which, paid to the aforesaid shepherd by the hand of John Clerk for the term of the Annunciation of the Blessed Virgin Mary [*25 March*], 15s. And to the same by the hand of William Elsy for the term of the Nativity of St John the Baptist [*24 June*], 15s. Total paid, 30s.

And 21s. are owed to the same shepherd. Total paid to the same shepherd

---

[79] Assumed to be the feast of the Nativity of St John the Baptist.

on 27 November in the 1ˢᵗ year of King Henry VIII [*1509*]. And thus equals.

Thorpe Episcopi. Account of Walter Ballez, shepherd there, from the feast of the Nativity of the Lord in the 24ᵗʰ year of King Henry VII to the feast of Michael the Archangel next following, in the 1st year of King Henry VIII [*25 December 1508 to 29 September 1509*]. And in the 5ᵗʰ year of lord Robert [*Catton*], Prior.

He responds for the tally of wethers. The same shepherd responds for the remainder of the account immediately preceding, 1,087. Of which:

From the stock of the monastery and the Cellarer. From remainder, 982 of the stock of the monastery and 44 of the Cellarer. Total wethers, 1,026.

Of which, sent to the kitchen of the convent just before the feast of the Nativity of the Lord in the 24th year of King Henry VIII [*25 December 1508*] , 20. And sent to the said kitchen around the feast of the Epiphany of the Lord next following [*6 January 1509*], 30. And sent to the said kitchen on the Saturday before Whit-Sunday following [*26 May 1509*], 2. And sent to John Bronde of Catton immediately after the following feast of St John the Baptist [*24 June 1509*] on the orders of the lord Prior, to be consumed by the gild of St John of Catton, 3. And in murrain, the pelts thereof sent to the stockman, 20. And remaining there, 951.

Wethers from the stock of the lord Prior. From remainder of the stock of the lord Prior, as appears in the preceding account, 61. And remaining there, 61.

Total head of sheep now remaining there, 1,012. Of which, 831 [*are the*] stock of the monastery, 61 of the lord Prior, 120 of the Cellarer.

Cullet. And from agistment of 80 sheep as contracted with the shepherd, nothing in money. But for the agistment of 36 wethers from the stock of Leonard Spencer *18d.* from the feast of the Nativity of St John the Baptist in the 1ˢᵗ year of King Henry VIII [*24 June 1509*] to the feast of St Michael the Archangel [*29 September*] next following, price for each ½d. Total, 18d.

Manure. And the aforesaid shepherd with the aforesaid sheep manured on the land of Robert Clere, knight, and of John Kypping of Freethorpe, 16 acres simply manured, of which 8 acres manured for the aforesaid lord Robert Clere, knight, within the vill of Southwood. And 8 acres for the portion of the aforesaid John Kypping within the said vill of Freethorpe, from the feast of St Matthew the Apostle in the 1ˢᵗ year of King Henry VIII [*21 September 1509*] until the feast of St Nicholas the Bishop then next following [*6 December 1509*], amounting to eleven weeks to be paid for the said manure, beyond the agistment of the aforesaid ewes in aid [*auxilium*] of the stipend of the said shepherd and above the board [*ac super mensam*] of the said shepherd provided by [*alloc'*] the said lord Robert Clere, knight, and John Kypping, 6s. 8d. Total, 6s. 8d.

Between the Master Cellarer and the aforesaid Walter Balles, shepherd there, on 28 November in the 1st year of King Henry VIII [*1509*].
For his stipend for three terms finishing at the feast of Michael the Archangel in the 1st year of King Henry VIII [*29 September 1509*], 45s. Item, he claims for his livery this year *5s.* also for oil to grease the sheep *18d.*, 6s. 6d. Total claim, 51s. 6d.
Of which, paid to the aforesaid shepherd as the same shepherd confirms on the day and year aforesaid in reward and sustenance for part of his stipend for two terms finishing at the feast of St John the Baptist in the 1st year of King Henry VIII [*24 June 1509*] by the hand of the Master from November on two occasions, namely the first time for the term of the Annunciation of the Blessed Virgin Mary [*25 March*] above past, 11s. 8d. And the second time for the term of the Nativity of St John the Baptist [*24 June*], 13s. 4d. And withheld from cullet *18d.* and manure *6s. 8d.,* as appears above, 8s. 2d.
And 18s. 4d. are owed to the same shepherd. Which is paid to the aforewritten shepherd on 28 November in the year above [*1509*] in the presence of the stockman. And paid to the said Walter on the fourth Sunday of the Advent of the Lord [*23 December 1509*] for part of 15s. for the term finishing at the Nativity of the Lord in the next future, 5s. And paid to the same on the feast of the Circumcision of the Lord in the 1st year of King Henry VIII [*1 January 1510*] in full payment of his stipend for the term finishing at the Nativity of the Lord [*25 December 1509*] as claimed, 10s. And thus equals.

Newton. Account of John Smyth, shepherd there, from the feast of the Nativity of the Lord in the 24th year of King Henry VII to the feast of St Michael the Archangel next following in the 1st year of King Henry VIII [*25 December 1508 to 29 September 1509*]. And the 5th year of lord Robert [*Catton*], Prior.
He responds for the tally of wethers. The same accountant is charged and responds for the tally of the preceding account, 621. Of which:
Wethers. From remainder, 420. Of which, sent to the kitchen of the monastery on diverse occasions this year before Michaelmas in the 1st year of King Henry VIII [*29 September 1509*], <140> 87. And sent to the said kitchen immediately after the feast of St Michael the Archangel abovesaid, 60. And sold to Thomas Deye of Norwich, butcher, 81 price for each <16d.> 20d. *£6 13s. 4d.* And sent to the fold of Eaton under the custody of John Sturmyn, 7. And in murrain, the pelts thereof sent to [*?John*] Staunford, 39. And remaining there, 146.
Ewes. From remainder, 5. And remaining there, 5. And received from the fold of Monks' Grange, 120. And from the fold of Thorpe Episcopi, 120. And from the fold of Sedgeford, 120. And remaining there, 365.

Riggs. From remainder, 148. Of which, <sent> sold to John Mekylbergh of Thurlton, 42 *62s. 8d.* And sent to the kitchen to feed the *famuli* of the manor of Newton during the harvest, 3. And sold to Thomas Deye of Norwich, butcher, 40, price for each 20d., 66s. 8d. And sent to the kitchen of the monastery before the feast of St Michael the Archangel in the 1st year of King Henry VIII [*29 September 1509*], 53. And thus equals.

Rams. From remainder, 48. And received from the fold of Hindringham, 12. Total head, 64, of which sent to the fold of Eaton under the custody of John Sturmyn, shepherd there, 64. And thus equals.

Total head of sheep now remaining there, 511. Of which, 146 wethers, 365 ewes. And thus he made the tally in the vigil of St Andrew in the 1st year of King Henry VIII [*29 November 1509*].

Manure. And the aforesaid shepherd with the aforesaid sheep manured 12 acres, lying in one piece, of the demesne land of the manor of Newton, part of 80 acres of land lying near Kyrby simply manured. Nothing, because the money is assigned to [*blank*] Algor, farmer of the manor there, as part of his lease. Total, nothing.

Between the Master Cellarer and the aforesaid John Smyth, shepherd there, in the vigil of St Andrew in the 1st year of King Henry VIII [*29 November 1509*].

First, the same shepherd claims for his stipend for <one whole year> three terms of the year finishing at the feast of Michael the Archangel in the 1st year of King Henry VIII [*29 September 1509*], <26s. 8d.> 20s. And the same shepherd claims 3 quarters 4 bushels of mixture,[80] and 3 quarters 4 bushels of malt, granted out of custom for *Le Mettecorn*,[81] without any cash value. And for oil to grease the sheep there, 13d. Total claim, excluding the *Metcorn*, <27s. 9d.> 21s. 1d.

Of which, paid to the said shepherd as the same shepherd confirms on the vigil of St Andrew in the aforesaid year in reward and sustenance by the hand of the Master of Normans[82], 13s. 4d. And owed to the same shepherd, 7s. 9d. And the same claims for his livery this year, 5s. And thus owed now to the aforesaid shepherd, 12s. 9d. Which is paid to the said shepherd on the vigil of St Andrew [*29 November*]. And thus equals.

DCN 64/10: 25 December 1530 to 25 December 1531.

Hindringham. The account of William Maye, shepherd of the lords

---

[80] An equal mixture of wheat and rye, also known as maslin.

[81] Le Mettecorn/Metcorn is clearly some form of customary payment to workers, probably at the harvest.

[82] Normans Hospital in Norwich.

Robert and William, Priors[83] of the cathedral church of the Holy Trinity, Norwich, there during the year ending at the Nativity of the Lord in the twenty third year of King Henry VIII.

He responds for the tally. The same shepherd is charged for the remainder from the previous year, 922. Of which:

Sent to the sheep fold of Lomnours, 181 wethers. Sent to the sheep fold of Lathes, 120 ewes. Sent to the sheep fold of Eaton, 120 ewes. And at another time sent to the said sheep fold of Eaton, 60 ewes. And also at a subsequent time sent to the sheep fold at Lomnours, 60 wethers. And in murrain, the pelts thereof sent to Richard Salter, 217. And in murrain at another time, whereof the pelts for this remain in the custody of the shepherd, 17. And deficient [*charged*] upon William Maye himself, 8. And remaining there, 139.

Lambs [born] this year. Born of the said ewes there, beyond all barren sheep, none.

And afterwards received from the fold of Eaton, 389. And afterwards received from the fold of Lathes, 260, [*total*] 649.

Total head of sheep remaining there, 788. And thus the tally is made by William Maye.

Manure. The aforesaid shepherd with the aforesaid sheep flock manured the land of Thomas Large, 2½ acres for 2s. 6d.; and of Richard Jolle, 3 acres for 3s.; and of William Bryde, 2½ acres for 2s. 6d. Total acres, 8, total sum of money, 8s.

Cullet. And received from John Manne for agistment of 58 sheep and lambs, Richard Maye for agistment of 100, John Lamberd of Binham, 20, and for the sheep of William Mason, 80. Total head, 258 sheep. Total sum of money, 10s. 9d.

Hurdles. From remainder from the previous year, four dozen. And bought by the same William Maye, shepherd there, two dozen. And thus remaining in total, 6 dozen. Of which, bought by William Maye two dozen, 2s. 6d., and one iron sowel [*iron saule*].[84]

From whynnes [saliunc'] sold.[85] From 360 whynnes sold at 6d. per 120, total for the same whynnes, 18d.

Concerning the Master Cellarer and William Maye.

The same accountant is charged beyond the account[86] for the arrears of deficient sheep from the year before charged upon William Maye himself,

[83] William Castleton replaced Robert Catton as Prior during this year.

[84] For sowel, see Glossary.

[85] Whin (Latin, *saliunca*) was a bundle of heathland plants, usually gorse and furze, which was sold as a fuel.

[86] The phrase 'beyond [or upon] the account' (*super compotum*) refers to the practice of making final, often minor, adjustments to the account at the point of audit.

nothing. But he is charged for six dozen hurdles and one iron sowel. For sheep, upon his aforesaid deficiency of 8 sheep at 12d. each, total stands at 8s. Manure, *8s.* cullet, *10s. 9d.* whynnes,* 10s. 3d.*, [*total owed*] 28s. 3d., in addition to the hurdles and *le iron saule*. And over and above the 17 pelts, which remain in the custody of the shepherd himself.

Of which, the aforesaid accountant claims as [*his*] stipend for the year ending at the next Nativity, according to the said accountant, 60s., beyond the 15s. paid to the same by Robert Thwaytez at the Lent court session, also the 15s. paid to the same at the feast of the Nativity of St John the Baptist, also the 15s. paid to the same by the hand of Andrew Robyns at the Martinmas [*11 November*] court session: to the same, in addition to the aforesaid, 15s. He also claims allowance for one barrel of bitumen bought by himself from John Kynges of Wiveton, 5s. [*He also claims*] for grease, 2s., and ruddle, 2d., bought to treat and mark the sheep, [*total*] 2s. 2d. [*He also claims*] for his livery, for the whole year, 5s. [*He also claims*] for the two dozen hurdles, 2s. 8d., and for the iron sowel, 2s., [*total*] 4s. 8d.

Sum of the claims, 31s. <8d.> 9d.

[*The rest of this account is missing*]

DCN 64/11: 25 December 1530 to 25 December 1531.

[*Northflock in Sedgeford*]. [*The account of*] John Wraske and Nicholas Brown, shepherds of lord William, Prior of the Cathedral Church of the Holy Trinity, Norwich, [*from the feast*] of the Nativity of the Lord in the 22nd year of King Henry VIII [*25 December 1530*] through to the same feast thereafter in the next year following, the 23rd of the same lord King. And the first of lord William Castylton, the aforesaid Prior.

They respond for the tally. The same shepherds render account for the remainder from the previous year, 1,012.

Of which, none were sold. But sent to Nicholas Brown, shepherd there before shearing, 748. And in murrain, 240, whereof the pelts were sent to Richard Salter. And in murrain at another time, 19, whereof the pelts were sent to Richard Salter, over and above the single pelt given to John Goold by the aforesaid Richard Salter. And deficient charged upon the aforesaid John Wraske, 5 wethers.

And thus remaining this year in the charge of the aforesaid Nicholas Brown, 748.

Of which, sent to the fold at Lomnours and Plumstead, 121 wethers. And sent to the fold of Eaton, 60 ewes. And in murrain, the pelts thereof sent to Richard Salter, 11. And thus remaining clear, in the custody of the same Nicholas Brown, 556, of which 496 are wethers and rams, and 60 ewes.

And the said Nicholas Brown receives from the fold of Gnatingdon from lambs, 403.

Total head of sheep remaining there, 959, of which 496 wethers and rams, 60 ewes, 403 lambs. And thus the tally is made by the aforesaid Nicholas Brown, shepherd there.

Manure. The aforesaid shepherds with the sheep flocks there for the duration of this account have manured for Thomas Hargate, Geoffrey Mannyng and Nicholas Smyth, farmers of the demesne land there, 60 acres. And nothing paid for this manure, because the aforesaid manure is included in their lease according to the contract as before. And also manured by the aforesaid shepherds there, 2 acres, for which nothing is paid as agreed with the stockman. Total, nothing.

Cullet. From agistment for foreign stock, beyond the 40 included in the contract of the stockman, and beyond the 120 in the contract of the shepherds there this year, nothing.

Hurdles. From remainder from the previous year, nothing. One iron sowel remaining, and the hurdles belong to the farmers there.

Concerning the Master Cellarer and the aforesaid shepherds, namely John Wraske and Nicholas Brown, [*who*] are charged beyond the account [*super compotum*] for the arrears of the preceding year, for deficient sheep, for manure, and cullet this year. Nothing.

From John Wraske, shepherd there, for deficient sheep this year, 5 wethers charged upon him.

Total above [*supra*].

Item, John [*Wraske*] mentioned above claims in allowances for his stipend toward the half year ending at the feast of the Nativity of St John the Baptist [*24 June*] past, beyond that paid by the hand of John Goold, 30s. It is paid. Similarly, the said John Wraske is allowed for his livery for the said time, 2s. 6d. And the same John claims allowance for hurdles bought at the said time, 12d.

And Nicholas Brown, shepherd there, claims 30s. for his stipend for half the year, beyond the 5s. paid to him by the hand of the lord at the court [*held at the feast*] of St John [*27 December*], and the 5s. to the same Nicholas paid at the court [*held at the feast*] of St Martin [*11 November*] by John Goolde. [*Net*] 20s.

And the same Nicholas claims for his livery at the same time, 2s. 6d. And also for the wattle bought by himself at the same time, 8d. And he also claims for the ruddle [*le redyng*] bought by himself to mark his sheep, 2d. Total, 26s. 10d.

2. CENTRALISED STOCK ACCOUNTS OF THE MONASTERY[87]

DCN 62/16: Account of 1 December 1488.

Sheep of the monastery. General account of the shepherds of the lord Prior of Norwich in a view taken on the morrow of the feast of St Andrew the apostle in the 4th year of King Henry VII [*1 December 1488*]. Remaining under custody in the following folds and places, namely:
Eaton. Under the charge and custody of Robert Grene there remain 720. Of which, 1 wether, 715 ewes, 4 lambs.
Carleton. Under the charge and custody of Thomas Carter there remain 160 hoggs.
Lathes. Under the charge and custody of John Maykyn there, 769 ewes.
Lomnours. Under the custody of Robert Rudkyn there, 771. Of which, 746 ewes, 25 lambs.
Newton. Under the charge of John Sire there remain 582, of which 447 ewes, 135 rams and riggs.
Heigham. Under the charge of Thomas Baxter there remain 705. Of which, 673 wethers, 32 rams.
Sedgeford. Under the custody of Roger Wrask there remain 373. Of which, 313 wethers, 60 ewes with the farmer.
Cullet there 729.
Hindringham. Under the custody of Robert Hardewyne there remain 845 hoggs.
Total head of sheep, 4,925. Of which, 1,434 wethers, 2,290 ewes, 1,034 hoggs and lambs, 167 rams and riggs.

DCN 62/17: Account of 25 December 1490.[88]

[*The top of the manuscript is torn, so the place and first part of the entry are missing, but it is probably Catton*] <...under the custody of John Brond ...844 ewes, 3 lambs, of which [*torn, but probably 820 ewes and 3 lambs*] of the monastery. 24 ewes of pure stock of the lord Prior.
Eaton. Under the custody of Thomas Baxter, 769. Of which, 1 wether, 767

---

[87] See Introduction, p. 10.

[88] This untitled document appears on a separate piece of parchment enrolled within NRO DCN 62/17, following the individual shepherds' accounts for the year ending at 30 November 1490 (pp. 24-6). The totals from those shepherds' accounts are similar to the totals in this account, close enough to suppose that this is a draft centralized stock account for 25 December 1490. The whole is lightly crossed out with a single large cross.

ewes, 1 lamb. Of [*these, belonging to*] the monastery, 697, 1 wether, 1 lamb, 695 ewes. Stock of the lord Prior, 72 ewes.

Thorpe Market. Under the custody of Thomas Baxter [*sic*], 769, of which the monastery, 19 ewes, 750 lambs.

Heigham [*next Norwich*]. Under the custody of Thomas Baxter [*sic*], 741, of which the monastery, 48 rams, 693 wethers.

Lomnours. Under the custody of Robert Rudkyn, 760, all ewes of the monastery.

Newton. Under the custody of William Staunford, 548. Of which, 63 rams, 419 wethers. Of these [*wethers*], 60 belong to the lord [*Prior*].

Sedgeford. Under the custody of Roger Wrask, 860. Of which, 90 ewes, 30 belonging to the lord [*Prior*], 60 to the monastery. 770 wethers, of which 69 to the lord [*Prior*], 701 to the monastery.

Hindringham. Now nothing from the old fold of 46. But from the new fold under the custody of John Suffolk, 691. Of which 631 lambs of the monastery, 60 lambs of the lord [*Prior*].

[*No grand total is given, but in the margin is written*] 5,639 of the monastery, 365 of the lord Prior.>

[*On the top of the individual shepherd's account for Sedgeford in this year, the following sentence appears*] Still of Lathes at the feast of St Andrew 6 Henry VII [*30 November 1490*].

Of which the tally of John Bronde, shepherd there. Total head remaining as the stock of the lord, 846, of which 843 ewes, 3 lambs of this year.

DCN 62/16: Account of 25 December 1491.

General sheep of the monastery of Norwich copied from the accounts [*transumpte extra compos'*] of the shepherds remaining at the feast of the Nativity of our Lord in the 7th year of King Henry VII. Namely, at:

Thorpe Market. None, because the fold there lately leased from Richard Randes has been relinquished.

Heigham next to Norwich. None, because the fold there, recently leased from the abbey of St Benedict and John Appilyerd, has been relinquished this year.

Eaton. Under the charge and custody of Thomas Baxter there remain 882. Of which, 174 wethers, 708 ewes.

Lomnours. Under the charge and custody of Robert Rudkyn there, 941. Of which, 936 ewes, 5 lambs of this year.

Lathes. Under the charge and custody of John Bronde there, 839. Of which, 836 ewes, 3 lambs of this year.

Newton. Under the charge of Robert Howlynes, farmer, there remain 540, of which 80 rams and 460 wethers.

Sedgeford. Under the charge and custody of Roger Wrask, beyond 60 with the farmer there, 1,061. Of which, 1,023 wethers, 38 rams and riggs.
Hindringham. Under the charge and custody of John Suffolk, there remain 881. Of which, 10 ewes, 871 lambs.[89]
Little Ryburgh. Agisting within the cullet [*infra colliettam agistmenti*] of Robert Silvester, there remain 126 ewes.
Sparham. Agisting within the cullet of lord Fitzwauter there, under custody of Robert Gynne, remain 120 wethers.
Total head of sheep, 5,436. Of which, 1,787 wethers, 118 rams and riggs, 2,616 ewes, 26 gerks, 879 lambs.

The particular sheep [*oves particulares*] belonging to the lord Prior remaining in the folds written above. Namely, at:
Sedgeford. 115 wethers.
Eaton. 37 ewes.
Lathes. 2 wethers and 52 ewes.
Hindringham. 35 lambs of this year.
Newton. 74 wethers, also the farmer has outside the account, 32 ewes.
Total head, 315. Of which, 191 wethers, 89 ewes, 35 lambs.

DCN 62/16: Account of 9 December 1493.

General sheep counted and remaining on individual accounts produced by the shepherds of the flocks and folds of the monastery of Norwich, limited to the following vills and flocks for one whole year ending on the morrow of the Conception of the Blessed Virgin Mary [*9 December*] in the year 1493. And the 9th year of King Henry VII.
Newton. Under the charge and custody of Robert Howlynes, farmer there, beyond 32 included within his lease and beyond the particular sheep of the lord Prior, 396 wethers.
Lathes. Under the charge and custody of Thomas Beny, shepherd there, 908. Of which, 907 ewes, 1 lamb.
Lomnours. Under the charge and custody of William Albon, shepherd there, 793. Of which, 60 ewes, 733 wethers.
Sedgeford. Under the charge and custody of Roger Wrask, shepherd there, 1,129. Of which, 537 wethers, 40 rams, 552 ewes.
Eaton. Under the charge and custody of Thomas Baxter, shepherd there, 972. Of which, 961 ewes, 11 lambs.
Hindringham. Under the charge and custody of John Dowdy, 896. Of which, 4 wethers, 9 ewes, 883 lambs.

[89] Marginal note: 'Of which, Robert Hoo now renders account for two years, 46. Of which 20 wethers, 26 hoggs for gerks.'

Hethersett. Under the charge and custody of Thomas Rede, shepherd there, 647. Of which, 40 wethers, 607 lambs.
Cringleford. In agistment in the custody of the fold there, 325. Of which, 262 wethers, 63 rams.
Total head of sheep in all the flocks of the monastery, above those remaining with the farmers by indenture, 6,066. Of which, 1,972 wethers, 103 rams, 2,489 ewes, 1,502 lambs.

The sheep belonging to the lord Prior remaining in the folds written above. Namely, at:
Eaton. 73. Of which, 63 ewes, 10 lambs.
Hindringham. 40. Of which, 20 hoggs and gerks, 20 lambs.
Lathes. 39. Of which 2 wethers and 37 ewes.
Newton. 171 wethers.
Hethersett. 30 lambs.
Total all head [*of sheep*], 353. Of which, 173 wethers, 100 ewes, 20 hoggs, 60 lambs.

DCN 62/16: Account of 9 December 1494.

General sheep counted and remaining on individual accounts produced by the shepherds of the flocks and folds of the monastery of Norwich, limited to the following vills and flocks for one whole year ending on the morrow of the Conception of the Blessed Virgin Mary [*9 December*] in the year of our Lord 1494. And the 10th year of King Henry VII.
Lathes. Under the charge and custody of Thomas Beny, 818. Of which, 813 ewes, 5 lambs.
Newton. Under the charge and custody of Robert Howlyns, 403 wethers.
Eaton. Under the charge and custody of Thomas Baxter, 954. Of which, 951 ewes, 3 lambs.
Hindringham. Under the charge and custody of John Dowdy, 852. Of which, 4 wethers, 37 ewes, 811 lambs.
Lomnours. Under the charge and custody of William Albon, 781 wethers.
Sedgeford. Under the charge and custody of Roger Wrask, 1,062. Of which, 1 wether, 27 rams, 1,032 ewes, 2 lambs.
Bintree. With Robert Godwyne, 40. Of which, for custody [*pro Cus'*], 20. And thus he is charged for 20 lambs.
Wood Norton. Agisting with Thomas Martynes, 170 lambs.
Sedgeford Westmanor. Agisting in the Westmanor there, 125 wethers.
Intwood. Agisting with Robert Lilye, 475. Of which, 1 wether, 474 hoggs and gerks.
Plumstead. Agisting with Thomas Sprotte, 363 wethers.

Carleton. Agisting with Robert Long, 319 lambs.

Lomnours. Fattening [*impingnend'*] in a close of the lord there to the benefit of the lord, 27 wethers.

Total of all head of sheep, 6,473. Of which, 1,806 wethers, 27 rams, 2,833 ewes, 477 hoggs and gerks, 1,330 lambs.

The sheep belonging to the lord Prior within these flocks are as written below:

Lathes. 38, of which 2 wethers and 36 ewes.

Newton. 181 wethers.

Eaton. 68 ewes.

Hindringham. 22 lambs.

Intwood. Those from Hethersett, 30 gerks.

Carleton. 42 lambs.

Total head of sheep, 381, of which 183 wethers, 104 ewes, 30 gerks, 64 lambs.

DCN 64/2: Account of 25 December 1495.

General sheep counted and remaining, according to the accounts of the shepherds of the monastery of Norwich, in the following vills and flocks for one whole year ending at the Nativity of our Lord in the year of our Lord 1495. And the 11th year of King Henry VII, and the 7th year of lord William Spynk, Prior. That is to say, at:

Sedgeford. Under the charge and custody of Roger Wrask, 1,370. Of which, 1 wether, 43 rams, 1,326 ewes.

Hindringham. Under the charge and custody of John Dowdy, 831. Of which, 40 ewes, 791 lambs.

Newton. Under the charge and custody of Robert Howlynes, 453 wethers.

Eaton. Under the charge and custody of Thomas Baxter, 1056 ewes.

Lathes. Under the charge and custody of Robert Long, discharged from Thomas Beny, 788 ewes.

Lomnours. Under the charge and custody of William Albon, 860 wethers.

Intwood. Under the charge and custody of Robert Lelye for agistment, 363 wethers.

Wood Norton. Under the custody of Thomas Martyns for agistment, 364 lambs.

Catton. Under the custody of Richard Isbelles there, 577 lambs.

Crouchstoke [*Stoke Holy Cross*]. Under the custody of William Giles for agistment, 431 wethers.

Plumstead. Under the custody of Thomas Sprot for agistment, 70 wethers.

Total of all heads of sheep, 7,163. Of which, 2,178 wethers, 3,210 ewes, 1,732 lambs, 43 rams.

Particular sheep of the lord Prior remaining in the folds below written. That is to say at:

Hindringham. Under the custody of the shepherd there, 50. Of which, 10 ewes, 40 lambs.

Newton. Under the custody of the farmer there, 181 wethers.

Eaton. Under the custody of the shepherd there, 94 ewes.

Lathes. Under the custody of the shepherd there, 37. Of which, 1 wether, 36 ewes.

Intwood. Under the custody of Robert Lely, no return [*non responc'*], 10 ewes.

Catton. Under the custody of the shepherd there, 60. Of which, 40 wethers, 20 lambs.

Total of all head, 432. Of which, 222 wethers, 150 ewes, 60 lambs.

DCN 62/18: Account of 25 December 1496.

General sheep counted and remaining, according to the accounts of the shepherds of the monastery of Norwich, in the following vills and flocks for one whole year ending at the Nativity of our Lord in the year of our lord 1496. And the 12th year of King Henry VII, and the 8th year of lord William Spynk, Prior. That is to say, at:

Sedgeford. Under the charge and custody of Robert Mayne, 1,327. Of which, 1 wether, 42 rams, 1,280 ewes, 4 lambs.

Hindringham. Under the charge and custody of John Dowdy, 704. Of which, 25 ewes, 679 lambs.

Lomnours. Under the charge and custody of William Albon, 801 wethers.

Lathes. Under the charge and custody of Robert Long, 748 ewes.

Newton. Under the charge and custody of Robert Howlynes, 424 wethers. And in the close of the lord called Buttes there, 3 weak wethers.

Eaton. Under the charge and custody of Thomas Baxter, 906. Of which, 23 rams, 1 wether, 882 ewes.

Catton. Under the charge and custody of John Barsham, 556. Of which, 71 ewes, 250 wethers, 235 lambs. [*...slight damage*] 2 wethers and 2 ewes remain there as stray.

Cawston. Under the charge and custody of *the shepherd* [*of*] Thomas Woodhous esquire, 492 wethers.

Wood Norton. Under the custody of Thomas Martyns, 98 wethers.

Crouchstoke [*Stoke Holy Cross*]. Under the charge of William Giles for agistment, 146 wethers.

Hemsby. Under the charge of John Botolf, farmer there, for stock, 60 wethers.

Hindringham. Under the charge of John Clerk, farmer there, for stock, 60 wethers.

Total of all heads of sheep, [*blank, actual number is 6,325*]. Of which, 65 rams, 2,336 wethers, 3,006 ewes, 918 lambs.

The sheep belonging to the lord Prior in these flocks are as written below, namely at:
Lomnours, under the custody of the shepherd there, 10 wethers.
Lathes, under the custody of the shepherd there, 27. Of which 1 wether, 26 ewes.
Newton, under the custody of the farmer there, 181 wethers.
Hindringham, under the custody of the shepherd there, 56. Of which, 10 ewes, 16 wethers, 30 lambs.
Eaton, under the custody of the shepherd there, 108 ewes.
Catton, under the custody of the shepherd there, 70. Of which, 50 wethers, 10 ewes, 10 lambs.
Total of all head, 452, of which 258 wethers, 154 ewes, 40 lambs.

DCN 62/19: Account of 25 December 1497.

General sheep counted and remaining on the accounts of the shepherds of the monastery of Norwich limited to the following vills and flocks for one whole year ending at the Nativity of our Lord in the year of our Lord 1497. And the 13th year of King Henry VII. And the 9th year of lord William Spynk, Prior.
Sedgeford. Under the custody of John Carman, shepherd, 1,360. Of which, 1 wether, 1,359 ewes.
Lomnours. Under the custody of Robert Hekelton, 818 wethers.
Eaton. Under the custody of Thomas Baxter, 852. Of which, 24 wethers, 23 rams, 741 ewes, 64 lambs.
Lathes. Under the custody of Robert Long, 781. Of which, 671 ewes, 110 lambs.
Newton. Under the custody of Robert Howlynes, 295 wethers, with 8 in Buttes close.
Hindringham. Under the custody of John Sparhauk, 873. Of which, 64 ewes, 74 wethers, 735 lambs.
Fring. Under the custody of William Page, 1,023. Of which, 393 wethers, 116 ewes, 34 rams, 480 lambs.
Total of all head of sheep, 6,002. Of which, 57 rams, 1,605 wethers, 2,951 ewes, 1,389 lambs.

Particular sheep of the lord Prior remaining in the folds written above, namely at:
Lomnours, under the custody of the shepherd there, 10 wethers.

Lathes, under the custody of the shepherd there, 1 wether. 26 ewes under the custody of the shepherd there, and received from Catton after shearing, 20 [*total*] 46. 14 lambs received from birth of ewes this year, and remaining.

Newton. From remainder there, 181 wethers. And received from Catton, 50. Of which, sold before shearing, 40. And remaining, 191.

Eaton. And remaining, 130 ewes. And remaining, 60 lambs.

Hindringham. And remaining, 56, of which, 10 ewes, 16 wethers, 30 lambs. And sent to Fring.

DCN 64/2: Account of 25 December 1498.

General sheep counted and remaining, according to the accounts of the shepherds of the monastery of Norwich, limited to the following vills and flocks for one whole year ending at the Nativity of our Lord in the year of our Lord 1498. And the 14th year of King Henry VII, and the 10th year of lord William Spynk, Prior.

Fring. Under the custody of Ed. Brook, 1,308. Of which, 913 wethers, 34 rams, 361 lambs.

Hindringham. Under the custody of John Sparhauk, 772. Of which, 15 ewes, 757 lambs.

Sedgeford. Under the custody of John Rose, accounted by the stockman, 1,537. Of which, 1 wether, 1,536 ewes.

Lathes. Under the custody of Robert Long, 768 ewes.

Newton. Under the custody of Robert Howlynes, 157 wethers.

Eaton. Under the custody of Thomas Baxter, 927. Of which, 24 wethers, 23 rams, 782 ewes, 98 lambs.

Lomnours. Under the custody of Robert Hekilton, 743 wethers.

Total of all head of sheep, 6,212. Of which, 57 rams, 1,838 wethers, 3,101 ewes, 1,216 lambs.

The sheep belonging to the lord Prior in these flocks are as written below, namely at:

Newton, 128 wethers.

Eaton, 171, of which 131 ewes, 40 lambs.

Lomnours, 10 wethers.

Fring, 56, of which, 10 ewes, 46 wethers.

Total head of sheep, 365, of which 184 wethers, 141 ewes, 40 lambs.

Beyond which, remaining as stock of the monastery in the hands of the farmers of certain manors as contracted, outside the account, 180 ewes.[90]

---

[90] The Priory included some sheep as part of the lease of the arable demesne of these manors.

Total, 180 ewes, of which with the farmers of the manors of Hindringham 60, Sedgeford 60, Hemsby 60.

DCN 62/16: Account of 25 December 1499.

General sheep counted and remaining on individual accounts produced by the shepherds of the flocks and folds of the monastery of Norwich, limited to the following vills and flocks for one whole year ending at the Nativity of our Lord in the year 1499. And the 15th year of King Henry VII, and the 11th year of lord William Spynk, Prior. That is to say, at:

Hindringham. Under the charge of John Sparhawk, shepherd there, 843. Of which, 6 wethers, 55 ewes, 782 lambs.

Lathes. Under the charge of Robert Hekelton, 781. Of which, 769 ewes and 12 lambs.

Lomnours. Under the charge of Robert Long, 508 wethers.

Sedgeford. Under the charge of John Broun, 1,396. Of which, 1 wether, 1,374 ewes, 21 lambs.

Fring. Under the charge of Thomas Meye, 1,347. Of which, 34 rams, 1,313 wethers.

Newton. Under the custody of Robert Howlyns, 453 wethers.

Eaton. Under the custody of Thomas Baxter, 699 ewes.

Total of all head of sheep of the monastery, 6,027. Of which, 34 rams, 2,281 wethers, 2,897 ewes, 815 lambs.

The sheep belonging to the lord Prior in these flocks are as written below:

Lomnours. Under the custody of Robert Long, shepherd there, 118 wethers.

Fring. Under the custody of Robert Mayne, 58. Of which, 46 wethers, 10 ewes, 2 lambs.

Eaton. Under the custody of Thomas Baxter, 120 ewes.

Total head of sheep, 296. Of which, 164 wethers, 130 ewes, 2 lambs.

Beyond these are 180 ewes remaining as stock of the monastery in the hands of the farmers of certain manors by contract, outside the account. Total, 180 ewes, of which the farmers of the manors of Hindringham *60*, Sedgeford *60*, Hemsby, *60*.

DCN 62/16: Account of 25 December 1500.

General sheep counted and remaining on individual accounts produced by the shepherds of the flocks and folds of the monastery of Norwich, limited to the following vills and flocks for one whole year ending at the Nativity of our Lord in the year 1500. And the 16th year of King Henry VII, and the 12th year of lord William Spynk, Prior. That is to say, at:

Hindringham. Under the custody of John Sparhauk, 1,014. Of which, 10 wethers, 32 stock ewes, 125 crone ewes, 847 lambs.

Fring. Under the custody of Robert Mayne, 1,319. Of which, 34 rams, 1,285 wethers.

Sedgeford. Under the custody of the said Robert Mayne, 1,295. Of which, 1,286 ewes, 9 lambs.

Lathes. Under the custody of Robert Hekylton, 826 ewes.

Newton. Under the custody of Robert Howlynes, bailiff there, 325 wethers.

Lomnours. The way and liberty of fold there is leased to Richard Yuttes, paying each year £4.[91]

Eaton. Under the custody of Thomas Heyward, 938 ewes.

Sheep given by the lord Prior to lord Robert Walsingham, the new Master Cellarer, at the end of this account. From deficient sheep [charged] on Robert Howlynes in Newton, he agrees [*ei assumpt'*], 21 wethers.

From deficient sheep [charged] on Robert Long at Lomnours, he agrees, 8 wethers.

From deficient sheep [charged] on Robert Hekelton at Lathes, he agrees, 20 wethers.

From sheep remaining with the farmers of the manors, namely at Hindringham *60,* Sedgeford *60*, Hemsby *60*, and Newton *58*. Total 238 ewes.

Total head of sheep, 6,004. Of which, 34 rams, 1,649 wethers, 3,465 ewes, 856 lambs.

DCN 62/16: Account of 25 December 1501.

General sheep counted and remaining on individual accounts produced by the shepherds of the flocks and folds of the monastery of Norwich, limited to the following vills and flocks for one whole year ending at the Nativity of our Lord in the year 1501. And the 17th year of King Henry VII, and the 13th year of lord William Spynk, Prior. That is to say, at:

Hindringham. Under the custody of John Larke, shepherd there, 888. Of which, 32 ewes, 856 lambs.

Fring. Under the custody of Robert Mayne, shepherd there, 1,130. Of which, 34 rams, 54 wethers, 790 ewes, 252 lambs.

Sedgeford. Under the custody of the said Robert Mayne, 1,251. Of which, 1,238 wethers, 13 lambs.

---

[91] Marginal note: 'Empty, because leased at farm'.

Lathes. Under the custody of Robert Hekelton, 832. Of which, 822 ewes, 10 lambs.

Eaton. Under the custody of Thomas Heyward, 1,309. Of which, 1,308 wethers, 1 ewe.

Newton. Under the custody of Robert Howlyns, 277 wethers.

Of the sheep remaining with the farmers of the manors, namely at Hindringham *60,* Sedgeford *60,* Hemsby *60,* and Newton *58*. Total 238 ewes.

Total head of sheep, 5,925. Of which, 34 rams, 1,639 wethers, 3,121 ewes, 1,131 lambs.

DCN 64/5: Account of 25 December 1503.

General sheep counted and remaining on individual accounts produced by the shepherds of the flocks and folds of the monastery of Norwich, limited to the following vills and flocks for one whole year ending at the Nativity of our Lord in the year of grace 1503. And the 19th year of King Henry VII, and the 1st year of lord William Bakonesthorpe, Prior. That is to say, at:

Fring. Under the custody of John Morelond, shepherd there, 1,156. Of which, 945 ewes, 211 lambs.

Sedgeford. Under the custody of Nicholas Rust, shepherd there, 1,069. Of which, 949 ewes, 120 lambs

Hindringham. Under the custody of John Laxe, shepherd there, 945. Of which, 70 rams, 17 ewes, 41 hoggs, 817 lambs.

Lathes. Under the custody of Robert Long, now shepherd there, 880 ewes.

Eaton. Under the custody of John Sturmyn, shepherd there, 955. Of which, 954 wethers, 1 ewe.

Newton. Under the custody of Robert Howlynes, farmer there, 657 wethers. From the sheep remaining with the farmers of the manors, namely at Hindringham *60,* Sedgeford *60*, Hemsby *60*, and Newton *58*. Total 238 ewes.

Total head of sheep now remaining in the above mentioned vills and flocks, 5,900. Of which, 70 rams, 1,611 wethers, 3,030 ewes, 41 hoggs, 1,148 lambs.

DCN 62/23: Account of 29 September 1509.

General sheep counted and remaining on individual accounts produced by the shepherds of the flocks and folds of the monastery of Norwich in the following vills and flocks for one whole year ending at the feast of St Michael the Archangel in the year of our Lord 1509. And the 1st year of

King Henry VIII. And in the 5th year of lord Robert [Catton], Prior.[92]
Lathes. Under the custody of Robert Chamberleyn, shepherd there, 954. Of which, 949 ewes, 5 lambs.
Eaton. Under the custody of John Sturmyn, shepherd there, 849. Of which, 773 wethers, 3 ewes, 2 lambs, 71 rams.
Thorpe Episcopi [*next Norwich*]. Under the custody of Walter Balles, shepherd there, 831 wethers.
Under the custody of Thomas Newman, shepherd there, 725 ewes.
Hindringham. Under the custody of John Laxe, shepherd there, 903. Of which, 2 ewes, 1 wether, 900 lambs.
Newton. Under the custody of John Smyth, shepherd there, 511. Of which, 146 wethers, 365 ewes.
Sedgeford. Under the custody of John Pepyr, shepherd there, 1,305. Of which, 187 ewes, 18 rams, 1,100 lambs.
Gnatingdon. Under the custody of Nicholas Rust, shepherd there, 1,222. Of which, 1,221 ewes, 1 wether.
Thurlton. Under the custody of John Mekylbergh, 288. Of which, 241 ewes, 47 riggs.
Total of all heads of sheep of the monastery now remaining in the above mentioned vills and flocks, 7,588. Of which, 3,693 ewes, 1,752 wethers, 2,007 lambs, 89 rams, 47 riggs.

Sheep of the lord Prior counted and remaining on the account produced by Walter Balles, shepherd of the flock and fold of Thorpe Episcopi next to Norwich, limited to one whole year finishing at Michaelmas in the year of our Lord 1509. And the 1st year of King Henry VIII. And the 5th year of lord Robert, Prior. That is at,
Thorpe Episcopi [*next Norwich*]. Under the custody of Walter Balles, shepherd there, 61 wethers.

Sheep pertaining to the office of the Cellarer of the Cathedral Church of Norwich, counted and remaining on the above accounts produced by the shepherds named below, and limited to the following vills and flocks finishing at Michaelmas in the 1st year of King Henry VIII.
Thorpe Episcopi [*next Norwich*]. Under the custody of Walter Balles, shepherd there, 120 wethers.
Eaton. Under the custody of John Sturmyn, shepherd there, 120 wethers.
Total of all head of sheep now pertaining to the office of Cellarer, 240 wethers.

Account made between master lord George Hyngham master cellarer of

---

[92] Robert Catton became prior in 1505, Saunders, *Obedientary Rolls*, p. 191.

the monastery of Norwich and William Cleres supervisor and stockman of the flocks of the folds of the monastery aforesaid as for one whole year finishing at Michaelmas in the 1st year of King Henry VIII. And the 5th year of lord Robert, Prior.

First, the supervisor of stock is charged with certain pelts called *le mortis* received from diverse shepherds of the following folds.[93] That is, from the fold of:

Gnatingdon. Under the custody of Nicholas Rust, shepherd there, from murrain, 55.

Sedgeford. Under the custody of Robert Pepyr, from pelts in murrain 98, of which 23 from ewes and 75 from last year's lambs.

Newton. Under the custody of John Smyth, shepherd there, from pelts in murrain, 39 wethers.

Thorpe Episcopi [*next Norwich*] Under the custody of Walter Balles, shepherd there, 20 wethers.

Under the custody of John Hekylton, shepherd, 29 ewes.

Hindringham. Under the custody of John Laxe, shepherd there, 62 ewes.

Eaton. Under the custody of John Sturmyn, shepherd there, 16 wethers

Lathes. Under the custody of Robert Chaumberleyn, shepherd there, 57 ewes.

Total pelts called *le mortis* as above, 376. Of which, 164 ewes, 75 wethers, 137 of the previous year's lambs [*agni ultimo anno*]. Total cash for 376 pelts as above, at 15s. per 120, 47s.

Memorandum of sales of sheep of the monastery of Norwich in diverse folds and places to the underwritten people, named for information by Walter Cleres, stockman of the monastery aforesaid, on the Cellarer's account ending at Michaelmas [*29 September*] in the year of our Lord 1509 and the 1st year of Henry VIII. That is to say from the fold at:

Newton. First, sold to Thomas Dey of Norwich, butcher, 120, of which 80 wethers priced 20d. each, total £6 13s. 4d., and 40 riggs priced 20d. each, total 66s. 8d.

Eaton. Item, sold from the same fold to Thomas Leek of Norwich, butcher, 120 wethers at 20d. each, total £10.

Total head of sheep of the monastery sold to the people aforenamed, 240 at 20d. per head, and thus the total cash generated, £20.

Memo that certain deficient sheep [*are charged*] upon the shepherds in the folds written above according to the accounts finished at Michaelmas in

---

[93] This is the most detailed of the centralised stock accounts, recording information about the transfer of pelts from individual shepherds to the monastery's stockman, and the charge upon individual shepherds for deficient sheep. The cash generated from such charges is also recorded in Category Three accounts, e.g. pp. 88, 90.

the 1st year of King Henry VIII [*29 September 1509*], of which in the fold of:
Thorpe Episcopi [*next Norwich*]. On John Hekylton, shepherd of the flocks and
folds, 3 deficient ewes priced at 12d. per head, 3s.

Total head of deficient sheep [*charged*] on shepherds this year, 3.

Memo that certain sheep were delivered to the people written below from
the folds noted below [*and*] accounted on the account of the Cellarer
ending at Michaelmas in the 1st year of King Henry VIII, that is to say the
folds of:

Newton. Item, first, given to Robert Peers at the kitchen to feed the *famuli* of
the manor there during the harvest,[94] 3 riggs.

Item. to the kitchen of the convent before Michaelmas, 87 wethers, and 60
wethers after Michaelmas, total 147 wethers.

Item, to the kitchen of the monastery before Michaelmas, 53 riggs.

Thorpe Episcopi [*next Norwich*]. Item, given to the kitchen of the monastery,
52 wethers, and 3 to John Bronde, total 55 wethers.

Lathes. Item, given to the kitchen of the monastery by John Hekylton, 20
ewes.

Item, given to the kitchen of the convent, 20 ewes.

Item, given to the same kitchen, 22 lambs.

Sedgeford and Gnatingdon. Item, given to the kitchen of the manor for the
court [*held around the feast*] of John in the 1st year of King Henry VIII,[95] 3,
of which 1 wether and 2 lambs of this year.

Total head of sheep delivered as written above, 323.

Total head of sheep of the monastery, as in pelts called *les mortis* *376*, or
sales *241*, or deficient sheep *3*, or given the kitchen of the monastery
314, the kitchen of the manor of Newton *3*, the kitchen of the manor
of Sedgeford *3*, and given to John Bronde *3*. Total, 943 [*sic*].

Total head of all sheep of the monastery this year ending at the feast of
Michaelmas in the 1st year of King Henry VIII, with sheep sold *241*, and
pelts called *les Mortis* *376*, and deficient sheep *3*, and given to the
kitchens of the monastery *314*, Newton *3*, and Sedgeford *3*, and
John Bronde, *3*. Total, 8,531.

The charge of William Cleres supervisor of the stock of the monastery for
the year finishing at Michaelmas in the 1st year of King Henry VIII.

---

[94] The *famuli* were the full time workers on the lord's demesne manor, who received food,
cash and clothing as part of their remuneration package. See C. Dyer, 'Changes in Diet in the
Late Middle Ages: the Case of Harvest Workers', *Agricultural History Review*, 36 (1988), pp. 21-
37, which discusses examples from Sedgeford.

[95] Presumably the feast of the Nativity of St John the Baptist, so this would be held in late
June 1509.

First the same is charged with the price of 376 pells called *le mortez* price 15s. a hundred, total 47s. And the same is charged with money [*peceuniis*] received from the hands of William Elsy on the Wednesday immediately before the feast of the Nativity of St John the Baptist in the 1st year of King Henry VIII, 20s.

Total of the charge 67s.

Of which is allowed to the supervisor for the washing and shearing of the sheep of the monastery at Sedgeford and Gnatingdon with other small expenses there, as appears by his bill allowed upon the account, 20s. 7d. And to the same for washing and shearing of the sheep of the monastery at Hindringham with other small expenses there, 7s. 3d. And to the same for small expenses incurred at the time of the washing and shearing of the sheep in diverse folds near Norwich, 7d. And to the same for one dozen *le hirdell* bought for the fold of *le Lathes* price 18d. And to the same for one barrel of bitumen *4s. 4d.* bought from Richard Pynnes of Little Walsingham for the flock at Hindringham together with the carriage *1d.* there from Walsingham to Hindringham, 4s. 5d.

And the same claims for his stipend for three terms finishing at Michaelmas in the 1st year of King Henry VIII, 30s. And the same claims for driving the animals from one pasture to another *6s. 3d.* and for his livery *6s. 8d.*, 12s. 11d.

Total of the claims and allowances, 77s. 3d.

And 10s. 3d. is owed to the aforesaid stockman. Which is paid to him in the presence of Richard Boty and John Mekylbergh on the 4th December in the 1st year of King Henry VIII.

DCN 62/24: Account of 29 September 1510.

General sheep counted and remaining on individual accounts produced by the shepherds of the flocks and folds of the monastery of Norwich in the following vills and flocks for one whole year ending at the feast of St Michael the Archangel in the year of our lord 1510. And the 2nd year of King Henry VIII. And in the 6th year of lord Robert [*Catton*], Prior. That is to say, at:

Lathes. Under the custody of John Smyth, shepherd there, 910 ewes.

Eaton. Under the custody of Clement Alesson, shepherd there, 1,024. Of which, 70 rams, 75 riggs, 877 wethers, 2 ewes.

Thorpe Episcopi [*next Norwich*]. Under the custody of Thomas Newman, shepherd there, 784 ewes.

Under the custody of Walter Balles, shepherd there, 908. Of which, 17 rams, 891 wethers.

Newton. Under the charge and custody of John Love, alias Algore, farmer of the manor of the lord there, 300. Of which, 166 wethers, 134 ewes.

There under the charge of the said John Love, alias Algore, with the lease of the manor as appears in an indenture, 240 ewes.

Hindringham. Under the custody of John Laxe, shepherd there, 795. Of which, 4 wethers, 9 ewes, 782 lambs.

There under the charge of Thomas Mason, farmer there, as appears in an indenture, 82. Of which, 54 wethers, 28 hoggs.

Gnatingdon. Under the custody of Nicholas Rust, shepherd there, 1,283. Of which, 1 wether, 1,282 ewes.

Sedgeford. Under the custody of the aforesaid Nicholas Rust, shepherd there, 957 lambs.

Sedgeford Westmanor farmer's flock. Under the charge and custody of John Clerk, farmer of the manor of the lord, 447. Of which, 223 wethers, 224 ewes.

Hemsby. Under the charge of John Botolff, farmer there, as contracted as appears in an indenture, 60 ewes

Total head of sheep, 7,790. Of which, 87 rams, 2,216 wethers, 3,645 ewes, 1,739 lambs, 75 riggs, 28 hoggs.

Memorandum that last year 129 ewes within the total for the sheep of remainder were dead [*mortue fuerunt*] that were then made alive in the same last year [*de parte ovium rem' *tunc fact'* vivencium eodem ultimo anno*], as claimed by the release of diverse shepherds in their accounts this year [*two words are illegible*] was, that should be credited to them [*debunt esse eis ventate*].[96]

Particular sheep of the lord Prior, counted and return made by Walter Balles shepherd of the flock of Thorpe Episcopi by Norwich to the feast of the Nativity [*Ms crumpled*] in the year of the Lord within written, and in the year of the King within written. [*Total*] 61.

Particular sheep of the office of Cellarer of the cathedral church returned by the shepherds below written for the aforesaid year. That is to say at:

Thorpe Episcopi [*next Norwich*]. Under the custody of Walter Balles, shepherd there, 120 wethers.

Eaton. Under the custody of Clement Alesson, shepherd there, 120 wethers. Total head of sheep pertaining to the office of Cellarer, 240 wethers.

DCN 62/27: Account of 29 September 1514.

General sheep counted and remaining on individual accounts produced by the shepherds of the flocks and folds of the monastery of Norwich in the

---

[96] A difficult sentence and an unhappy translation. The general sense is clear, however, and indicates that sheep counted as alive the year before were actually dead, and the fact should be recorded accordingly.

following vills and flocks for one whole year ending at the feast of St Michael in the year of our Lord 1514. And the 6th year of King Henry VIII. And in the 10th year of lord Robert, Prior.

Sedgeford Northflock. Under the custody of Nicholas Rust, shepherd there, 1,096. Of which, 15 wethers, 1,081 lambs.

Gnatingdon. Under the custody of Thomas Perot, shepherd there, 1,257. Of which, 4 rams, 1 wether, 1,252 ewes.

Sedgeford Westmanor. Under the charge and custody of John Elger, farmer of the site of Westmanor there, as contracted as appears in an indenture, 120 ewes.

Hindringham. Under the custody of Robert Gowty, shepherd there, 796. Of which, 4 wethers, 22 ewes, 770 lambs.

There under the charge of Thomas Mason, farmer of the site of the manor there, as appears in an indenture, 82. Of which, 54 ewes, 28 hoggs.

Lathes. Under the custody of Thomas Rede, shepherd there, 897 ewes.

Eaton. Under the custody of John Foket, shepherd there, 803 ewes.

Newton. Under the charge and custody of John Love, alias Algore, farmer of the site of the manor there, 199. Of which 96 wethers, 103 ewes.

There under the charge of the said John Love, alias Algore, with the lease of the site of the manor there as appears in an indenture, 240 ewes.

Thorpe Episcopi [*next Norwich*]. Under the custody of Henry Balles, shepherd there, 875. Of which, 66 rams, 70 riggs, 739 wethers.

Under the custody of Walter Balles, shepherd there, 1,110. Of which, 2 rams, 1,108 wethers.

Thurlton. Under the charge of John Mekilbergh as appears in his account there, 40. Of which, 20 rams, 20 wethers.

Hemsby. Under the charge of John Broun, farmer of the site of the manor there, as contracted as appears in an indenture, 60 ewes.

Total heads of sheep, 7,575. Of which, 92 rams, 70 riggs, 1,983 wethers, 3,551 ewes, 28 hoggs, 1,851 lambs.

Particular sheep of the lord Prior counted and return made by Walter Balles, shepherd of the flock and fold of Thorpe Epsicopi next to Norwich, ended at the Nativity of the Lord in the year written above and the year of King Henry VIII written above [*25 December 1514*], 61 wethers.

Sheep pertaining to the office of the Cellarer of the Cathedral Church by the shepherds written above in the year abovesaid, that is at:

Thorpe Episcopi [*next Norwich*]. Under the custody of Walter Balles, one shepherd there, 120 wethers.

Under the custody of Henry Balles, the other shepherd there, 120 wethers.

Total head of sheep pertaining to the office of Cellarer, 240 wethers.

DCN 62/28: Account of 29 September 1515.

General sheep counted and remaining on individual accounts produced by the shepherds of the flocks and folds of the monastery of Norwich in the following vills and flocks for one whole year ending at the feast of St Michael in the year of our Lord 1515. And the 7th year of King Henry VIII. And in the 11th year of lord Robert [Catton], Prior.

Gnatingdon. Under the custody of Thomas Perot, shepherd there, 1,316. Of which, 4 rams, 1 wether, 1,311 ewes.

Sedgeford Northflock. Under the custody of Nicholas Rust, shepherd there, 1,089. Of which, 16 wethers, 16 ewes, 1,057 lambs.

Sedgeford Westmanor. Under the charge and custody of John Elger, farmer there, as contracted as appears in an indenture, 120 ewes.

Lathes. Under the custody of Richard Deynes, shepherd there, 988 ewes.

Eaton. Under the custody of John Foket, shepherd there, 947 ewes.

Newton. Under the charge and custody of John Love, alias Algoore, farmer of the site of the manor there, 325. Of which, 214 wethers, 111 ewes.

There under the charge of the said John, with the farm of the site of the manor there, as contracted as appears in an indenture, 240 ewes.

Thorpe Episcopi [next to Norwich]. Under the custody of Henry Balles, shepherd there, 870. Of which, 2 rams, 868 wethers.

Under the custody of Walter Balles, shepherd there, 1,199. Of which, 2 rams, 1,197 ewes.

Hindringham. Under the custody of Robert Gowty, shepherd there, 844. Of which, 9 wethers, 9 ewes, 826 lambs.

Thurlton. Under the charge of John Mekilbergh, as appears in his account of the third year preceding, 40. Of which, 20 rams, 20 wethers.

Hemsby. Under the charge of John Broun, farmer of the site of the manor, as contracted as appears in an indenture, 60 ewes.

Total[97] head of sheep 8,120. Of which, 92 rams, 50 riggs, 28 hoggs, 2,211 wethers, 3,856 ewes, 1,883 lambs.

Particular sheep of the lord Prior counted and return made by Walter Ballez, shepherd of the flock of Thorpe Episcopi, ending at the Nativity of the Lord in the said year. And the year of the King written above, 61 wethers.

Sheep pertaining to the office of the Cellarer of the Cathedral Church, return made by the shepherds written below in the year aforesaid. That is to say, at:

Thorpe Episcopi [next to Norwich]. Under the custody of Walter Balles, one

---

[97] The capital S of *Summa* is ornate.

shepherd there, 120 wethers. Under the custody of Henry Balles, the other shepherd there, 120 wethers.
Total head of sheep pertaining to the office of the Cellarer, 240 wethers.

DCN 62/29: Account of 29th September 1517.

General sheep counted and remaining on individual accounts produced by the shepherds of the flocks and folds of the monastery of Norwich in the following vills and flocks for one whole year ending at the feast of St Michael the Archangel in the year of our Lord 1517. And the 9th year of King Henry VIII. And in the 13th year of lord Robert [Catton], Prior.
Gnatingdon. Under the custody of Nicholas Ruste, shepherd there, 1,378. Of which, 1,363 ewes, 15 lambs.
Northflock in Sedgeford. Under the custody of Robert Papere, shepherd there, 1,027. Of which, 20 rams, 80 wethers, 103 ewes, 824 lambs.
Sedgeford Westmanor. Under the charge and custody of Thomas Alynne, farmer there as contracted as appears in an indenture, 120 ewes.
Lathes. Under the custody of John Flyte, shepherd there, 991 ewes.
Eaton. Under the custody of William Grene, shepherd there, 840 ewes.
Newton. Under the charge and custody of John Love, alias Algore, farmer of the site of the manor there, 334. Of which, 187 wethers, 147 ewes.
There under the charge of the said John, farmer of the site of the manor there as contracted as appears in an indenture, 240 ewes.
Thorpe Episcopi [next to Norwich]. Under the custody of Thomas Ballez, shepherd there, 859. Of which, 44 riggs, 815 wethers.
Under the custody of Walter Ballez, shepherd there, 1,014. Of which, 2 rams, 1,012 wethers.
Hindringham. Under the custody of John Laxe, shepherd there, 882. Of which, 13 wethers, 21 ewes, 848 lambs.
There under the charge of Robert Pedder, farmer of the site of the manor there as appears in an indenture, 82. Of which, 54 ewes, 28 hoggs.
Thurlton. Under the charge of John Mekilburgh, as appears in his account there five years previously, 40. Of which 20 rams, 20 wethers.
Hemsby. Under the charge of John Broun, farmer of the site of the manor there as contracted as appears in an indenture, 60 ewes.
Spixworth. Under the custody of John Hekelton, shepherd there, 468. Of which, 40 rams, 20 riggs, 360 wethers, 48 ewes.
Total of all heads of sheep of the monastery now remaining in the above mentioned vills and flocks, 8,335. Of which, 82 rams, 64 riggs, 28 hoggs, 2,487 wethers, 3,987 ewes, 1,687 lambs.

Sheep of the lord Prior counted and return made by Walter Ballez, shepherd of the flocks of Thorpe Episcopi with Lomnours, at the feast of the Nativity of our Lord in the year of King Henry above said [*25 December 1517*], 61 wethers.

Sheep pertaining to the office of the Cellarer of the Cathedral Church of Norwich, counted and remaining with the shepherds named below, and limited to the following vills and flocks finishing at Michaelmas in the said year of King Henry VIII [*29 September 1517*].

Thorpe Episcopi [*next to Norwich*]. Under the custody of Walter Ballez, shepherd there, 120 wethers. Under the custody of Thomas Ballez, shepherd there, 120 wethers.

Total, 240 wethers.

DCN 62/16: Account of 25th December 1523.

General sheep counted and remaining, according to the particular accounts of the shepherds and the responses of the shepherds of the flocks and folds of the monastery of Norwich, limited to the following vills and flocks for one whole year ending at the Nativity of our Lord in the year of our Lord 1523. And the 15th year of King Henry VIII. And the 19th year of lord Robert [*Catton*], Prior. Namely, at:

Hindringham. Under the custody of Robert Gowty, shepherd there, 941. Of which, 2 wethers, 108 ewes, 831 lambs.

There under the custody of Robert Pedder, farmer of the site of the manor there as appears in an indenture, 82. Of which, 54 ewes, 28 hoggs.

Gnatingdon. Under the custody of Nicholas Rust, shepherd there, 1,395. Of which, 1 ram, 1,394 ewes.

Northflock in Sedgeford. Under the custody of Nicholas Rust, shepherd there, 400 lambs.

Sedgeford Westmanor. Under the charge of Henry Russell, farmer of the site of the manor there, as appears in an indenture, 120 ewes.

Lathes. Under the custody of Robert Beny, shepherd there, 1,085. Of which, 1 wether, 1,069 ewes, 15 lambs.

Thorpe Episcopi [*next to Norwich*]. Under the custody of the said Robert Beny, shepherd there, 860. Of which, 18 hoggs, 74 rams, 768 wethers.

Thorpe Episcopi with Lomnours. Under the custody of Walter Ballez shepherd there, 1,174. Of which, 3 rams, 20 riggs, 1,151 wethers.

Spixworth. Under the custody of John Hekylton, shepherd there, 864. Of which, 57 riggs, 807 wethers.

Hellesdon. Under the charge of William Hermere, farmer there, 10. Of which, 8 ewes, as in the [*account*] two years previously, 2 lambs.

Foulsham. Under the charge of Simon Oldryng there, as in the preceding year, 34. Of which, 7 wethers, 27 ewes.

Hemsby. Under the charge of Isabella, lately wife of John Broune, widow of the farmer of the site of the manor there, as contracted by an indenture, 60 ewes.

Thurlton. Under the charge of the executors of the will of John Mekylbergh, as appears in account of the said John in the 11th year previously, 40. Of which, 20 rams, 20 wethers.

Newton. Under the charge of John Howlynez, farmer of the site of the manor there as contracted by indenture, price per hundred £8 by agreement of the said John in the [*account*] two years earlier, 240 ewes.[98]

There in the farm of the said John Howlynez paying for the farm annually by the hundred, 179. Of which, ewes by the hundred valued at £8 by agreement with the said John in the [*account*], 177. Lambs valued at 6d. per head by agreement as above, 2.

There <in the farm> *under the charge* of the said John Howlynez for agistment received by us until Michaelmas forthcoming, just as then were charged at 2d. per head, 545.[99] Of which, 4 wethers, 541 ewes.

Salhouse, with John Corbelle. Under the charge of the said John Corbelle, 65 crone wethers.

Total head of all sheep, 8,094.

Of which, 42 rams, 151 riggs, 28 hoggs, 2,831 wethers, 3,792 ewes, 1,250 lambs.

The particular sheep of the said Prior counted and return made by Walter Ballez, shepherd of the flock of Lomnours with Great Plumstead, to the feast of the Nativity of our Lord, in the year of our Lord and the year of the King above mentioned [*25 December 1523*], 61 wethers.

---

[98] The language employed here is terse and so the meaning is not very clear. An agreement had been struck between John and the monastery in 1521 ['the account two years earlier'], and the details were recorded in that account: unfortunately, it is not extant. Essentially, John, as part of his lease of the manor of Newton, takes direct control of some of the monastery's sheep, paying at the rate of £8 per 120 sheep. John presumably gains the benefit of the manure and fleeces. The cash paid by John for this rental agreement is also recorded in the centralised revenue accounts, see pp. 87, 89.

[99] Howlyns, as lessee of the manor of Newton, pays the monastery to have the use of its flocks at Newton for his own benefit, as an adjunct to his lease. Yet this entry reveals that the monastery also has an arrangement whereby it can rent back some pasture grounds in Newton from Howlyns on an *ad hoc* basis. Hence the monastery pays Howlyns to look after an additional 545 sheep over the summer months on its own pastures at Newton. The costs of this arrangement are recorded in the centralised revenue accounts, p. 90. This is a complex, but presumably flexible, arrangement, which implies a good working relationship between the monastery and Howlyns. Howlyns is previously described as the bailiff of Newton, so he was once an employee of the monastery.

DCN 64/2. Account of 25th December 1524.

General sheep counted and remaining, according to the particular accounts of the shepherds and the responses of the shepherds of the flocks and folds of the monastery of Norwich, limited to the following vills and flocks for one whole year ending at the Nativity of our Lord in the year of our Lord 1524. And the 16th year of King Henry VIII. And the 20th year of lord Robert [*Catton*], Prior. Namely, at:

Lathes. Under the custody of Robert Beny, shepherd there, 1,067. Of which, 1 wether, 1,041 ewes, 25 lambs.

Newton. Under the charge of John Howlyns for agistment from the lord received by him to Michaelmas next for 543 head of wethers and ewes, as they were then brought [*per ipsum recipiend' ad Michaelem pro futur' prout tunc product' fuerunt pro capite...*]. Of which, 486 wethers, 57 ewes.

There in the farm of the said John Howlyns 179, paying for the lease each year [*at a rate*] per 120 [*sheep*]. Of which, 177 ewes valued at £8 per hundred as in the agreement with the said John in the account three years earlier. And 2 lambs which are valued at 6d. per head, as in the agreement as above etc., 2.

There under the charge of John Howlyns, farmer of the site of the manor there, as contracted through an indenture at a price of £8 per 120, as agreed with the said John in the third account previously, 240 ewes.

Eaton. Under the custody of Thomas Wake, shepherd there, 1,078. Of which, 682 ewes, 396 lambs.

Gnatingdon. Under the custody of John Barwik, shepherd there, 1,387 ewes.

Northflock in Sedgeford. Under the custody of Nicholas Rust, shepherd there, 927. Of which, 20 rams, 870 wethers, 37 riggs.

Sedgeford Westmanor. Under the charge of Henry Russell, farmer of the site of the manor there, as appears in an indenture, 120 ewes.

Hindringham. Under the custody of Robert Gowty, shepherd there, 1,030. Of which, 6 wethers, 14 ewes, 1,010 lambs.

There under the custody of Robert Pedder, farmer there, as contracted by an indenture, 82. Of which, 54 ewes, 28 hoggs.

Taverham. Under the charge of Robert Wattes, farmer of the manor there, for agistment until Michaelmas next in the future, regarding the head of sheep which came to him from Thorpe Episcopi, 360 wethers.

Lomnours with Great Plumstead. Under the charge of Robert New*m*an, shepherd there, 1,158. Of which, 1 ram, 3 riggs, 1,153 wethers, 1 lamb.

Hellesdon. Under the charge of William Hermere, as previously, 10, [*of which*] 8 ewes, 2 lambs.

Salhouse. Under the charge of John Corbowe, as in the previous year, 65. Thereof charged in the account of Robert Beny at Thorpe Episcopi, that is laid out in the account of the said Robert this year, 3. And thus far remains at Salhouse, 62 crone wethers.

Hemsby. Under the charge of Isabella Browne, widow of the farmer of the site of the manor there, as contracted by an indenture, 60 ewes.

Foulsham. Under the charge of Simon Oldryng, as in the previous [*account*], 34. Of which, 7 wethers, 27 ewes.

Thurlton. Under the charge of the executors of of the will of John Mekylbergh, as previously, 40. Of which, 20 rams, 20 wethers.

Total head of sheep, 8,377.

Of which, 41 rams, 40 riggs, 28 hoggs, 2,965 wethers, 3,878 ewes, 1,425 lambs.[100]

The particular sheep of the said Prior counted and responded by Walter Ballez, shepherd of the flock of Lomnours with Great Plumstead, to the feast of the Nativity of our Lord, in the year of our Lord and the year of the King above mentioned, 61 wethers.

---

[100] The total number given for each of the manors adds up to 8,380, although the summary line here gives 8,377. The difference is explained by the entry for Salhouse, which accounts for three wethers separately.

3. CENTRALISED ACCOUNTS OF INCOME AND EXPENDITURE[101]

DCN 64/6. 29th September 1525 to 29th September 1526

The account of lord Robert Catton, Prior of Norwich, for each and every issue and expense of all the sheep belonging to the office of the Master Cellarer, from the feast of St Michael the Archangel in the year of our lord, 1525. And in the seventeenth year of the reign of King Henry VIII, through to the same feast of St Michael thereafter, in the next year following, the eighteenth of the same reign of the King. And in the twenty second year of the aforesaid Prior, lord Robert.

Receipts from issues of the same sheep.
From 541½ stone of wool sold this year at various prices, £71 16s. 0d.[102] From the locks [*flectis*] produced from the same wool, 2s. 8d. From the sale of sheep, £55 18s. 6d. From the sheep and lamb pelts resulting from murrain in our flocks this year, £4 4s. 7½d. And from John Hughlyns, farmer of Newton for the lease of 179 ewes, valued at 33s. 4d. per 120, thus total 49s. 8½d. And from the cullet of the folds of Hindringham *9s. 10d.* and Eaton *5s. 11½d.*, beyond the contracts of the stockman and the shepherds, 15s. 9½d. From the cullet of our other folds, beyond the contracts of the Master of Magdalene [*Mawdelene*], the stockman and the shepherds, nothing. From the manure of the fold of Hindringham *4s.* and Lomnours with Great Plumstead *3s. 6d.*, 7s. 6d. From the manure of the other folds this year, beyond the contracts of our various farmers, as appears in the auditor's book [*per librum auditoris*], nothing.
Total receipts, £135 14s. 9½d.

Expenditure on the said sheep.
In pasture for our sheep at Lomnours and Great Plumstead, £6 12s. 2d. In pasture for the sheep at Monks' Grange[103], over and above certain lands manured for the Master of Magdalene according to the contract, 53s. 4d. In pasture for the sheep at Eaton, 72s. In pasture for the sheep at Hindringham, 65s. 3d. In pasture for the sheep of the Northflock at Sedgeford, 65s. 7d. In pasture for the sheep at Gnatingdon, 69s. 4d. In pasture for certain sheep at Newton, as appears in the auditor's book, £4

---

[101] See Introduction, pp. 11–12.
[102] The sale of wool at various prices is indicative of multiple sales to a number of merchants.
[103] *Grangias Monachorum*: in Pockthorpe.

11s. 6½d. In washing and shearing our aforesaid sheep, 66s. 8d. In driving sheep from pasture to pasture, 22s.[104] In the stipend of the stockman, 40s. In his livery[105] [*in liberatura sua*], 16s. In the stipends of the shepherds, namely of John Barwyk at Gnatingdon *60s.*, Nicholas Ruste for custody of the Northflock in Sedgeford *60s.*, Robert Gowty at Hindringham *53s. 4d.*, Robert Bene at Lathes *53s. 4d.*, Thomas Wake at Eaton *53s. 4d.*, and Robert Newman at Lomnours and Great Plumstead *60s.,* £17. And to the same shepherds for their livery, as appears in the auditor's book, 31s. 8d. In hurdles *24s.*, pitch and bitumen *46s. 2d.*, the ruddling boles, *3s. 6d.*, and grease *7s. 4d.* for the sheep, £4 1s. 3d. And in various other small expenses regarding our aforesaid sheep this year, as appears in the book of the accountant, 7s. 8d.
Total payments, £57 14s. 5½d.

And thus remains clear, £78 0s. 3½d. It is assigned to the said accountant in part payment for grain bought by him, as appears in the account of the office of the Master Cellarer this year.[106] Thus equals.

DCN 64/7. 29th September 1526 to 29th September 1527

The account of lord Robert Catton, Prior of Norwich, for each and every issue and expense of all the sheep belonging to the office of the Master Cellarer, from the feast of St Michael the archangel in the year of our lord, 1526. And in the eighteenth year of the reign of King Henry VIII, through to the same feast of St Michael thereafter, in the next year following, the nineteenth of the same reign of the lord King. And in the twenty third year of the aforesaid Prior, lord Robert.

Receipts from issues of the same sheep
From 503 stone of wool sold this year at various prices, £74 3s. 8d. From the sale of sheep this year, £40 11s. 7d. From the sheep and lamb pelts resulting from murrain in our flocks this year, £7 12s. 4d. And from John

---

[104] See Introduction, p. 13.

[105] The Priory's employees were given an annual clothing allowance, which would have incorporated the Priory's insignia.

[106] This reference is confusing. Strictly speaking, the accountant is the Prior, for this is the Prior's account. Yet this same account is clear that these are the sheep of the Master Cellarer. If the sheep belong to the Master Cellarer, it is odd that the Prior should be drawing up the account and that the office of Prior should be the beneficiary of the healthy financial surplus. In fact, the surplus is allocated to the office of the Master Cellarer to buy grain for the monks, and the surplus is also accounted for in the annual account of the Master Cellarer. This is an example of the lack of clear lines of accountability within the management structure of the Priory, see Introduction, pp. 4–5.

Hughlyns, farmer of Newton for the lease of 179 ewes, valued at 33s. 4d. per 120, thus total 49s. 8½d. And from the cullet of the fold of Hindringham, 7s. 1½d. From the cullet of the other folds, beyond the contracts of the stockman and the shepherds, nothing this year. From the manure of the folds of Hindringham *7s. 3d.*, Lomnours *5s. 10d.*, and Eaton *6s.*, 19s. 1d. From the manure of the other folds, over and above certain lands of ours manured for the Master of Magdalene, and various of our farmers as contracted, nothing.
Total receipts, £126 3s. 6½d.

Expenditure on the said sheep
In pasture for our sheep at Lomnours and Great Plumstead, £6 12s. 2d, at Monks' Grange *53s. 4d.*, over and above certain lands manured for the master of Magdalene each year as contracted, at Eaton *65s. 4d.*, at Hindringham *65s. 3d.*, at Sedgeford for the Northflock *60s. 10½d.*, at Gnatingdon *66s. 8d.*, and at Newton *£4 11s. 6½d.*, [*total*] £26 15s. 2d. In washing and shearing our aforesaid sheep, 60s. In driving the same sheep from pasture to pasture, 20s. 6d. In the stipend of the stockman, 40s. In his livery this year, nothing. In the stipends of the shepherds, namely of Gnatingdon *60s.*, of Sedgeford with the Northflock *60s.*, of Hindringham *60s.*, of Lathes *53s. 4d.*, of Eaton *60s.*, of Lomnours and Great Plumstead *60s.*, and of Newton *66s. 8d.*, [*total*] £21. And to the shepherds for their livery, 35s. 10d. In hurdles *35s. 1d.*, pitch and bitumen *53s.*, the ruddling *14d.*, and grease *9s. 1d.* for the sheep, £4 18s. 4d. And in various other small expenses regarding our aforesaid sheep this year, with the tips [*regardis*] given to our shepherds at various times this year, as appears in the book of the accountant, 9s. 8d.
Total payments, £60 19s. 6d.

And thus remains clear, £65 4s. ½d. It is assigned to the aforesaid accountant for grain bought by the same, as appears in the account of the office of the Master Cellarer this year. Thus equals.

DCN 64/8. 29th September 1529 to 29th September 1530

The account of lord Robert Catton, Prior of Norwich, for each and every issue and expense of all the sheep belonging to the office of the Master Cellarer, from the feast of St Michael the archangel in the year of our lord, 1529. And in the twenty first year of the reign of King Henry VIII, through to the same feast of St Michael thereafter, in the next year following, the twenty second of the same reign of the lord King. And in the twenty sixth year of the aforesaid Prior, lord Robert.

Receipts from issues of the same sheep.
From 494 stone of wool issuing from all our sheep this year, sold to William Wattes of Mattishall, at £18 10s. per 120, over and above 13s. 4d. allocated to the same William, total £75 9s. 10d.[107] From the locks [*le lockys*] produced from our folds at Sedgeford, Gnatingdon and Hindringham, nothing in money, because included in the contract with the same William Wattes. And from the locks produced from our own folds around Norwich, nothing in money, because they are reserved for mattresses and other necessities for our rooms. From the sale of sheep and lambs, plus certain deficient sheep [*charged*] upon our shepherds, as is more fully evident in the auditor's book this year, total £73 1s. 1d. Of which received this year, £71 12s. 10d. And thus still owed by William Halle, late shepherd at Hindringham for settlement of certain sheep [*charged*] on the same William as deficient, just as his account for this year acknowledges [*satislignet*], 28s. From the sheep and lamb pelts resulting from murrain in our sheep flocks, as appears in the auditor's book this year, 78s. 3d. From John Hughlyns, farmer of the manor of Newton for the lease of 179 ewes, valued at 33s. 4d. per 120, thus total 49s. 8½d. From the cullet of the folds of Eaton *14s.*, Gnatingdon *10s.,* and Lathes *20d.*, 25s. 8d. And from the cullet of our other folds this year, as appears in the book of our auditor, beyond the contracts of our stockman and shepherds, nothing. From the manure of the fold of Eaton, 12d. And from the manure of our other folds this year, beyond the contracts of the farmers of Magdalene and Gnatingdon, as also appears in the same book, nothing.
Total receipts, £154 17s. 3½d.

Expenditure on the said sheep
In pasture for our sheep, namely at Lomnours and Great Plumstead *111s. 8d.*, at Monks' Grange *53s. 4d.*, at Eaton *65s. 4d.*, at Hindringham *54s. 1d.*, at Sedgeford for the Northflock *68s. 10½d.*, and at Gnatingdon *67s. 8d.*, £21 0s. 11½d. And paid to John Hughlyns, farmer of the manor of Newton for agistment of 720 wethers of our own sheep for one whole year, £6. And payment to the churchwardens [*iconomis*] of the church of Binham for the farm of one acre of land lying in the sheep pasture at Hindringham for seven years, ending at Michaelmas in the 21st year of the reign of our lord King, at 8d. per annum, total 4s. 8d. In washing and shearing our sheep this year, with various other expenses, 73s. 2d. In driving the same sheep from pasture to pasture, 22s. In the stipend of the stockman, 40s. And in money allowed to him for his livery this year, 13s. 4d. In the stipends of our shepherds, namely at Gnatingdon *60s.*, at the Northflock in Sedgeford *60s.*, at Hindringham *60s.*, at Lathes *53s.*

---

[107] The sale of wool is now to a single merchant at a fixed price, and includes a customary inducement (or *avantagium*) to the purchasing merchant for a wholesale transaction.

4d.*, at Lomnours and Great Plumstead *60s.*, and at Eaton *66s. 8d.*, £18. And to the same shepherds for their liveries, 30s. In hurdles *46s. 11d.*, pitch and bitumen *107s. 4d.*, the ruddling, *3s. 2d.*, and grease *8s.* for our sheep, £8 5s. 5d. In hunting foxes and other harmful animals at various times this year, 5s. 6d. In various small expenses incurred this year concerning our sheep *2s. 6d.*, with the tips given to our shepherds at various times *2s. 4d.*, 4s. 10d.
Total payments, £62 19s. 10½d.

And thus remains clear, £91 17s. 5½d. It is assigned to the said accountant in part payment for grain bought this year by the same accountant, just as is fully laid out in another account of the office of the Master Cellarer this year. And thus equals.

DCN 64/9. 25th March 1531 to 29th September 1531

The account of lord William Castelten, Prior of Norwich, for each and every issue and expense of all the sheep belonging to the office of the Master Cellarer, from the feast of the Annunciation of St Mary the Virgin in the year of our lord, 1532 [recte 1531]. And in the twenty second year of the reign of King Henry VIII, through to the feast of St Michael thereafter, in the next year following, the twenty third of the same reign of the lord King. And in the first year of the aforesaid Prior, lord William.

Receipts from issues of the same sheep
From 518 stone of wool issuing from all our sheep this year, sold to Master Spryng of Lavenham, at £20 per 120, total £87 12s. 8d. From the locks produced from the same sheep, nothing in money, because included in the contract with the same Master Spryng. From the sale of sheep and lambs, plus certain deficient sheep [charged] upon our shepherds, as appears and acknowledged in the auditor's book for this year, total £40 4s. 6d. Of which received, £38 14s. 3d. And thus still owed by John Wace, our shepherd at Eaton for part payment of certain sheep [charged] to him as deficient, just as his account for this year acknowledges, 30s. 3d. From 844 sheep and lamb pelts resulting from murrain in our sheep flocks, as appears in the auditor's book this year, sold to William Salter at 18s. for 120, total £6 6s. 7d. From the cullet of the folds of Hindringham *10s. 9d.*, Eaton *6s. 10½d.*, and Lathes *20d.*, as appears in the auditor's book this year, 19s. 3½d. From the cullet of our other folds this year, as appears in the auditor's book, beyond the contracts of our stockman and shepherds, nothing this year. From the manure of the fold of Hindringham, 8s. And from the manure of our other folds, beyond the

contracts of the farmers of Magdalene and Gnatingdon, as also appears in
the same book, nothing this year.
Total receipts, £134 0s. 9½d.

Expenditure on the said sheep
In pasture for our sheep, namely at Lomnours and Great Plumstead *£6
1s. 0d.*, at Monks' Grange *63s. 4d.*, at Eaton *65s. 4d.*, at
Hindringham *54s. 1d.*, at Sedgeford for the Northflock *62s. 2d.*, and at
Gnatingdon *60s. 4d.*, £21 6s. 3d. Payment to John Hughlyns, farmer of
our manor of Newton for agistment of 720 wethers of our own sheep
through one whole year, £6. And to the same for the agistment of certain
of our other sheep there for a certain time, as appears more fully in the
auditor's book for the last year, 20s. 3d. Paid to Miles Hubberd esquire, for
the farm of one acre of land lying for pasture for our sheep at Lomnours
and Great Plumstead for two years, ending at Michaelmas in the 22nd year
of the reign of our lord king, 2s. In washing and shearing our sheep, with
various other expenses concerning the same sheep of ours, 75s. 10½d. In
driving the same sheep from pasture to pasture, 23s. 2d. In the stipend to
John Bronde senior, our stockman, *40s.*, with his livery for one whole
year *13s. 4d.*, 53s. 4d. In the stipends of our shepherds, namely at
Hindringham *60s.*, at Gnatingdon *60s.*, and at the Northflock in
Sedgeford *60s.*, for one whole year, £9. And in the stipends of our other
shepherds, namely at Monks' Grange *40s.*, at Lomnours and Great
Plumstead *45s.*, and at Eaton *50s*, for three quarters of the year, £6
15s. 0d. And in the liveries of our aforesaid shepherds for one whole year,
30s. In hurdles *42s. 4d.*, pitch and bitumen *31s. 6d.*, the ruddling, *2s.
3½d.*, and grease *8s. 2d.*, for our sheep, £4 4s. 3½d. In hunting foxes
and other harmful animals at various times this year, 8s. 4d. In various
other small expenses incurred this year concerning our sheep *2s. 8d.*,
with the tips given to our shepherds at various times this year *3s.*, 5s. 8d.
Total payments, £58 4s. 2d.

And thus remains clear, £75 16s. 7½d. It is assigned to the said
accountant in part payment for grain bought this year by the same
accountant, just as is fully laid out in another account of the office of the
Master Cellarer this year. And thus equals.

DCN 64/12. 29th September 1533 to 29th September 1534

The account of lord William Castelten, Prior of Norwich, for each and
every issue and expense of all the sheep belonging to the office of the
Master Cellarer, from the feast of St Michael the Archangel in the year of

our lord, 1533. And in the twenty fifth year of the reign of King Henry VIII through to the same feast of St Michael thereafter, in the next year following, the twenty sixth of the same reign of the lord King. And in the fourth year of the aforesaid Prior, lord William Castelten.

Receipts from issues of the same sheep
From 345 stone of wool issuing this year from all our sheep pertaining to the said office, sold to Master Spryng of Lavenham in the county of Suffolk, price per stone 3s. 6d., total £60 18s. 0d. From the locks produced from the same sheep, nothing this year. From 384 sheep and lamb pelts resulting this year from murrain in all our sheep flocks, as appears in the auditor's book this year, sold to John Baker of Norwich at 20s. for 120, total 64s. From the sale of sheep and lambs, plus certain deficient sheep charged upon our shepherds this year, and as appears in the book of our auditor aforesaid, total £51 19s. 5d. From the cullet of the fold of Hindringham 7s. 6d. From the cullet of our other folds this year, as also appears in the book of our auditor aforesaid, beyond the contracts of our stockman and shepherds, nothing this year. From the manure of our folds, beyond the contracts of the farmers of Magdalene and Gnatingdon, as also appears in the same book, nothing this year.
Total receipts, £116 8s. 11d.

Payments of the said sheep
In pasture for our sheep at Lomnours and Great Plumstead *£6 1s. 0d.*, at Monks' Grange *73s. 4d.*, at Eaton *67s. 4d.*, at Hindringham *55s. 1d.*, and at Gnatingdon in Sedgeford *60s.*, £18 16s. 9d. Payment to John Hughlyns, farmer of our manor of Newton for agistment of certain of our sheep there this year, £6. In the stipend of our stockman, with his gift, 53s. 4d. In the stipends of our shepherds, namely at Gnatingdon *73s. 4d.*, at Hindringham *60s.*, at Lomnours and Great Plumstead *60s.*, at Lathes *53s. 4d.*, and at Eaton *£4*, £16 6s. 8d. In gifts for the aforesaid shepherds, 25s. In washing and shearing our sheep this year, with the other expenses incurred regarding the same, £4 7s. 4d. In driving the same sheep from pasture to pasture, 14s. 4d. In hurdles *37s. 4d.*, pitch and bitumen *27s. 8d.*, the ruddling, *3s. 5½d.*, and grease *6s. 4d.*, for our sheep this year, 74s. 9½d. In Lent sheep called le Rammes bought from Leonard Spencer, gentleman [*generoso*], £4. And in various other small expenses incurred this year concerning our sheep, and above the said tips given to our shepherds, 9s. 6d.
Total payments, £58 7s. 8½d.

And thus remains clear, £58 1s. 2½d. It is assigned to the said accountant in part payment for grain bought by the same accountant, just as is fully laid out and acknowledged in another account of the office of the Master Cellarer. And thus equals.

GLOSSARY

Agistment The provision of grazing for animals, usually on someone else's land involving a financial charge.

Crone An old sheep, usually a female.

Cullet Sheep of other people grazing with the flock of another person, usually the manorial lord.

Deficient sheep Sheep charged personally against the shepherd because of its loss through negligence or theft.

Demesne The land within the manor allocated to the lord for his own use.

Equals Adds up to the first figure given.

Ewe Female sheep after its second shearing.

Farmer In the strict medieval sense, a tenant holding land on a leasehold agreement: a farm is therefore land held through a lease.

Gerk, gimmer Female sheep aged one year, i.e. between its first and second shearing.

Hogg, hoggaster Castrated male sheep aged one year, i.e between its first and second shearing.

Hurdle Light and portable wattle fencing used to pen sheep; also known as clattes.

Lamb Male or female sheep before its first shearing (a lamb would not be sheared in its first season).

Livery The identifying uniform worn by household members or employees of a lord.

Locks The wool which had fallen from the sheep.

Magdalene St Mary Magdalene hospital, Sprowston near Norwich.

Markinglamb Lambs gifted to shepherds at the time of the marking with red dye.

Maslin, mixture An equal mixture of wheat and rye.

Murrain A generic word for the diseases afflicting sheep. An excellent summary of the specific diseases is provided in R. Trow-Smith, *A History of British Livestock Husbandry to 1700* (London, 1957), pp. 153–60.

Pelt The skin of a dead sheep. The pelt of an adult sheep that had died before shearing (*pellis lanuta*) contained the thickest wool, and was therefore the most valuable. Lamb pelts, and adult pelts from a sheep that had died soon after shearing, were worth less. See Bailey, *Marginal Economy?*, p. 126.

Ram Uncastrated male sheep after its first shearing.

Rigg Adult male sheep, half castrated or born with one testicle.

Ruddle Red dye used to mark sheep.

Shack Feed for livestock on the stubble of the open fields after the harvest.

Sowel An iron stake, used to fix hurdles or tether animals.

Stockman The stockman was probably in charge of preparing and supervising livestock destined for the monastic kitchens, Welch, 'Sheep Accounts', p. 25.

Tally The process of reckoning, counting or scoring sheep (or other livestock or commodities), which implies the use of a stick or counting device.

Wether Castrated male sheep after its second shearing.

Whynnes, whin Heathland plant, usually gorse.

APPENDIX: CATALOGUE OF ACCOUNTS
USED IN THIS EDITION.

All documents are deposited in the Norfolk Record Office.

DCN 62/16 Centralised stock accounts for 1 December 1488; 25 December 1491; 9 December 1493; 9 December 1494; 25 December 1499; 25 December 1500; 25 December 1501; 25 December 1523.

DCN 62/17 Individual stock accounts for Newton, Heigham and Sedgeford 1489–90.
Centralised stock account for 25 December 1490.

DCN 62/18 Individual stock accounts for Catton, Eaton, Hindringham, Newton, Plumstead, Lathes, Lomnours, Sedgeford, Cawston, Intwood, Wood Norton and Stoke Holy Cross, 1495–6.
Centralised stock account for 25 December 1496.

DCN 62/19 Individual stock accounts for Lomnours, Stoke Holy Cross, Cawston, Sedgeford, Wood Norton, Hemsby, Hindringham, Eaton, Lathes, Newton and Catton, 1496–7.
Centralised stock account for 25 December 1497.

DCN 62/22 Individual stock accounts for Thorpe Episcopi, Hindringham, Lathes, Gnatingdon, Sedgeford Westmanor, Newton and Eaton, 1504–5.

DCN 62/23 Individual stock accounts for Sedgeford, Gnatingdon, Thorpe Episcopi and Newton 1508–9.
Centralised stock account for 25 December 1509.

DCN 62/24 Centralised stock account for 29 September 1510.

DCN 62/27 Centralised stock account for 29 September 1514.

DCN 62/28 Centralised stock account for 29 September 1515.

DCN 62/29 Centralised stock accounts for 29 September 1517.

DCN 64/1 Individual stock accounts for Lathes 1484–5; Eaton 1489–90; Thorpe Market 1489–90; Lathes 1489–90; Newton 1492–3; Lathes 1492–3; and Lomnours 1492–3.
(The original roll is fragile and this edition is taken from a photocopy.)

DCN 64/2 Centralised stock accounts for 25 December 1495; 25 December 1498; 25 December 1524.

DCN 64/3 Individual stock account for Eaton (fragile and not possible to reproduce). Not included in this edition.

DCN 64/4 Individual stock accounts for Hindringham, Fring, Sedgeford and Lathes 1499–1500.

DCN 64/5 Centralised stock account for 25 December 1503.

DCN 64/6 Centralised revenue account, 1525–6.

DCN 64/7 Centralised revenue account, 1526–7.

DCN 64/8 Centralised revenue account, 1529–30.

DCN 64/9 Centralised revenue account, half year 1531.

DCN 64/10 Individual stock account for Hindringham, 1530–1.

DCN 64/11 Individual stock account for Sedgeford, 1530–1.

DCN 64/12 Centralised revenue account, 1533–4.

Income Tax Assessments of Norwich, 1472 and 1489

EDITED BY MAUREEN JURKOWSKI

Introduction

The documents edited here comprise two assessments of the population of Norwich for taxes on income levied by the governments of Edward IV and Henry VII in 1472 and 1489. Not only do they provide rare information about the wealth and income of the inhabitants of what was then one of England's largest provincial cities, but because the assessors were not required to submit copies of their assessments to the royal Exchequer, these documents are among the few extant assessments made for either tax. Indeed, Norwich is the only locality in England from which assessments survive for both taxes. As such, they provide unique information about the assessment and administration of these two taxes, both of which have been widely neglected by historians. For Norwich itself, they bridge a long gap in our knowledge of the city's taxable population and wealth, since they are the only tax assessments made of the city's inhabitants between 1451 and 1524 still substantially intact.[1]

Fifteenth-Century Income Taxes

The income taxes of 1472 and 1489 followed a long line of experimental taxes levied on income in the fifteenth century, beginning in 1404. To understand their development it is necessary first to trace briefly the history of taxation in medieval England. In theory, medieval kings were expected to live off their own resources and periodic levies of taxes on the wealth or income of the king's subjects were considered extraordinary measures taken only in exceptional circumstances. Taxes were collected almost always for war, and never without the consent of a representative body of the taxpayers, as established by *Magna Carta* in 1215. In practice, of course, such taxation had become virtually constant by the middle of the fourteenth

---

[1] For the assessment of the income tax of 1450, see R. Virgoe, 'A Norwich Taxation List of 1451', *NA*, 40 (1988), pp. 145-54 (reprinted in C. Barron, C. Rawcliffe and J.T. Rosenthal, eds, *East Anglian Society and the Political Community of Late Medieval England. Selected Papers of Roger Virgoe* (Norwich, 1997), pp. 65-78), and for the Tudor subsidies of 1524-7, see J. Pound, *Tudor and Stuart Norwich* (Chichester, 1988).

century, but the king still had to obtain individual grants of taxation from parliament in order to levy the taxes.

The most usual form of taxation of lay men and women (who were taxed separately from the clergy) was the 'fractional tax' on moveable goods. Assessed by specially-appointed commissioners, a fractional tax took a fractional part (for example, one-ninth) of an individual's personal property, exclusive of the bare necessities of life, such as food, clothing, beds, and tools. Beginning in 1188 with the 'Saladin tithe', fractional taxes became common in the thirteenth century, and were levied with great frequency from the 1290s to pay for Edward I's wars. By this time it had become customary to levy a higher rate in boroughs and cities, where moveable wealth was concentrated, than in the countryside. In 1334 these rates became permanently fixed at one-fifteenth in rural areas and one-tenth in urban communities, when it was decided that rather than require fresh assessments to be made and returned to the royal Exchequer for each new levy of a 'fifteenth and tenth', it would be far simpler if every township and borough was assigned an overall quota, based on what the locality had paid at the last levy of the tax, in 1332.[2] Much easier to administer, the fifteenth and tenth guaranteed the Crown an overall yield of about £37,000 each time it was levied.

The quota system was no doubt more efficient for the central government in the short term, but over time the fifteenth and tenth became a less effective tax of the nation's wealth. It failed to take account of changes in the geographical distribution of wealth and the inflationary pressures which reduced the value of the £37,000. The Crown was able to compensate partly for this decline in value by levying multiple fifteenths and tenths (when parliament would grant them), and in 1433 remissions for hardship were introduced to adjust the tax burden according to shifts in the distribution of wealth. A rebate of £4,000, raised to £6,000 in 1446, was subtracted from each parliamentary grant of a fifteenth and tenth and re-distributed to the poorer towns to aid them in meeting their quotas.[3] Until about 1468, the re-distribution of the rebates was determined by the Commons (i.e., the elected parliamentary representatives) after each individual subsidy grant, but thereafter the amount of rebate for each township also became fixed. This solution proved less than ideal, not least because it reduced the amount of revenue accruing to the king. By the beginning of

[2] M. Jurkowski, C.L. Smith and D. Crook, *Lay Taxes in England and Wales 1188-1688*, PRO Handbooks no. 31 (Kew, 1998), pp. xxvi-xxxiv. For the quotas, see R.E. Glasscock, *The Lay Subsidy of 1334* (British Academy, Records of Social and Economic History, new series, ii, 1975).

[3] For the apportionment of reductions in Norfolk in 1449 see: W. Hudson, 'The Assessment of the Townships of the County of Norfolk for the King's Tenths and Fifteenths as Settled in 1334', *NA*, 12 (1895), pp. 246-94.

the fifteenth century, therefore, the king's advisors were anxiously seeking new ways of taxing the income and wealth of the laity and they devised a series of directly-assessed, experimental taxes on income (chiefly from land which, in theory, was not taxed by fifteenths and tenths).[4] All of these income taxes were highly unpopular with the Commons, who preferred a system of taxation which let them determine who and what was taxed in their own localities.

The first such income tax was the subsidy of £12,000 granted in 1404 for a military expedition to France, which, in certain respects, proved to be a forerunner of the income taxes of 1472 and 1489. Individuals were taxed in 1404 on either their land or goods, but not both, and two different rates were levied on land, according to type of tenure. Land held by military service (i.e., knights' fees and portions of knights' fees) was taxed at the higher rate of 20s. per knight's fee, and land held by other types of tenure, worth 20s. or more annually (in net value), was taxed at the rate of 12d. for every pound in value. Individuals whose land was valued at under the minimum threshold (or level) of liability of 20s., but who owned goods worth £20 or more, did not pay tax on their land, but instead paid this same tax of 12d. per pound on their goods.

Where this tax anticipated those of 1472 and 1489 was in the stringent conditions imposed by the Commons on its administration. They legislated that the tax receipts were to be paid not into the Exchequer, where they might be squandered on assignments to the king's favourites and creditors, but to four trusted 'treasurers of war', who would both receive and disburse these proceeds as they were intended. The Commons also showed concern that the tax should not form a precedent for future grants of taxation and insisted that no record of the levy be preserved on the parliament roll. They forbade, moreover, the return of the commissioners' assessments of the taxpayers to the Exchequer, lest the information contained within them become a matter of record. The tax proved highly unpopular and yielded only about £5,000 of the £12,000 expected to be raised.[5]

A tax levied on annual income from land of £20 or more in 1411, although less contentious, raised no more than £2,000 for the Crown's coffers.[6] In 1428 a tax on land held by military service (the minimum level

---

[4] In actual fact, the basis of assessment in some regions was land, while in some towns, wages may also have been assessed: M. Jurkowski, 'Parliamentary and Prerogative Taxation in the Reign of Edward IV', *Parliamentary History*, 18 (1999), p. 279, n. 53.

[5] Jurkowski, *et al.*, *Lay Taxes*, pp. 74-5; T. Kido, 'English Land Taxes of 1404', in R. Pérez Bustamante, ed., *Estudios de Historia del Derecho Europeo Homenaje al professor G. Martínez Díez*, (Madrid, 1994), i, pp. 325-9, 334-5.

[6] Jurkowski, *et al.*, *Lay Taxes*, pp. 78-9. The assessments are printed in *Inquisitions and Assessments Relating to Feudal Aids* (6 vols., London, 1899-1920), vi, but none have survived from Norwich.

of liability being one-quarter of a knight's fee), levied in conjunction with another on parishes, promised a bigger yield, and it did raise £12,291 for the Crown, but this sum still fell far short of the £37,000 which would have been provided by the traditional fifteenth and tenth.[7] In 1431, when crown officials attempted to levy a tax on income from land at higher rates and with much lower minimum thresholds of liability, making thus many poorer taxpayers liable to pay, there was considerable resistance during the assessment process and the tax had to be cancelled in the following parliament and replaced by a fifteenth and tenth. The Commons also demanded that all traces of its levy be erased from the record, lest it prove a precedent for future taxes.[8]

In 1435 the minimum threshold of liability (£5 annual income from lands), that had been found so objectionable in 1431, proved more acceptable when a graduated tax with the same minimum threshold, levied at three rates on land and goods, and (for the first time) on fees and labourers' wages, was voted to the king. This was a far more ambitious and complex tax than those which had gone before, but its yield was still less than £9,000.[9] The income tax of 1450 took the same form, but attempted to extend the levy to a larger proportion of the population and increase the rate of taxation on taxpayers in the middle income bracket. For previous income taxes, only landowners of freehold lands had been liable, but in 1450 land held by copyhold and customary tenure was also taxed, as were estates owned communally (by cities, towns, guilds and other corporations) and income from offices of £200 and over. A lowering of the minimum threshold of liability on income from land to 20s. per annum, and the tax on annual wages of £2 or more was much resented in the shires. The assessment and collection process met with considerable resistance and coincided with the uprising known as Cade's Rebellion, forcing the government to raise the two minimum thresholds of liability on land and wages to 40s. and £3, respectively, in an amendment to the subsidy act made in parliament later in the same year. This concession to public opinion reduced the yield to about £7,303, far less than anticipated.[10]

[7] Jurkowski, et al., Lay Taxes, pp. 85-6. Most of the assessment of Norwich is printed in Feudal Aids, iii, pp. 603-6, from TNA PRO, E 179/149/105, but another small part of it (in E 179/149/104, m. 2d) is not.

[8] Jurkowski, et al., Lay Taxes, pp. 88-9. Many of the surviving assessments are printed in Feudal Aids, but there are no extant returns from Norwich or Norfolk.

[9] Jurkowski, et al., Lay Taxes, pp. 91-2. No assessment survives from Norwich, but a list of individuals from the city who failed to appear before the commissioners and assessors is on TNA PRO, E 179/240/269, rot. 5.

[10] Jurkowski, et al., Lay Taxes, pp. 102-4; R. Virgoe, 'The Parliamentary Subsidy of 1450', Bulletin of the Institute of Historical Research, 55 (1982), pp. 125-38. Dr. Virgoe printed the assessment of Norwich from what is now TNA PRO, E 179/238/78, part 3: 'Norwich Taxation List of 1451', pp. 145-54.

The income tax of 1450 had been granted specifically to finance the sending of reinforcements to Normandy and, as in 1404, mistrust of the government had led the Commons to appoint four treasurers of war to receive and disburse its proceeds. In April 1453, with much of the proceeds still uncollected and with the military situation becoming ever more desperate, the Commons granted another experimental tax on income even more closely linked with a planned military campaign. This tax was to be levied only if the king personally led an expedition to France, and since this did not come to pass, it was never collected.[11] In 1472, however, when Edward IV needed to raise large sums to finance his own French campaign, he procured a grant from parliament of an identical tax.

The Income Tax of 1472

Parliament assembled on 6 October 1472, and, after much discussion, on 30 November the Commons granted the king a subsidy to pay the wages of 13,000 archers for one year, at a rate of 6d. per day, which amounted in all to £118,625. The 13,000 archers were apportioned among the counties, cities and boroughs of England. Each locality was expected to support its quota of archers, the allocation having been based upon the total amount of tax paid there for a fifteenth and tenth.[12] This hefty sum was to be raised by means of a tax of one-tenth of the income from all lands, tenements, rents, fees, annuities, offices, corrodies[13] and pensions, less outgoings (*ultra reprisas*, i.e., the net income) for one year. It was to be paid by the owners or occupiers of lands, whether held jointly, severally, in fee simple or fee tail, for themselves, or by others to their use. For the first time, remarkably, there was no minimum threshold of liability, and the taxable year began at the feast of the Circumcision of the Lord (1 January) 1472. The Lords made their own grant of this tax, as they had in 1404,[14] the proceeds of which were to be administered separately.

The Commons took control of the administration of the tax to an unprecedented degree, imposing conditions even stricter than those laid down in 1404. The commissioners appointed in each county to oversee its levy received their formal commissions from Chancery, but most of their instructions were contained, significantly, in the parliamentary act itself. They could employ 'all maner [of] weyes and meanes after their discretion

---

[11] Jurkowski, *et al.*, *Lay Taxes*, pp. 105-6.

[12] In the counties one archer was assigned for every 50 marks, but in the cities and boroughs the ratio was higher and varied from place to place: R.S. Schofield, 'The Geographical Distribution of Wealth in England, 1334-1649', *Economic History Review*, 2nd ser., 18 (1965), pp. 488-9.

[13] A corrody was a form of pension, paid in kind, by religious houses.

[14] *Rotuli Parliamentorum* (7 vols., London, 1767-77), iii, pp. 545-7.

possible' to ascertain tax liability, and avail themselves of the services of sheriffs, mayors, bailiffs, constables and other royal officials whenever necessary. As in 1404, the Commons forbade the return of the commissioners' assessments to the Exchequer, although defaulting taxpayers and collectors could be prosecuted by the Exchequer to recover arrears. After making their assessment, the commissioners were to draw up indentures with the collectors whom they appointed and instruct them to deliver the proceeds not to the Exchequer, but to designated local repositories, such as castles or monasteries, where they would be safely held until authorization was given by the Commons for their delivery to either the Exchequer or the king. This authorization was not to occur until orders were given to muster troops for the expedition; if the campaign was not underway by Michaelmas 1474, the tax grant would be cancelled and the money returned to the taypayers.[15] The Lords' grant laid down similar conditions, with the proceeds to be received by the archbishop of Canterbury and three other lords at St Paul's Cathedral, where the tax money would be held.[16] In both cases, the tax was to be collected in one payment, on 3 February 1473.

After the Commons had granted the income tax to the king, parliament was not dissolved, as normally, but was instead prorogued until 8 February 1473, five days after payment of the tax was due, when the Commons were to be informed of the total receipts by certificates sent from the shires. In this second session of parliament, the Lords presented a bill arguing that the tax money collected from the nobility be transferred immediately from St Paul's to the treasurer of England so that the necessary arms and ammunition could be procured well before the king sailed, and this was agreed.[17] Reports of problems in levying the tax granted by the Commons had meanwhile begun to issue from the counties, namely a widespread refusal to receive the tax money in the designated repositories. A measure was thus passed in the second parliamentary session mandating that any repository keeper still refusing to receive the proceeds after 1 March 1473 would be forced to pay the king an equivalent sum. On the final day of this session, 8 April 1473, it was reported that not all of the returns from the counties had been received and the total projected yield was still therefore unknown. With payment of the wages of the 13,000 archers necessary before the king sailed, the Commons agreed to grant the king an additional tax of a fifteenth and tenth also to be held in the designated repositories. Parliament was again prorogued until more information about the yield of the income tax had been received.

---

[15] *Rot. Parl.*, vi, pp. 4-6.
[16] For a copy of the Lords' grant, see: BL, Cotton MS Cleo. F vi, f. 212.
[17] Jurkowski, 'Parliamentary Taxation', pp. 275-83.

It was not until 18 July 1474, at the end of a sixth parliamentary session, that the Commons were at last informed of the total proceeds of the income tax. Only £31,410 14s.1½d. had reportedly been received, with returns still lacking from five northern counties and a few other places. The prohibition on the return of assessments to the Exchequer means that for knowledge of how much was assessed in each locality we are reliant upon a schedule, now in the Surrey Record Office, but probably once in the possession of a member of parliament.[18] Its bottom section has been torn off, but fortunately the tear occurs just after it reveals that the total amount assessed in the city of Norwich was £139 14s.4d.[19], nowhere near the £1,104 2s.6d. needed to finance the city's quota of 121 archers.[20] The overall yield nationally fell far short of what was required, and was suspiciously close to the £31,000 normally raised by the levy of a fifteenth and tenth (minus the standard deduction of £6,000), which suggests that this was all that the assessors were willing to assess or the taxpayers would pay. For the king's purposes, however, it was inadequate, and the expedition had to be postponed and additional taxes levied. The northern counties which had not collected the income tax were instructed that they had to provide a total of £5383 15s. to pay their quota of archers, and the Commons granted the king the £51,147 4s.7¾d. still needed, to be apportioned among each locality in England. Norwich was expected to provide £172 4s.1d., nearly 150% more than it had raised in 1473. The text of the tax grant instructed the commissioners that they were to levy the tax upon individuals who had paid little or nothing for either the income tax or the fifteenth and tenth, and collect it in two tranches (on 24 June and 11 November 1475), to be stored again in local repositories.[21]

Parliament was once more prorogued until 23 January 1475, a week before payment of the first quarter's wages of the archers was due and the troops were to muster. In the meantime, on 28 November 1474, ten receivers were appointed to gather the receipts of the income tax held in local repositories and bring them to the Exchequer.[22] When parliament reconvened in its seventh session on January 1475, however, it was found that the receivers had not been able to lay their hands on much of the £31,410 14s.1½d. reportedly raised. Some of the tax money had never found its way into the designated repositories, while in other cases its custodians

[18] Woking, Surrey History Centre, Loseley MSS, LM/1498/A, printed in Jurkowski, 'Parliamentary Taxation', p. 288.

[19] Jurkowski, 'Parliamentary Taxation', p. 288.

[20] *Rot. Parl.*, v, p. 232; Surrey History Centre, 'LM/1498/A (dorse); Jurkowski, 'Parliamentary Taxation', p. 277.

[21] *Rot. Parl.*, vi, pp. 113-19; Jurkowski, 'Parliamentary Taxation', p. 280.

[22] John Sorell, an Exchequer official, was to retrieve the tax money from the East Anglian counties, including the city of Norwich, probably being held in the abbey of Bury St. Edmunds: *CPR 1467-77*, p. 496.

would not hand it over. Around Easter 1475, therefore, it was ordered that the county sheriffs proclaim openly that all collectors or keepers of the proceeds of the income tax bring them to the Exchequer by 14 May 1475, and most of the outstanding money arrived at Westminster in the next few months.[23] It also emerged in this seventh parliamentary session that the subsidy of £51,147 4s.7¾d. had proved unleviable, the commissioners having reported that they found their task of targeting specific taxpayers too 'diffuse and laborious'. The Commons and king thus agreed by indenture to convert this tax into its equivalent in fifteenths and tenths (one and three-quarters). It was only then, on 14 March 1475, that the longest parliament held to-date was dissolved.[24]

On 4 July 1475 Edward IV finally sailed with the largest army that had ever invaded France,[25] but when the support expected from his Burgundian allies failed to materialize, he allowed himself to be bought off. The treaty of Picquigny was signed on 29 August, whereby he agreed to withdraw his forces to England in exchange for payment by the king of France of a lump sum equivalent to £15,000 and a life annuity of £10,000. Popular disturbances followed the return and disbanding of the army, and on 6 October 1475, amidst seething resentment, the king was forced to remit the three-quarters of a fifteenth and tenth not yet collected.[26]

The Income Tax of 1489

None of these problems deterred Henry VII from levying a very similar income tax to finance his own foreign campaign in 1489. The grants of 1453 and 1472 had established precedents for the tax and, with the great reluctance of the Commons to grant directly-assessed taxes, it was always easier to secure agreement to a tax which had been levied before, however objectionable, than for novel taxes. The king and his ministers probably also believed that with some amendments to the 1472 act they could improve both the yield and administration of the income tax.

At a meeting of the king's great council in December 1488 an expedition

[23] Only £2,071 18s.9½d. was still unrecovered in July 1475: Jurkowski, 'Parliamentary Taxation', p. 281. Sorell received £3,933 7s.10d. from the East Anglian counties (presumably including Norwich) in Michaelmas term 1474 and a further £235 3s.8½d. in Easter term 1475: TNA PRO, Exchequer, Treasury of Receipt, Tellers' Rolls, E 405/54, rot. 7; E 405/60, rot. 4.

[24] Jurkowski, 'Parliamentary Taxation', pp. 282-3.

[25] For this expedition, see: J.R. Lander, 'The Hundred Years' War and Edward IV's 1475 Campaign in France', in his *Crown and Nobility, 1450-1509* (London, 1976), pp. 234-41 (first published in A.J. Slavin, ed., *Tudor Men and Institutions. Studies in English Law and Government* (Baton Rouge, Louisiana, 1972)).

[26] *Rot. Parl.*, vi, pp. 113-21, 150-3; Jurkowski, 'Parliamentary Taxation', p. 283.

to aid the duchess of Brittany in a war against the French was approved. The duchess agreed to reimburse the king for the wages of an English army of up to 10,000 men and allow him to occupy two Breton towns as security, but he had to find the initial funds for the campaign, which were estimated to be about £100,000.[27] Parliament was convened on 13 January, and some weeks later, on 23 February 1489, the Commons agreed to provide £75,000 of the £100,000 by a tax on income, with the remaining £25,000 to be raised from the clergy.[28] As in 1472, the Lords and Commons made separate grants of the tax of one-tenth of a year's net income from all lands, tenements, fees, annuities, corrodies and pensions. No assessments were to be returned to the Exchequer, as before, and the proceeds were to be held at designated repositories until the king authorised their release. The latter condition was imposed because of uncertainty about the length of the campaign. If it lasted less than a year, and, indeed, Henry VII's agreement with the duchess specified a campaign of only nine months, then the tax would be pro-rated and the difference returned to the taxpayers. If it lasted for more than a year, the same tax would be levied again annually, for up to two subsequent years. Three northern counties which had not paid the 1472 tax were made officially exempt.[29]

The most important innovation since 1472 was the addition of a tax of 20d. on every 10 marks'[30] worth of goods and chattels (that is, one-eightieth part). Ten marks was the minimum threshold of liability for the tax on goods, and taxpayers were to be assessed only where they resided, although this limitation did not apply to the tax on land. In Norwich it meant that the assessment of individuals for the goods which they owned throughout the city appears under the wards in which they lived. Exempt from assessment were all items of clothing, household utensils, plate, coin, and ships and their tackle, and no member of the nobility was to be taxed on his or her goods. The stock of merchants, craftsmen, hostillers, brewers and retailers was to be included, but the wares of merchants from the Hanseatic League, Castile and the Italian cities of Venice, Genoa, Florence and Lucca (whose trade the king wished to encourage) were not. Whereas the tax on land was to be paid in two instalments, on 1 May and 1 November 1489, the subsidy on goods was to be collected in full with the first payment. There were also measures to correct abuses which had hampered collection in 1472; harsh penalties would be imposed upon

---

[27] For this military campaign, see: J.M. Currin, '"The King's Army into the Partes of Bretaigne": Henry VII and the Breton Wars, 1489-1491', *War in History*, 7 (2000), pp. 379-412.

[28] For the clerical subsidy of £25,000, see: *The Register of John Morton, Archbishop of Canterbury 1486-1500*, ed. C. Harper-Bill (Canterbury & York Society, lxxv, 1987), i, pp. 29-47; *CFR 1485-1509*, pp. 109-10.

[29] Namely, Northumberland, Westmorland and Cumberland.

[30] £6 13s. 4d.

anyone who refused to receive the proceeds in the designated repositories, and against tax commissioners and collectors who were dilatory, negligent or dishonest.[31]

The process of assessment was to have been completed by Easter (20 April), but it was undoubtedly delayed in Norwich, since the commissioners did not appoint the collectors until 27 July. Such a delay was by no means unusual, since the levy, coming hard on the heels of two fifteenths and tenths granted in December 1487, was greatly resented by the taxpayers. In Yorkshire, where support for the Yorkist cause had spawned two uprisings in 1486 and 1487, a major rebellion erupted in late April after the earl of Northumberland informed a group of protesters that, unlike their northern neighbours, Henry VII had refused them an exemption. The king mustered all the forces at his disposal (perhaps as many as 10,000 men) to put down the revolt, and most of the rebels surrendered on 20 May. All that the revolt achieved (apart from giving Henry VII a fright) was a delay in the collection of the tax.[32]

We know more about the delays in Norfolk and Suffolk than elsewhere in the country because of the unique survival of an account book.[33] This document was undoubtedly drawn up by Exchequer officers attempting to determine the arrears still due in March 1492 from the abbot of Bury St Edmunds, whose abbey was the designated repository for the proceeds collected in Norfolk, Suffolk and the city of Norwich. From this book, which lists the dates of deposits made with the abbot, we know that the earliest was made on 6 May and that most of the proceeds arrived at the abbey in late May and June. On 9 July the sheriff of Norfolk and Suffolk, Robert Lovell, conveyed the £683 which he had retrieved from the abbot to the Exchequer, with an armed guard of twelve men,[34] but these receipts did not include the tax money from Norwich. The full amount due for the first payment (£19 7¼d. for lands, and £17 5s.6d. for goods) was not deposited with the abbot until 31 July 1489.[35]

There is less information about receipts from the rest of the country, but from those recorded in the tellers' rolls of the Exchequer, it is clear that although some collectors paid their receipts directly into the Exchequer, most deposited them, as directed, in local repositories. In Michaelmas term 1489 the king sent letters under his signet to sixty-one sheriffs and local

[31] *Rot. Parl.*, vi, pp. 421-4; Jurkowski, *et al.*, *Lay Taxes*, pp. 122-4; R. Schofield, *Taxation under the Early Tudors 1485-1547* (Oxford, 2004), pp. 74-9.

[32] For the revolt, see: M.J. Bennett, 'Henry VII and the Northern Rising of 1489', *EHR*, 105 (1990), pp. 34-55; M.A. Hicks, 'The Yorkshire Rebellion of 1489 Reconsidered', *Northern History*, 22 (1986), pp. 39-62.

[33] This book is damaged and has been split into two pieces. The bulk of it is TNA PRO, E 179/280/27, and E 179/240/272 is what remains of its outer leaf.

[34] TNA PRO, Exchequer, Treasury of Receipt, Miscellaneous Books, E 36/130, f. 40.

[35] TNA PRO, E 179/280/27.

collectors, ordering them to bring the tax receipts to Westminster, and thereafter many collectors paid their receipts directly into the Exchequer.[36] It was perhaps one of the local collectors in Norwich who brought to Westminster the full amount due for the second payment of the tax (£19 7¼d.), probably in the autumn of 1489 or winter of 1490. Robert Lovell received at least £464 directly from local collectors in Norfolk and Suffolk, most of it in the first four months of 1490. At least another £82 from these counties were paid to unnamed royal commissioners and further receipts were made by the earl of Oxford and others.[37]

When parliament reconvened in February 1490, however, not all of the certificates of the amounts assessed and collected around the country had been returned, and the total proceeds could only then be estimated at around £27,000. This was, of course, well short of the £75,000 granted, and parliament agreed to the levy of a fifteenth and tenth to make up some of the difference.[38] Contemporaries cited two reasons for the disappointing yield: the high costs of collecting the tax and underassessment by the commissioners.[39] The costs of retrieving the tax money from local repositories did prove expensive in many cases, since the expenses of those who conveyed it to Westminster had to be paid and these were sometimes considerable. Sir Hugh Luterell, for example, incurred expenses of £25 in transporting the tax money from Somerset and Dorset to the Exchequer in Michaelmas term 1489.[40] In the end, receipts were carried to Westminster by all and sundry: receivers, commissioners, collectors, and sometimes the keepers of repositories themselves, such as William Bodenham, cellarer of the abbey of Bury St Edmunds, who paid into the Exchequer at least £391 11s.¼d. of the tax money collected in Suffolk in Michaelmas 1489.[41] It is possible, in fact, that the assessment rolls from the city of Norwich, the town of Great Yarmouth and the Norfolk hundreds of Blofield, Clavering, Earsham, East Flegg, Happing and Humbleyard survive, uniquely, among the Exchequer records because Bodenham brought them to Westminster with the tax money.[42] It seems more likely, however, that the rolls came to the Exchequer as part of an investigation into arrears that occurred in

---

[36] TNA PRO, E 405/78, rot. 4. A further round of letters was sent out in Easter term 1490: TNA PRO, E 36/124, ff. 52v, 62v.

[37] TNA PRO, E 179/280/27; E 179/240/272.

[38] *Rot. Parl.*, vi, pp. 438-9.

[39] Schofield, *Taxation under the Early Tudors*, p. 79.

[40] TNA PRO, E 405/78, rots. 6, 7.

[41] The abbot was reimbursed 26s.8d. for the cellarer's expenses: TNA PRO, E 405/78, rot. 15d; E 179/280/27; E 179/240/272.

[42] As suggested by Schofield: Schofield, *Taxation under the Early Tudors*, p. 243, n. 38. For these assessments, see: TNA PRO, E 179/240/272 (Great Yarmouth); E 179/149/184 (Blofield); E 179/154/711 (Clavering); E 179/149/188 (Earsham); E 179/149/185 (East Flegg); E 179/149/186 (Happing); E 179/151/353 (Humbleyard).

1492, especially since Bodenham appears to have carried only the receipts from Suffolk with him. On the question of underassessment, these rolls and the comparison made below of the Norwich assessments of 1472 and 1489 have much to tell us.

Comparison and Analysis

The two assessments of taxpayers in Norwich edited here are, in general, very similar to each other. They have much in common and both differ markedly from the assessment of 1451, which offers little basis of comparison with either. The income tax of 1450 taxed only individuals drawing income from land of £2 or more, or receiving fees, annuities or wages of £3 or more, while there was, in theory, no minimum threshold of liability in 1472 or 1489.[43] The assessment roll of 1451 is not organised topographically, but according to the social status of the taxpayers, and most crucially, taxpayers' property in Norwich was not assessed alone, but in combination with all their holdings throughout England. Thus, for example, the assessment of John Paston, esquire, at £66, even if it were accurate (and there is every reason to believe that it is not), is a valuation of all of his estates and tells us little about his Norwich property.[44] By contrast, the basis of assessment of the income taxes of 1472 and 1489 (apart from the additional tax on goods in 1489) was the same, and very helpfully the assessment rolls of both are organised firstly by ward, and then (usually) by parish. There are, however, many significant differences between them.

First of all, although the 1489 assessment is full and complete, only about half of the 1472 assessment survives, in six separate rolls, in the city archives. From Conesford, only the assessments of the sub-wards of South Conesford and Berstrete with Trowse, remain, and from the ward of Mancroft only the assessment of the largest parish of St Peter Mancroft is extant. Nothing survives from the parish of St Stephen and very little from St Giles.[45] From Wymer ward, only the assessment of the four parishes of East Wymer sub-ward (St Peter Hungate, SS Simon and Jude, St George Tombland and St Martin at Palace) survive; the sub-wards of West and

[43] In practice, the commissioners do not appear to have assessed any holdings worth less than 25d. per annum in 1472; in 1489 no tenements valued at less than 10d. were taxed.

[44] Virgoe, 'Norwich Taxation List', p. 71, and for the doubtful accuracy of Paston's assessment, p. 67. The tenement of his widow Margaret in the parish of St. Peter Hungate, the site of which (on Elm Hill) is now marked with a plaque, was valued in 1472 at 40s.: see below at p. 133.

[45] Only two individuals were assessed in St Giles in 1472 (see p. 132 below) compared to fifty in 1489. One of the two was John Selot, master of St Giles' Hospital (C. Rawcliffe, *Medicine for the Soul* (Stroud, 1999), pp. 256-7), and the heading 'St Giles' is possibly an error for the parish of St Helen's in which the Hospital lay.

Middle Wymer are wanting. From Over the Water (or Ultra Aquam), only the assessment rolls of Coslany sub-ward (parishes of St Michael Coslany, St Mary Coslany and St Martin at Oak) are extant. The rolls of the other two sub-wards of Fyebridge and Colegate have perished (see Fig. 2).

Secondly, the 1489 assessment is in its final redaction, taking the form of an indenture between the commissioners and the collectors which provides the latter with only a list of names and the amount of tax to be collected from each person. Organised topographically, it begins in the south with the ward of Conesford and proceeds clockwise in a circle around the castle, ending with the ward of Ultra Aquam in the northeastern part of the city. Even though the assessment appears to list individual tenements, because the taxpayers' names are recorded only once in each parish/ward it is not entirely clear (as it usually is in the 1472 assessment) whether the assessment is of a single tenement or of all a taxpayer's holdings in the parish/ward.[46] In two wards (Conesford and Ultra Aquam), moreover, the assessment roll is not always subdivided by parish.[47]

The 1472 assessment rolls, however, represent one or the other (or, in one case, both) of the two stages of the assessment process: the ward inquests and the final indentures drawn up between the commissioners and the collectors. For the most part, the ward inquests record the assessment of each individual tenement (or messuage)[48] made by twelve or more named jurors of the ward, and give the impression of proceeding house-by-house; in only a few instances are all a taxpayer's holdings in the parish given in one entry.[49] In a handful of other cases, it is clear that both the occupant/lessee and owner of the tenement were assessed,[50] but by and large it appears to have been the owner, as the recipient of the income from the property, who was taxed. The inquests list the assessed value of each tenement, but not the tax payable. Only in the finalised indentures is the tax to be collected listed, together with the assessed value. For South Conesford with Trowse, both the ward inquest and the indenture survive, in two separate rolls, which have been collated here together. For Berstrete, only the ward inquest remains, and for the extant portions of Mancroft, Wymer and Ultra Aquam, only the indenture.[51]

[46] In the comparison below, nevertheless, they have been counted as individual tenements.

[47] The parishes of the north and south wards of Conesford are all listed together under the heading 'Conisford' and the parishes of St Michael Coslany, St Mary Coslany and St Martin at Oak, all in the sub-ward of Coslany, appear together under 'Coslany'.

[48] A tenement was a general term for any landed property; a messuage was a dwelling house, with the plot of land on which it stood, its courtyard (or curtilage) and outbuildings.

[49] All the lands and tenements in the parish of St John Timberhill owned by Walter Geffreys are listed, for example, in one entry at the head of the list, and in the same parish is one entry for 'divers tenements of Thomas Elys, alderman'.

[50] Most notably, Margaret Appleyard and her tenants in various parishes.

[51] Additional information about some of the tenements assessed in Conesford and Berstrete

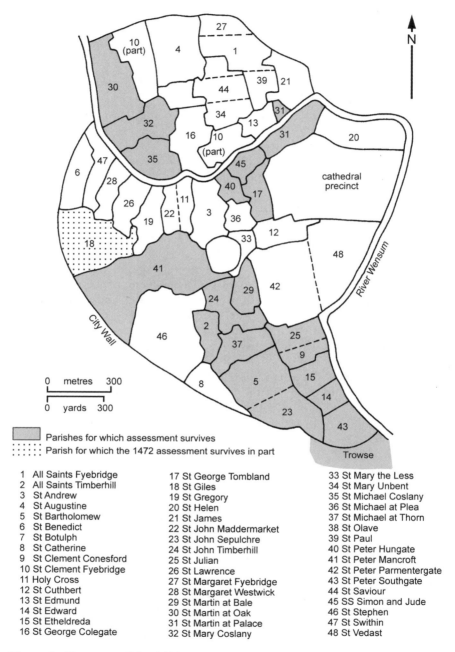

Figure 2. Coverage of the 1472 assessment.

N

0 metres 300
0 yards 300

Parishes for which assessment survives
Parish for which the 1472 assessment survives in part

1 All Saints Fyebridge
2 All Saints Timberhill
3 St Andrew
4 St Augustine
5 St Bartholomew
6 St Benedict
7 St Botulph
8 St Catherine
9 St Clement Conesford
10 St Clement Fyebridge
11 Holy Cross
12 St Cuthbert
13 St Edmund
14 St Edward
15 St Etheldreda
16 St George Colegate

17 St George Tombland
18 St Giles
19 St Gregory
20 St Helen
21 St James
22 St John Maddermarket
23 St John Sepulchre
24 St John Timberhill
25 St Julian
26 St Lawrence
27 St Margaret Fyebridge
28 St Margaret Westwick
29 St Martin at Bale
30 St Martin at Oak
31 St Martin at Palace
32 St Mary Coslany

33 St Mary the Less
34 St Mary Unbent
35 St Michael Coslany
36 St Michael at Plea
37 St Michael at Thorn
38 St Olave
39 St Paul
40 St Peter Hungate
41 St Peter Mancroft
42 St Peter Parmentergate
43 St Peter Southgate
44 St Saviour
45 SS Simon and Jude
46 St Stephen
47 St Swithin
48 St Vedast

Finally, and most obviously, there is the striking difference in the total amount assessed for each tax. As stated above, the total assessed in 1472 was £139 14s.4d., and the total in 1489 was £56 6s.8½d. (£38 1s.2½d. on income and £17 5s.6d. on goods), which was even less than the £79 14s.11d. which the city normally paid for a fifteenth and tenth.[52] When we compare closely the two assessments printed below we can see the two main reasons why there was such a discrepancy in the two totals (see Table 1). Firstly, far fewer tenements were taxed in 1489 in most of the wards and parishes which can be compared. In the parish of St Peter Mancroft, for example, only seventy-one tenements were assessed in 1489, as compared to 106 in 1472 (33% fewer). In the three parishes in the ward of Ultra Aquam which can be compared, namely St Michael and St Mary Coslany, and St Martin at Oak, the drop from 124 assessed tenements in 1472 to only sixty-five in 1489 (48% fewer) is all the more striking because significant economic and demographic growth in this area of the city is thought to have occurred in the last quarter of the fifteenth century, due to the expansion of the worsted cloth industry.[53] Similarly, fewer tenements were assessed in Berstrete (132 compared with ninety-three, 29.5% fewer) and Trowse (eighteen compared with twelve, 50% fewer). In the sub-ward of East Wymer, however, only four fewer tenements (7%) were assessed in 1489 (fifty-seven compared with fifty-three).[54]

It might have been possible to interpret the lower number of tenements taxed in 1489 as evidence of an increased prosperity and industrial activity which led to the amalgamation of small tenements into larger units were it not for the fact that the decreased number of tenements was accompanied by a decline in the amounts assessed, although this decline did not corre- spond closely with the rate of decrease in the number of tenements. In St Peter Mancroft, where there were about a third fewer tenements in 1489 than in 1472, the tax payable on income from tenements and rents (that is, excluding the annuities charged on the city's fee farm there) was £19 4s.7d. in 1472, as opposed to the £6 3d. payable in 1489, a drop of 68%. In Coslany, the drop in tax paid again exceeded the 48% decline in tene- ments assessed; the tax payable was £13 4s.¼d. in 1472, as opposed to £4 14d. in 1489, another decline of over two-thirds (68%). In Berstrete, the fall in tax paid was even more dramatic. The decline from £10 8s.7d. to £2 5s.5½d. represents a decrease in rental income here of 78%, far more

can be found in an assessment of assize and landgable rents due to the city from this ward which was made on 1 Nov. 1474, now NRO, Norwich City Records, Case 7, shelf i.

[52] Jurkowski, 'Parliamentary Taxation', p. 289.

[53] C. Rawcliffe and R. Wilson, eds, *Medieval Norwich* (London and New York, 2004), p. 217.

[54] Unfortunately, it is not possible to compile comparative figures for South Conesford sub- ward because the 1489 roll lists the assessments of the north and south wards of Conesford together.

than the fall in taxable tenements of only 29.5%. Similarly, the 50% decrease in taxable tenements in Trowse was far outstripped by the fall in tax paid – from 19s.½d. to 3s.4d. (82% less) – and the same situation prevailed in East Wymer. Although only four tenements fewer (7%) were assessed in 1489 than in 1472, the fall in tax paid there was more than 80% (£11 19s.10d. was assessed in 1472 and £2 3s.2d. in 1489).

All of these figures recording the fall of landed income at a much higher rate than the decline in numbers of tenements suggest consistent under-assessment rather than a massive fall in income from property in Norwich. This is shown most conclusively by comparing the individuals assessed. A comparison, firstly, of the names of the individuals assessed for both taxes in most of the parishes and sub-wards yields a high rate of 'persistence' in the ownership of tenements from 1472 to 1489 (see Table 1).[55] In Berstrete sub-ward forty-five of the ninety-three taxpayers (48%) assessed there (or, ostensibly, their heirs or widows) in 1489 are listed in the assessments of both years, and in every case the individual assessments were dramatically lower than in 1472, suggesting a stagnating housing market and a real fall in economic prosperity. Similarly, in Coslany sub-ward thirty-five of the sixty-five individuals (54%) assessed in 1489 were there in 1472. In most cases, the numbers of individuals assessed here dropped sharply between 1472 and 1489, but there were a few examples where the valuations declined only slightly, and the tenements of three taxpayers (Bartholomew Kyng, Thomas Wilkyns and John Knowte) were assessed at exactly the same amount. The valuation of John Dowse junior's property here actually increased from 40d. to 60d., perhaps representing an additional property which he had acquired in the intervening period. The obvious conclusion to draw in this ward, however, is that the value of tenements here had declined markedly.

Elsewhere in the city the persistence rate from 1472 to 1489 was lower. In the parish of St Peter Mancroft only nineteen of the seventy-one individuals assessed (27%) in 1472 were the same as in 1489, and although there had been an overall marked decline (68%) in the value of tenements here, this fall was not universal. A few individual valuations remained the same or were only slightly less, and the assessment of one person (John Quynton) rose from 16d. to 2s. The impression given here, however, is that this parish, located around the city's market, remained, as it had been since at least the early fourteenth century, one of the more demographically fluid areas of the city, with much opportunity for casual labour.[56] In the sub-ward of East Wymer, only sixteen of the fifty-three taxpayers (30%) were

[55] For the distinction between rates of 'persistence' and 'turnover', see: E. Rutledge, 'Immigration and Population Growth in Early Fourteenth-Century Norwich: Evidence from the Tithing Roll', *Urban History Yearbook* (1988), p. 22.

[56] Rutledge, 'Immigration and Population Growth', p. 23.

TABLE 1: *Comparison of 1472 and 1489 Assessments*

Parish/ Sub-Ward	Individuals			Amounts			Same	
	1472	1489	%	1472	1489	%	Number	%
Trowse	18	12	-50	19s.¼d.	3s.4d.	-82.5	2	16.5
Berstrete Sub-ward	132	93	-29.5	£10 8s.7d.	£2 5s.5½d.	-78	45	48
St Peter Mancroft	106	71	-33	£18 15s.8½d.	£6 0s.3d.	-68	19	27
East Wymer Sub-ward*	57	53	-7	£11 19s.10d.	£2 3s.2d.	-82	16	30
Coslany Sub-ward**	124	65	-48	£13 4s.¼d.	£4 1s.2d.	-69	35	54

* Parishes of St Martin at Palace, St Peter Hungate, St George Tombland and SS Simon & Jude.
** Parishes of St Michael Coslany, St Mary Coslany and St Martin Coslany.

the same in 1472 and 1489, which would suggest a more lively housing market, had there not been such a dramatic decline in both overall and individual assessments here; only one tenement (that of William Fuller in the parish of SS Simon and Jude) was valued at the same amount. Clearly, however, a number of craftsmen serving the nearby cathedral priory continued to reside in the parishes of this sub-ward, as suggested by their names, for example, Robert, Richard and Mariona Marbeler, and Richard Goldsmyth. The latter was taxed on both his tenement and his goods here in 1489, while a John Orgonmaker, paying 3s.4d. for his goods in 1489, resided then in another of the East Wymer parishes.

A similar picture of low persistence rates of population and dramatic decline in property values is painted in Trowse, where only two of the twelve individuals (16.5%) were the same in 1472 and 1489, and the values of their tenements had fallen drastically in both cases. It should also be noted that only three individuals in Conesford, Berstrete and Trowse together were assessed on their goods there in 1489, which suggests that Conesford ward was not a desirable neighbourhood in which the wealthier members of the city's population chose to live.[57]

Was this decline real or was it a case of large scale underassessment? It is difficult to be absolutely certain about this. The few instances where individual valuations stayed the same, or even rose, suggest that the commissioners did indeed make assessments in some degree of compliance with their instructions, but examples can also be found which provide evidence to the contrary. Consider, for instance, the assessments of Geoffrey Sperlyng, who was taxed in both 1472 and 1489 for the same tenements. Sperlyng is known today to literary and codicology scholars as a scribe, together with his son Thomas, of his own copy of the *Canterbury Tales*,[58] but in his own time he rose to prominence firstly as an estate servant of the wealthy Norfolk landowner Sir John Fastolf (d. 1459), and after the latter's death, as a city official, residing in one of the two adjoining tenements in Coslany which he had acquired from Sir John's estate.[59] In 1472 he was assessed for four tenements which he owned in Coslany: the messuage in St Mary Coslany where he resided (valued at £1 16s.8d.), the second messuage acquired from Fastolf in St Martin Coslany (valued at 10s.), a messuage in St Mary Coslany formerly owned by 'R. Wode' (valued at £1 6s.8d.) and a messuage in the same parish 'lately...of Wyghton' (valued at £3 6s.8d.). By 1489, however, his tene-

---

[57] This was still true in 1524-5: Pound, *Tudor and Stuart Norwich*, p. 35.

[58] The text is on ff. 1-115 of Glasgow University Library, Hunterian MS U.I.1.

[59] He was city auditor by 1464, clerk of St George's gild from 1469, and common clerk of the city from 1471 to 1490: R. Beadle, 'Geoffrey Spirleng (c. 1426-c.1494): a Scribe of the *Canterbury Tales* in his Time', in P.R. Robinson and R. Zim, eds, *Of the Making of Books: Medieval Manuscripts, Their Scribes and Readers: Essays Presented to M.B. Parkes* (Aldershot, 1997), pp. 116-46.

ments in these parishes had plummeted in total value from £7 to £1, even though we know from his will of 1494 that he then still owned the first two tenements, at the very least.[60] His son Thomas' property in Berstrete (in the parish of St Bartholomew) had also declined in value from 20s. in 1472 to 5s. in 1489. It seems unlikely that the value of the Sperlyngs' tenements could have fallen so drastically over this period, and other such individual comparisons would undoubtedly invite the same conclusion.

It is in the assessment of the goods of the residents of Norwich in 1489, however, that the most conclusive proof of underassessment can be found. Since taxpayers were taxed on their goods only in their place of residence, the 1489 assessment potentially has much to tell us about patterns of residence in Norwich, but, in fact, very few individuals were assessed for their goods (see Table 2). The minimum threshold of liability of 10 marks was not especially high, and although many personal possessions such as clothing, household utensils, plate and coins were exempt, the stock of merchants and craftsmen (where their capital was invested and their wealth was concentrated) was included in the assessment. Only 107 persons in all, however, were assessed for their goods, and most of them paid the lowest rate of 20d. The highest number assessed in any one parish (St Peter Mancroft) was ten, although in some parishes the assessment of goods was grouped together with the other parishes of the sub-ward, and it is impossible to know from this document alone, therefore, in which parish the taxpayers assessed on their goods resided.[61] As noted above, in the whole of Conesford ward and Trowse only three individuals paid, all at the lowest rate, and, most significantly, in eight parishes no one at all was assessed on goods. Evasion and underassessment are the most likely reasons for this low number of taxpayers. The pattern of assessment of goods does, on the whole, however, correspond with that of the assessment of property holdings in the city, and both must be, to some extent, a measure of the distribution of income and wealth throughout the various parishes and wards of Norwich.[62]

In conclusion, we must be prepared to believe that there had been some decline in the prosperity of the economy of Norwich in the latter part of the fifteenth century, at least in some parts of the city, despite archaeological evidence of a building boom in high quality buildings between 1475

[60] In 1494 he also owned tenements in the parishes of St Giles and St George Colegate: NRO, NCR, City Court Rolls, Case 1/29, m. 65d. The latter is almost certainly the same tenement in Colegate which was assessed in 1489 at 6d.: see below, p. 153.

[61] For example, in St John Maddermarket, Holy Cross, St Andrew and St Michael at Pleas (all in Middle Wymer sub-ward), where thirty-four persons altogether paid tax on their goods.

[62] Both are generally consistent with the findings of Dr. Pound, based on his analysis of the subsidy rolls of 1524-5: Pound, *Tudor and Stuart Norwich*, pp. 32, 35.

TABLE 2: *Assessment of Goods in 1489*

Ward/Sub-Ward/Parish	No. of Taxpayers
Conesford Ward	
North and South Conesford Sub-wards, Berstrete Sub-ward and Trowse	3
Mancroft Ward	
St Peter Mancroft	10
St Stephen	8
St Giles	0
Wymer Ward	
West Wymer Sub-ward	
St Gregory	2
St Lawrence	3
St Margaret Westwick	1
St Swithin	1
St Benedict	0
Middle Wymer Sub-ward	
St John Maddermarket, Holy Cross, St Andrew and St Michael at Plea	34
East Wymer Sub-ward	
St Peter Hungate, SS Simon & Jude, St George Tombland and St Martin at Palace	16
Over the Water Ward	
Coslany Sub-ward	22
Colgate Sub-ward	0
Fyebridge Sub-ward	
St Clement Fyebridge	0
St Saviour	0
All Saints Fyebridge	0
St James Pockthorpe	0
St Edmund	7
St Paul	0

and 1525[63] and a general rise in the city's population over the period 1377 to 1525,[64] although it seems likely that the large-scale underassessment practised by the city tax commissioners gives an exaggerated impression of this decline. Decay in some areas of the city and moderate growth in others is probably closer to the truth and these assessment rolls can help, considered together with archaeological and other documentary evidence, in identifying where both occurred.[65]

Editorial note

Both documents are in Latin and have been translated fully into English. All sums, similarly, have been converted from Roman to Arabic numerals, but the original units of currency of pounds, shillings, pence and marks (one-mark being equivalent to two-thirds of a pound or 13s.4d.) have been retained. The 1489 assessment is contained on a single roll, and the 1472 assessment, which is on six rolls, has been arranged in this edition in the same order as the 1489 assessment.

---

[63] B. Ayers, 'Understanding the Urban Environment: Archaeological Approaches to Medieval Norwich', in C. Harper-Bill, ed., *Medieval East Anglia* (Woodbridge, 2005), pp. 80-1; A. Dyer, *Decline and Growth in English Towns 1400-1640* (Cambridge, 1995), p. 26; G. Astill, 'Archaeology and the Late-Medieval Urban Decline', in T.R. Slater, ed., *Towns in Decline, AD 100-1600* (Aldershot, 2000), p. 226; M.D. Lobel and W.H. John, eds, *The Atlas of Historic Towns: Bristol, Cambridge, Coventry, Norwich* (3 vols., London and Baltimore, 1975), ii, p. 17; G.N. Barrett, 'The Great Hall, Oak St., Norwich', *NA*, 41 (1991), pp. 203-4.

[64] A. Dyer, '"Urban Decline" in England, 1377-1525', in Slater, ed., *Towns in Decline*, pp. 273, 275, 284-5.

[65] For contemporaneous urban decay and growth in the same cities, see K.D. Lilley, 'Decline or Decay? Urban Landscapes in Late-Medieval England', in Slater, ed., *Towns in Decline*, pp. 248-56.

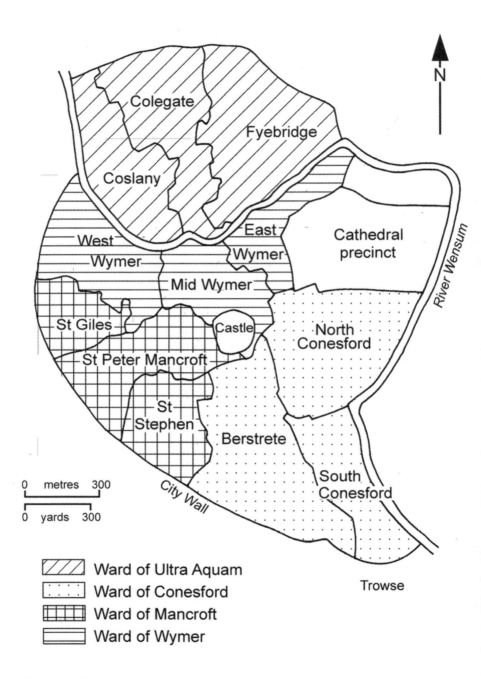

Figure 3. The wards of medieval Norwich.

NORWICH INCOME TAX ASSESSMENTS, 1472 AND 1489

1472 ASSESSMENT[1]

[Ward of Conesford]

[Rolls 1 and 2. Sub-]Ward of South Conesford with Trows[2]

Inquisition taken on Tuesday after the feast of Hilary the bishop in the twelfth year of the reign of Edward the fourth after the conquest [19 January 1473] at the Guildhall of the city of Norwich, before Roger Best, mayor, John Butte, William Skipwith and other commissioners of the said lord king, by virtue of two letters patent of the same king addressed to them, assigned to inquire, search and take cognizance of and upon the value of the issues and profits of one year only beginning at the feast of the Circumcision of the lord [1 January] last past from all manner of lands, tenements, rents, fees, annuities, offices, corrodies and pensions which any person of this realm, being or not being a lord of parliament of the said lord king, has, holds, possesses or occupies within the said county, jointly or severally, in fee simple or tail or otherwise, according to the force, form and effect of a certain act granted and ordained in the parliament of the said lord king beginning and held at Westminster on the sixth day of October last past and prorogation to the eighth day of February next coming having been made and proclaimed, on the oath of upright and lawful men of the various wards and parishes in this present schedule and in various bills annexed separately to the present schedule of their specific names, namely on the oath of Henry Hyrne, John Harman, Richard Wesill, Richard Grene, Nicholas Deye, Thomas Holueston, John Hood, Robert Boys, Simon Hogan, John Clement, John Johnson, Walter Wellis, Richard Couper, John Oldman, living in the parishes of St Peter de Southgate, St Edward, St Etheldreda, St Clement, St Julian and Trowse within the ward of South Conesford aforesaid, who say on their oath that:

---

[1] NRO NCR, Case 7 shelf i.

[2] The two assessments for South Conesford and Trowse have been collated together here. The transcript is taken mainly from the ward inquest (A) but the amounts payable in the right-hand column, together with the totals, come from the final indenture (B). B follows the same form as the returns for the sub-wards of East Wymer and Coslany below pp. 132-8.

Parish of St Peter de Southgate [*Value*] [*Tax*][3]

Who say on their oath [*sic*] that the value of the issues and profits of the tenement of John Hood within the said parish of St Peter being within the aforesaid ward was assessed for the said year ending at the said feast of the Circumcision of the lord, rents and services therefrom alone having been deducted

	13s.4d.	16d.
And of the messuage(s) land(s) and tenement(s) of John Couper there for the same period[4]	13s.4d.	16d.
Messuage[5] of John Cobbe	10s.	12d.
Messuage of Thomas Hulueston[6]	13s.4d.	16d.
Messuage of John Patryk[7]	13s.4d.	16d.
Messuage of Richard Wesill	20s.	2s.
Messuage of Matilda Hampson	13s.4d.	16d.
Four rental properties of John Candeler	25s.	2s.6d.
Messuage of Roger Clerk	17s.11d.	21½d.
Messuage of Margaret Reder[8] and Ed. Reder	17s.11d.	21½d.
Messuage of John Roke	11s.1½d.	13¼d.
Messuage of John Codlyng	13s.4d.	16d.
Messuage of Thomas Aleyn	10s.	12d.
Messuage of John Lyster[9]	5s.	6d.
A certain enclosure of William Wylles[10]	5s.	6d.
Messuage of Thomas Wysman[11]	10s.	12d.
Messuage of Robert Coke, 'hosier'	14s.6d.	17d.
[*Total*]:		22s.7¼d.

Parish of St Edward   *Value*   *Tax*

And further the said jurors say that the value of the issues and profits of the Master of the hospital of St Giles being within the said parish of St Edward within the said ward was assessed for the said year ending at the said feast of the Circumcision, rents and services only having been deducted therefrom[12]

	nothing because in mortmain	
Messuage of Robert Boys	4s.4d.	5¼d.
Messuage of Augustine Boys	5s.	6d.
Messuage of William Rothe,[13] vacant in the said year	nothing	

---

[3] Original in B: *Decima pars.*

[4] Most subsequent entries on roll A begin with 'And of' and end with 'there for the same period'.

[5] Most entries on rolls A and B give no ending to *mesuag'*, making it unclear whether a singular or plural is intended.

[6] Holuoston, in B.	[7] Patrike, in B.	[8] Rader, in B.	[9] Luster, in B.
[10] Willes, in B.	[11] Wyseman, in B.	[12] Not in B.	[13] Not in B.

Messuage of Joan Stalon	20s.	2s.
Messuage of John Mottes	6s.8d.	8d.
Messuage of Henry Cok[14]	20s.	2s.
[Total]:		5s.7¼d.

Parish of St Etheldreda

	Value	Tax
Messuage of Thomas Perot, chaplain[15]	20s.	2s.
Messuage of William Willes	40s.	4s.
Messuage of the abbot of Wymondham	18s.6½d.	22¼d.
'Le kylne' of Nicholas Rodclyf[16]	46s.8d.	4s.8d.
Messuage of John Clement	20s.	2s.
Messuage with one 'le kylne' *of John Damson*[17]	60s.	6s.
Messuage lately of[18] Robert Toppe, alderman	13s.4d.	16d.
[Total]:		21s.10¼d.

Parish of St Clement

	Value	Tax
And that the value of the issues and profits of messuage(s) of John Roke there for the same period	10s.	12d.
Messuage of Walter Welles	16s.	19¼d.
Messuage of Oliver Shurlok	33s.4d.	3s.4d.
Messuage of Hawis Balyngate[19]	10s.	12d.
Messuage of John Johnson	20s.	2s.
Messuage of John Wrave	16s.8d.	19d.
Messuage of William Pepir[20]	10s.	12d.
[Total]:		11s.7¼d.

Parish of St Julian

	Value	Tax
And that the value of the issues and profits of messuage(s) of John Oldman[21] there for the said time	5s.	6d.
Messuage of Thomas Wysdam[22]	40d.[23]	4d.
Messuage of Henry Woode,[24]	6s.8d.	8d.
[dorse] Messuage of Thomas Elys, alderman	26s.8d.	2s.8d.
Messuage of Edmunda[25] Wichingham	20s.	2s.
Messuage of Henry Smyth	13s.4d.	16d.
Messuage of John Wrave	4s.	4¾d.
Messuage of Robert Coke, hosier	6s.8d.	8d.
Messuage of John Couper	15s.	18d.

---

[14] Coke, in B.   [15] Thomas Perette, clerk, in B.   [16] Radclyf, in B.
[17] Danson *alias* Damyson, in B.   [18] executors of, in B.   [19] Hawesia Byllingate, in B.
[20] Peper, in B.   [21] Oldeman, in B.   [22] Wisdam *alias* Wiseman, in B.
[23] 3s.4d., in B.   [24] Wode, in B.   [25] Emma, in B.

One limekiln of William Aubry[26]	5 marks[27]	6s.8d.
[*Total*]:		16s.8¼d.

Concerning the quarter[28] of Trows	*Value*	*Tax*
And the value of the messuage of Ed. Staley there for the aforesaid period	30s.	3s.
Messuage of John Blake[29]	30s.	3s.
Messuage of John Barker	10s.	12d.
Messuage of Nicholas Deye[30]	10s.5d.	12½d.
Messuage of *Nicholas* <Richard> Grene[31]	13s.4d.	16d.
Messuage of Ed. Elys	4s.7d.	5½d.
Messuage of Stephen Childe	4s.2d.	5d.
Messuage of William Swayn	11s.½d.	13¼d.
Messuage of Nicholas Dikkes	4s.4½d.	5¼d.
Messuage of Walter Fornfeld	5s.	6d.
Messuage of William Koye	12s.6d.	15d.
Messuage of Henry Belcungre[32]	7s.6d.	9d.
Messuage of William Smyth	7s.6d.	9d.
Messuage of John Stakke	6s.8d.	8d.
Messuage of Hugh Lowes[33]	4s.7d.	5½d.
Messuage of Bartholomew Matheu[34]	4s.4½d.	5¼d.
Messuage of William Halles, chaplain	4s.4d.	5¼d.
Messuage of John Fader, esquire	20s.	2s.
[*Total*]:		19s.¼d.

Sum total of this indenture:	£4 17s.5¼d.

And that no spiritual or temporal lord, being a lord of parliament, had, held or possessed within the said year any lands or tenements, rents, fees, annuities, offices, corrodies or pensions not held in mortmain within the aforesaid parishes.

[*Roll 3. Sub-ward of*] Berstrete

Inquisition taken there on the aforesaid day and place before the said commissioners by virtue of the said king's letters patent, on the oath of Robert Fissher, Robert Eston, John Carrowe, John Thakker, Richard Osbern, William Mundes, John Thixill, Robert Stubberd, Henry Glovere, John Michilles, John Arpyngham, William Busshop, Thomas Gardener, William Hewe and Thomas

---

[26] Awbrey, in B.   [27] 66s.8d., in B.   [28] *Vicus.*   [29] Blak, in B.
[30] Dey, in B.   [31] *Breme* <Grene> in B.   [32] Belcongre, in B.
[33] Loweys, in B.   [34] Mathew, in B.

Mosse, living in the following parishes: St Sepulcre, St Bartholomew, St Michael, St Martin, St John and All Saints.

Parish of St [*John*] Sepulcre [*Value*]

Who say upon their oath that the value of the issues and profits of one messuage with annexed enclosure of Edward Magnus being within the said parish was assessed for one year ending at the feast of the Circumcision of the lord the said twelfth year of the lord king, rents and services alone having been deducted therefrom 33s.4d.

And of one messuage and enclosure there of John Thrower
for the same period[35] 13s.4d.
One tenement of John Gower 10s.
One tenement of William Bukley 12s.6d.
One tenement of William Talyour 15s.
One messuage with rental property adjoining of
John Carrowe 66s.8d.
One messuage of [*blank*] Poley 'gentilman' 13s.4d.
One messuage of Robert Thakker 13s.4d.
One tenement of Alice Hatter, widow 8s.4d.
One tenement of William Yekisworth & Thomas Cok 10s.
One messuage with rental property annexed of
Robert Herman 33s.4d.
One tenement of William Yekisworth & Thomas Cok 6s.8d.
One tenement of William Curteys 15s.
One tenement of *John* <William> Seman 2s.6d.
One tenement of Robert Cok 20s.
One tenement of Thomas Seman 10s.
One tenement of John Perbroun 5s.
One messuage of Robert Machon & William Blithe 21s.8d.
One tenement of John Buxton 3s.4d.
One tenement of John Thakker 20s.
One tenement of Thomas Toke 3s.4d.
One tenement of Alice Bonde 3s.11½d.
One messuage of Robert Fissher 40s.
One tenement of Thomas Alicok 6s.8d.
One messuage with enclosure of Margaret Fissher, widow 30s.

Parish of St Bartholomew [*Value*]

And of one tenement of John Manghteld in the said
parish for the aforesaid period 6s.8d.

---

[35] Most subsequent entries on this roll begin with 'And of' and end with 'for the aforesaid period'.

One *messuage* <tenement> of Richard Westerne,
   'baxter'   33s.4d.
One messuage of Robert Lounde   33s.4d.
One tenement of Robert Poule, 'marchaunt'   7s.11<½>d.
One tenement of Thomas Hullok   12s.1<½>d.
One tenement of Richard Westerne & Simon Child   6s.8d.
One tenement of Thomas Spirlyng   20s.
One tenement of Nicholas Wright   6s.7½d.
One messuage with enclosure of John Broun, 'bocher'   30s.
One tenement of Simon Child, 'brasier'   13s.4d.
One messuage with enclosure of John Barbour, 'bocher'   40s.

Parish of St Michael [*at Thorn*]   [*Value*]
And of one messuage of William Kyngges, 'barker',
   in the said parish for the said year   20s.
One tenement of Henry Coket   7s.1d.
One tenement of John Barkelee   6s.8d.
One tenement of Robert Stubberd   16s.½d.
One tenement of William Kegell   10s.
One messuage with rental property of Ed. Colman,
   alderman   20s.
One messuage of Roger Batell   20s.
One tenement with enclosure annexed of Ed. Redknape,
   alderman   20s.
One tenement of William Hewe, 'bocher'   10s.
One tenement of John Spycer of Derham   10s.
One tenement of Thomas Fulkes   6s.8d.
One tenement of John Briggeham   6s.8d.
One tenement of John Thixel, carpenter   33s.4d.
One messuage with enclosure of William Mundes   60s.
One tenement of Adam Awbrey   6s.8d.
Rents which Margaret Appilyerd receives from two
   tenements of Robert Stubberd & William Kegell above 4s.

Parish of St Martin [*at Bale*]   [*Value*]
And of one messuage of Thomas Gardenere
   in the said parish for the aforesaid year   20s.
One tenement of John Lakenham   6s.8d.
One tenement of John Store   7s.11d.
One tenement of John Ryngolf   6s.½d.
One tenement of John Keryche   4s.5½d.
One *garden* <tenement> of Thomas Bewfeld   <3s.> 2s.11d.

One *garden* <tenement> of Master William Feld	2s.1d.
One tenement of Robert Byrd	6s.8d.
One tenement of Andrew Couperwrythe	30s.
One tenement of John Symunds, 'wrythe'	12s.1d.
One tenement of John Lucas	6s.8d.
One tenement of John Attilborow	6s.8d.
One tenement of Edmund Bullyng	13s.4d.
One *garden* <tenement> of Matilda Tomson	<3s.> 2s.11d.
<One tenement of the executors of John Gylberd>	
One *garden* <tenement> of Robert Aylmer	2s.1d.
One tenement of John Ultyng, 'bocher'	6s.<1d.> ½d.
One tenement of Thomas Byrde, 'sawer'	10s.
One tenement of Joan Cole, 'wedow'	5s.
One tenement of John Langges	17s.1d.
One tenement of John Stevenes	10s.
One tenement of Thomas Aungell	6s.8d.
One tenement of William Birde	6s.½d.
One tenement of William Pays	2s.1d.
One tenement of the prior of St Faith	12s.1d.
One tenement of Robert Mayour	12s.1d.
One tenement of Robert Davy	5s.
One tenement of Richard Rilkes	5s.
One tenement of John Ely, 'taillour'	13s.4d.
<One tenement of John Grey, chaplain>	<6s.8d.> because nothing above rent(s) payable
One garden of Henry Coket	10s.
One garden of Walter Skynner	3s.4d.
One messuage with rental property and enclosure of William Bisshop	53s.4d.

Parish of St John [*Timberhill*]   [*Value*]

And of all lands and tenements of Walter Geffreys in the aforesaid parish for the aforesaid period	£9
One messuage of Thomas Alicok	40s.
One messuage of John Erpyngham	40s.
One messuage of John Michels	20s.
One messuage of William Coket	33s.4d.
One messuage of Henry Thurton	20s.
One messuage of Henry Glover	23s.4d.
One tenement of Robert Eston	20s.
One messuage of Katherine Dunyng	30s.
One messuage of Joan Underwode, widow	20s.

One tenement of Thomas Pye	13s.4d.
One tenement of John Boston	13s.4d.
One tenement of William Lely	10s.
One tenement of William Glovere	6s.8d.
One tenement of John Unbeyne	6s.8d.
One tenement of Stephen Benys	6s.8d.
One tenement of Catherine Colough	10s.
Various tenements of Thomas Elys, alderman	23s.4d.
One tenement of Thomas Derham	10s.
One messuage of Richard Ray	20s.
One tenement of John Levot	3s.4d.
One tenement of John Fowlyn	3s.4d.

Parish of All Saints

Parish of All Saints	[*Value*]
One messuage of Thomas Bokenham, alderman	40s.
One messuage with enclosure of Ed. Redknape, alderman	20s.
One tenement of Andrew Kentyng	5s.10d.
One tenement of Thomas Godewyn	7s.11d.
One tenement of Stephen Brownyng	7s.11d.
Two tenements of Robert Isbell	18s.<7d.> 6½d.
One messuage of William Baly	13s.4d.
One messuage of Robert <G>Brigges	23s.4d.
One messuage of William Hewe	40s.
One messuage of John Levot	10s.
One messuage of Elizabeth Barvyle	6s.½d.
One tenement of John Lakenham	7s.11d.
One tenement of Walter Kempe	6s.½d.
One tenement of Ed. Dilham	13s.4d.
One messuage of Barbara Pycot, widow	20s.
One tenement of William Scarlet	5s.
One tenement of William Swetman, clerk	15s.
One tenement of Thomas Knyght	10s.
One tenement of Thomas Perte	6s.8d.
One tenement of Reginald Harneys	13s.4d.
One tenement of [*blank*] Kar	6s.8d.
One messuage of John Jamys, built in the said two parishes of St John & All Saints	42s.1d.
One tenement of Catherine Dunnyng & Nicholas Mayhewe	6s.8d.
One messuage of Thomas Moos	33s.4d.
One messuage of Katherine Chandeler & William Barker	6s.8d.

And that no lords spiritual or temporal, being lords of parliament, had, held or possessed [*as entry for the sub-ward of South Conesford, p. 124*]

[*Roll 4.*] Ward of Mancroft

Parish of St Peter [*Mancroft*]	Value	Tax[36]
From Thomas Elys alderman there taxed at 60s, of which the tenth part [*is*] 6s[37]		
Philip Curson	26s.8d.	2s.8d.
John Roos, esquire	40s.	4s.
The said Philip Curson	40s.	4s.
The wife of Pert, widow	35s.	3s.6d.
John Barbour	26s.8d.	2s.8d.
Thomas Antyngham	52s.6d.	5s.3d.
Robert Osberne	60s.13s.4d.	7s.4d.
William Styward	61s.8d.	6s.2d.
Lady Margaret Purdauns	£6 5s.	12s.6d.
Thomas Burgeys	28s.4d.	2s.10d.
Thomas Derham	50s.	5s.
The executors of John Gylbert	20s.	2s.
John Baldyswell	6s.8d.	8d.
John Tevell	62s.6d.	6s.3d.
William Bakon	43s.4d.	4s.4d.
The wife of Pert, widow	20s.10d.	2s.1d.
Robert Pert	30s.	3s.
Master William Feld	20s.	2s.
Thomas Tyrryngham	26s.8d.	2s.8d.
William London	12s.6d.	15d.
The wife of Dunnygges, widow	25s.	2s.6d.
Richard Anyell, alderman	5s.10d.	7d.
John Game	26s.8d.	2s.8d.
John Burgh	73s.4d.	7s.4d.
The wife of Ed. Turnour, widow	40s.	4s.
Robert Dryvarr, chaplain	40s.	4s.
John Elmeham	40s.	4s.
Godfrey Joy	78s.4d.	7s.10d.
John Parker	13s.4d.	16d.
Walter Wellys	60s.	<6s.> 4s.8d.
Lady Suffolk	17s.6d.	21d.
John Walden	30s.	3s.
Walter Byllern	20s.	2s.

[36] *Decima pars.*
[37] Subsequent entries on this roll follow the same form.

Robert Mortemer	18s.4d.	22d.
Robert Crosse	15s.	18d.
Edward Cutler, *alderman*	65s.10d.	6s.7d.
Robert Bomsted	26s.8d.	2s.8d.
John Swardarr	£4	8s.
Robert Swyll	11s.8d.	14d.
The wife of Shotysham, widow	25s.	2s.6d.
John Jenney, 'jantylman'	40s.	4s.
William Shelton	26s.8d.	2s.8d.
Edmund Bukenham, 'esqwyr'	23s.4d.	2s.4d.
John Hastynggs, 'sqwyr'	35s.	3s.6d.
Edmund Erle	45s.	4s.6d.
William Fuller, bachelor in laws	33s.4d.	3s.4d.
Bartholomew Erle	13s.4d.	16d.
Robert Godeman	10s.	12d.
Richard Herward	15s.	18d.
Robert Hempton	25s.	2s.6d.
John at Meer	25s.	2s.6d.
Robert Powle	40s.	4s.
Thomas Haugh	40s.	4s.
Thomas Burgeys	25s.	2s.7d.
Roger Broun	12s.6d.	15d.
Robert Osberne	25s.	2s.6d.
John Swanne	27s.6d.	2s.9d.
William Hawhes	15s.10d.	19d.
The wife of Knappys, widow	6s.8d.	8d.
The wife of Knape, widow	10s.	12d.
Richard Tudenham	13s.4d.	16d.
Thomas Dobbys	15s.	18d.
John Holle	22s.6d.	2s.3d.
John Spencer	28s.4d.	2s.10d.
Henry Wylton	26s.8d.	2s.8d.
Alice Burgeys	7s.6d.	9d.
Agnes Aleyn	£7	14s.
Margaret Assheman	6s.8d.	8d.
[*Total*]:		£11 12s.11d.
[*dorse*] John Furbyssher	50s.	5s.
Thomas Wymer	40s.	4s.
Thomas Burgeys	46s.8d.	4s.8d.
William Bonde	35s.	3s.6d.
Henry Bradfeld	40s.	4s.
John Sherman	40s.	4s.

Simon Hubberd	13s.12d.	13d.
John Denton	6s.8d.	8d.
Common messuage of the commonalty of Norwich	£6.11s.8d.	13s.2d.
Thomas Bomsted	50s.10d.	5s.1d.
Thomas Veyle	40s.	4s.
William Swayne, *alderman*	75s.	7s.6d.
The executors of Simon Munham, clerk	£8.11s.8d.	17s.2d.
Thomas Vyell	33s.4d.	3s.4d.
William London	70s.	7s.
The said William London	£5.6s.8d.	10s.8d.
John Quyntyn	13s.4d.	16d.
Master Wechyngham	71s.8d.	7s.2d.
Alexander Weston	20s.	2s.
William Skarlett	20s.	2s.
John Fen	27s.6d.	2s.9d.
William Pekysworth	22s.6d.	2s.3d.
Robert Lound	37s.6d.	3s.9d.
Robert Powle	13s.4d.	16d.
Thomas Kyllyngworth	5s.10d.	7d.
William Quyncy	26s.8d.	2s.8d.
John Lawes	26s.8d.	2s.8d.
Richard Ballys	20s.	2s.
The rector of St Botolph's	25s.	2s.6d.
Thomas Fawkener	6s.8d.	8d.
The said Thomas Fawkener	£4.6s.8d.	8s.8d.
Oliver House	20s.	2s.
William Calthorp knight, for rents received from various tenements for the year	10s.	12d.
Thomas Bumstede for rents which he receives from the mayor and commonalty of Norwich in the said parish	9s.8d.	11½d.
Margaret Appilyerd for rents received in the said parish	5s.4d.	6½d.
John Garbald for rent[38] which he receives from Margaret Purdans above	8s.	9½d.
Total:	£18 15s. <14s.> 8½d.	/£7 2s.8d./

Thomas Mongomoray, knight, for a certain annuity which he receives from the fee farm of the lord king in the said city issuing in the said year

	£40	£4

[38] *de redd' de redd'.*

William Lye, a valet of the lord king, for an annuity which he receives from the
said fee farm　　　　　　　　　　　　　£9 2s.6d.　　　18s.3d.
William Hargvyle, another valet of the lord king, for an annuity which he
receives from the said fee farm　　　　　£9 2s.6d.　　　18s.3d.
Roger Kelteshale, another valet of the lord king, for an annuity which he
receives from the said fee farm　　　　　£9 2s.6d.　　　18s.3d.
Henry Grey, knight, for an annuity which he receives from the said fee farm for
the said year　　　　　　　　　　　　£11 8s.1½d.　　22s.9¾d.
Robert Marchale, for an annuity which he receives from the said fee farm for
the said year　　　　　　　　　　　　£6 13s.4d.　　　13s.4d.
Thomas Grene, for an annuity which he receives from the said fee farm for the
said year　　　　　　　　　　　　　£6 13s.4d.　　　13s.4d.
Thomas Cambrigge, for rent which he receives from the messuage called le
Belle, namely　　　　　　　　　　　　12s.　　　　14½d.

[Ward of Wymer]

[Roll 5. Sub-ward of] Est Wymer within the ward of Wymer

This indenture attests to the true value of the issues and profits of all lands and
tenements, rents, fees, annuities, offices, corrodies and pensions not held in
mortmain which any person existing in this realm and not being a lord of
parliament has, holds and possesses in the following parishes, within the ward of
Wymer, for a year only, beginning at the feast of the Circumcision of the lord
in the twelfth year of the king's reign, as is openly revealed in various inquisitions made of them, namely:

Parish of St Giles	*Value*	*Tax*[39]
From John Selot, clerk, from his land(s) and		
tenements being within the said parish taxed at	34s.*2d.*	3s.5d.
<From John, prior of the cathedral church of		
Norwich, *because the fee belongs to the		
commonalty of Norwich and not to the prior*	5s.	6d.>

Parish of St Martin [at Palace]	[Value]	[Tax]
From William Calthorp, knight, for land(s)		
and tenement(s) there taxed at	60s.	6s.
From Reginald Harneys there similarly		
taxed at[40]	66s.8d.	6s.8d.
Robert Everhard	60s.	6s.

[39] See p. 110 n. 45; *decima pars.*　　　[40] Subsequent entries drop the 'similarly'.

Margery Skryvenere	45s.2½d.	4s.6¼d.
Peter Mego	30s.	3s.
Margaret Stowe	12s.9d.	15¼d.
Henry Hemysby	19s.9d.	23¾d.
Henry Cobald	13s.4d.	16d.
Richard Ferrour, alderman of Norwich	20s.	<16d.> 2s.
Cecilia Chittok, widow	£8 4s.8d.	16s.5½d.
John Blounvyle, notary	26s.8d.	2s.8d.
Isabel Jeve	20s.	2s.
William Barbour & William Gladon	20s.	2s.
John Elmham	66s.½d.	6s.7¼d.
John Hokkam	13s.4d.	16d.
Simon Petyte	20s.	2s.
Henry Curtes	13s.11d.	16¾d.
Thomas Percy	38s.8d.	3s.10½d.
Stephen Brasier	6s.8d.	8d.
Margaret Appylyerd, for rents which she receives from various tenants of the aforesaid tenements in the said parish	22s.8d.	2s.3¼d
Total:		£3 17s.5½d.

Parish of St Peter [Hungate]	[Value]	[Tax]
Edmund Frensh	39s.	3s.10¾d.
Margery White	16s.	19¼d.
Nicholas Yngham	£4	8s.
John Scolehous	23s.4d.	2s.4d.
John Elgyr	10s.	12d.
Robert Gosbek	15s.4d.	18½d.
Thomas Shiford	33s.4d.	3s.4d.
Margaret Paston	40s.	4s.
Total:		25s.8½d.

Parish of St George [Tombland]	[Value]	[Tax]
Thomas Storme, notary	£4 16s.	9s.7¼d.
John Kyllyngworth & Robert Bury	11s.	13¼d.
Thomas Crowte	72s.11d.	7s.3½d.
Robert Portelond	£6 2s.8d.	11s.3¼d.
Roger Best, alderman of Norwich	53s.10d.	5s.4½d.
Joan Bramerton, widow	nothing because in mortmain	
Joan, lately wife of Robert Toppe	£11	22s.
Robert Lounde	20s.	2s.
John Scolehous	26s.8d.	2s.8d.
William Amyot	14s.8d.	17½d.

John Ripon, esquire	28s.	<21½d.>
		2s.9½d.
Thomas Sheef	13s.4d.	16d.
Alice, duchess of Suffolk	51s.10d.	5s.2¼d.
Richard Herreys	15s.	18d.
Margaret Appilyerd, widow, for rent which she		
receives from tenements in the said parish		
to the sum of	6s.	7¼d.
Total:		£3 15s.2¼d.

Parish of SS Simon & Jude	[*Value*]	[*Tax*]
Stephen Brasire	72s.6d.	6s.3d.
John Cok, alderman of Norwich	£9 3s.4d.	18s.4d.
William Fuller	35s.	3s.6d.
Simon Cuttyng	10s.	12d.
Cecilia May	2s.6d.	3d.
Edmund Felmyngham, chaplain	26s.8d.	2s.8d.
The alderman & fraternity of St George	£4 18s.	9s.9¾d.
William Merres, chaplain	71s.4d.	7s.1½d.
William Halle, chaplain	20s.	2s.
Richard Baxter of Hempton	29s.	2s.10¾d.
Nicholas Lathe	40s.	4s.
Thomas Brusyerd	8s.	9¾d.
Thomas Percy	5s.	6d.
William Gyles	23s.4d.	2s.4d.
Total:		61s.5¾d.
		<59s.1¾d.>

Sum of the tenth part of this indenture: [*blank*]

Sum total: £11 <18s.> *19s.5d.*

[Roll 6. Ward of Ultra Aquam]

This indenture attests to the true value of the issues and profits of all lands and
tenements, rents, fees, annuities, offices, corrodies and pensions not held in
mortmain that any person being of this realm and not being a lord of parliament has, holds and possesses in the following ward of Ultra Aquam assessed
for one year ending at the feast of the Circumcision of the lord in the twelfth
year of the reign of king Edward the fourth, as is openly revealed in various
inquisitions made of them, namely:

[*Sub-ward of*] Coslany

Parish of St Michael [*Coslany*]	*Value*	*Tax*[41]
From Robert Bakton from land(s) and tenements in the said parish assessed at 30s of which the tenth part [*is*] 3s		
Walter Waron	26s.8d.	2s.8d.
Thomas Symondis	25s.	2s.6d.
Margery Knyght, lately the wife of John Knyght	23s.4d.	2s.4d.
Bartholomew Kyng, for a garden lately of Nicholas Hall	3s.4d.	4d.
William Lacy, for a messuage lately of John Skyn	6s.8d.	8d.
[*blank*] late the wife of Thomas Lyne	20s.	2s.
William Lacy, for the messuage in which he lives	13s.4d.	16d.
John Roose, for a messuage lately of John Boteler	6s.8d.	8d.
Richard Ferrour, alderman, for a tenement lately of John Hulnere	12s.1d.	14½d.
Thomas Jervys	8s.4d.	10d.
John Dewe	13s.4d.	16d.
John Lesour	25s.	2s.6d.
John Emmes	16s.8d.	20d.
Thomas Elys	20s.	2s.
Cecilia Kyndell, widow	30s.	3s.
Roger Ayleward	16s.8d.	20d.
John Rose, alderman	33s.4d.	3s.4d.
Richard Burdon	10s.	12d.
Augustine Elsy	30s.	3s.
William Roo	33s.4d.	3s.4d.
Elvicia Seggeford	8s.4d.	10d.
John Bisshop	40s.	4s.
Roger Jekkys	10s.	12d.
Richard Ferrour, alderman, for a tenement late of John Gilbert	58s.	5s.9½d.
Thomas Roller	16s.8d.	20d.
Robert Wode, 'coupere'	20s.	2s.
Richard Ferrour, senior	6s.8d.	8d.
John Hevenyngham, knight	13s.4d.	16d.
John Colman, for the messuage in which he lives	53s.4d.	5s.4d.

[41] *Decima pars.*

John Colman, for a messuage lately of Grantham	53s.4d.	5s.4d.
William Ferrour	26s.8d.	2s.8d.
William Davy	33s.4d.	3s.4d.
John Huberd	6s.8d.	8d.
Peter M*o*ose	51s.	5s.
Richard Ferrour, senior, for the tenement in which he lives	10s.	12d.
Richard Ferrour, alderman, for the messuage in which he lives	5 marks	6s.8d.
The same Richard Ferrour, for the messuage late of Richard Albon	40s.	4s.
John Banyard, esquire	13s.4d.	16d.
Gregory Clerk	53s.4d.	5s.4d.
Katherine Blak, widow	13s.4d.	16d.
Thomas Staley	40s.	4s.
William Smith for the messuage in which he lives	36s.8d.	3s.8d.
The same William, for the tenement late of Thomas Hayte	23s.4d.	2s.4d.
Robert Grome	13s.4d.	16d.
Richard Tedde	20s.	2s.
Total of the tenth part:		£5 14s. 6d.

Parish of St Mary [*Coslany*]	[*Value*]	[*Tax*]
William Swan	6s.8d.	8d.
William Munford	6s.8d.	8d.
Thomas Oudolf, chaplain	11s.8d.	14d.
John Denton, for the tenement late of Robert Palmere	40s.	4s.
Robert Hemmyng	13s.4d.	16d.
Henry Oudolfe	66s.8d.	6s.8d.
Geoffrey Spyrleng for the messuage late of R. Wode	26s.8d.	2s.8d.
Thomas Flaxman	8s.4d.	10d.
Laurence Russhworth	£4	8s.
Thomas Norman	13s.4d.	16d.
William Merrys, chaplain, for one quarter[42]	20d.	2d.
Robert Roose, for two quarters	8s.	9½d.
Nicholas Crombe	33s.4d.	3s.4d.
John Knorigth	16s.8d.	20d.

[42] Of the year.

Richard Burdon	20s.	2s.
Richard Wattys	33s.4d.	3s.4d.
Katherine Bertram	5s.	6d.
Christine Tele	5s.	6d.
Laurence Russhworth, for the tenement Bertram	13s.4d.	16d.
John Oudolf, chaplain	3s.4d.	4d.
Bartholomew Kyng	26s.8d.	2s.8d.
Geoffrey Spyrleng, for the messuage Wyghton	66s.8d.	6s.8d.
William Synne	15s.	18d.
Thomas Spencer	20s.	2s.
John Fraunces	30s.	3s.
John Brewyn	53s.4d.	5s.4d.
William Coke	24s.4d.	2s.4d.
[*Dorse*] John Denton, for the tenement late of Howard	60s.	6s.
The same for the messuage in which he lives	20s.	2s.
John Wymondham, esquire	40s.	4s.
James Gresham, for the messuage which he occupies sometimes[43]	10s.	12d.
Geoffrey Spyrleng, for the messuage in which he lives	36s.8d.	3s.8d.
John Avelyn, clerk, for a messuage, assessed for a <quarter>	10s.	12d.
Total of the tenth part:		£4 2s. 5½d.

Parish of St Martin [*at Oak*]

	[*Value*]	[*Tax*]
Thomas Wylkyns	30s.	3s.
John Feltwelle	10s.	12d.
Joan Glover, for a messuage	10s.	12d.
Richard Ferrour, for a messuage with rental property, late of John Coppyng	53s.8d.	5s.4½d.
Gregory Clerk, for a messuage late of Joan	11s.8d.	14d.
John Reynald	15s.	18d.
John Dows	3s.4d.	4d.
Richard Tomson	20s.	2s.
John Deye	15s.	18d.
Robert Parker	11s.8d.	14d.
Gregory Clerk, for messuage of Pigott	6s.8d.	8d.
Gregory Clerk, for the messuage of Joan Clerk	5s	6d.
John Brond	20s.	2s.

---

43 *Per vices per vices.*

Thomas Careawey	4s.	4³⁄₄d.
Robert Skowe, for messuage Abraham	4s.	4³⁄₄d.
Thomas Massenger <clerk>	11s.8d.	14d.
Richard Skowe, for messuage Dobilday	15s.	18d.
Brice Skowe, for messuage Samuell	15s.	18d.
Isabel Payn	6s.8d.	8d.
Robert Clifforth, for a garden	12d.	1¹⁄₄d.
Geoffrey Spyrleng, for an enclosed tenement	10s.	12d.
Gregory Clerk, for two tenements late of Joan Clerk	46s.7d.	4s.7d.
Richard Corpusty	20s.	2s.
John Wymer	33s.4d.	3s.4d.
Thomas Aleyn, for messuage Budde	26s.8d.	2s.8d.
Richard Skowe	20s.	2s.
Thomas Drantale	9s.8¹⁄₂d.	11¹⁄₂d.
Robert Regnalde	13s.4d.	16d.
Alice Dobilday	15s.	18d.
John Stalon	33s.4d.	3s.4d.
Adam Ive	10s.	12d.
Robert Skowe	16s.¹⁄₂d.	19³⁄₄d.
William Samuelle	13s.4d.	16d.
Alice Brond	5s.	6d.
[blank] late wife of W. Langham	16s.8d.	20d.
Robert Clifforth	15s.	18d.
John Stalon, for the messuage of John Brond	16s.	19¹⁄₄d.
John Chapman	30s.	3s.
William Martyn	5s.	6d.
Brice Skowe	23s.4d.	2s.4d.
Richard Gylberd	10s.	12d.
Augustine Boys, for one quarter	3s.11¹⁄₂d.	4³⁄₄d.
Augustine Boys	5s.	6d.
William Roo	3s.11¹⁄₂d.	4³⁄₄d.
Total:		£3 7s.³⁄₄d.

Sum total of this indenture: £13 4s.¹⁄₄d.

1489 ASSESSMENT[44]

[*rot. 1*] This indenture made on the twenty seventh day of July in the fourth year of the reign of Henry seventh after the conquest [*1489*] between John Rede and Richard Howard, sheriffs of the city of Norwich, Richard Balles, Robert Belton, Robert Cok and John Dowes, senior, the king's commissioners in the said city, assigned by virtue of letters patent of the same lord king addressed to them and others, both in the said city and in the county of Norfolk, to inquire, search and take cognizance both of the value of the issues and profits of one year only, and of all lands and tenements, rents, fees, annuities, offices, corrodies and pensions which any person of this realm of England, not being a lord of parliament, has, holds or possesses within the said city, jointly or severally, in fee simple or tail, and of the true value of the issues and profits of one year only of all manner of honours, castles, lordships, manors, lands, tenements, rents, fees, annuities, corrodies, pensions and fee farms, which anyone, [*not*] being a lord of parliament, has, holds or possesses to his own use or by any other person to the use of him or any of them, within the said city in fee simple or tail or else for term of life, and also of all and singular, not being lords of the parliament of the lord king, having goods and chattels to the value of 10 marks or more, according to the form and effect of a certain act of grant and ordinance made in the parliament of the same lord king at Westminster begun and held on the thirteenth day of January last past and prorogued until the fourteenth day of October next coming, on the one part, and Geoffrey Tevel, John Wilton, William Swanton, John Rightwys, William Ferrour, Thomas Glaumvyle, Robert Best, John Randolff, Thomas Sweyn, Thomas Davy, John Smyth, rafman, Thomas Hemmyng and John Baly, from the said city, on the other part, attests that by virtue of the said letters patent the said commissioners assigned the said Geoffrey Tevel, John Wilton, William Swanton, John Rightwys, William Ferrour, Thomas Glaumvyle, Robert Best, John Randolff, Thomas Sweyn, Thomas Davy, John Smyth, Thomas Hemmyng and John Baly, and each of them, to collect, levy and receive the half part of the sums of the annual value of all lands, tenements and other premises within the said city, with Trowse annexed to the same, and of all and singular persons, not being lords of the said parliament,

[44] TNA PRO E 179/149/187. The assessment is of three rotulets, sewn in the wrong order. The first rotulet contains the indented commission, and the other two contain the assessment. The assessment begins on what is now rot. 3 and ends on the dorse of rot. 2. It is written on large parchment sheets, each measuring about 2 feet x 2 feet, and is in four columns (numbered A-D here). There are six seal tags, but only traces of the seals remain. A full Latin typescript transcript of the document (with a few errors), made in 1953 by George Hunt Holley of Halesworth, Suffolk, is now NRO, Hamond of Westacre, HMN 7/324.

having goods and chattels to the value of ten marks or more, according to the form and effect of the said act, grant and ordinance, from all and singular persons separately and specified in certain schedules annexed to these presents, as is perfectly clear in the same schedules. The which half part of the issues and profits of the said lands and tenements and other premises so to be collected and raised by them, according to the form of the said act, totals the sum of £19 7¼d. And the which sum of the said goods and chattels valued at ten marks and more to be collected and levied from the said singular persons, according to the form and effect of the said act, totals the sum of £17 5s.6d. And when the same collectors have collected and levied those singular sums to be collected and levied by them, as is aforesaid, then they should pay the same sums to the said lord king without delay and under impending peril, and, moreover, do all and singular which is pertinent to it, according to the force, form and effect of the same act. For which it is ordered to them and each of them on behalf of the said lord king that they attend to the business diligently and that it be executed without delay under heavy penalty. And likewise to all constables, bailiffs and other lieges of the lord king in the said city that they be attentive, helpful, and obedient to the aforesaid collectors in execution of the afore-mentioned as is befitting, under the same penalty. In witness of which thing, the said commissioners affixed their seals to one part of this indenture with the said schedules annexed, to the other part of this indenture the said collectors affixed their seals. Given on the day and year aforesaid.

[rot. 3A]   **City of Norwich**

Inquisition or examination there in the Guildhall of the same city, taken on the eighth day of April in the fourth year of the reign of Henry seventh after the conquest [*1489*], before John Rede and Richard Howard, sheriffs of the same city, Richard Balles, Robert Belton, Robert Cokke and John Dowes, senior, commissioners of the said lord king within the said city, by virtue of letters patent of the said lord king addressed to them and others, to inquire, search and take cognizance of the tenth part of the value of one year only of all lands and tenements, and not having been given in mortmain, rents and services paid on them having been deducted, and of all and singular persons having goods and chattels to the value of ten marks and more within the same city or elsewhere, according to the form and effect of the said letters patent of the lord king.
By virtue of which said letters patent of the lord king we the said commissioners on the day and year aforesaid in the said Guildhall have assigned and deputed William Hayward, Robert Belle, John Preston, Thomas Drew, John atte Mere, William Howlot, William Holston, Thomas Large, Geoffrey Freman, Walter Wellys, William Swanton, John Herman, Nicholas Deye, Roger Ferrour, Robert Fissher, John Leek senior, Edmund Michell, John Leek junior, John Syxhill,

Henry Thurton, William Smyth, Robert Thorn and Thomas Gardener, jurors for the wards of Conesford and Berstrete within the same city, with Trous annexed to the same, to inquire, search and take cognizance of the business in the said wards and certify us of it, according to the form and effect of the said letters patent of the lord king.

Ward of Conesford and Berstrete with Trous

The which jurors on the twentieth of April in the said year in the said Guildhall certify to the said commissioners both the tenth part of the value of the aforesaid lands and tenements being within the said ward and the persons living within the said ward having goods and chattels to the value of ten marks and more within the said ward or elsewhere, to be levied and collected in the following way and form, namely...

Conesford

[*Tenth part of lands and tenements*]	[*Tax*]
John Brevetour for the tenth part of his lands and tenements there, beyond [outgoings], etc.[45]	4d.
John Oldman	3d.
Robert Edmundys	5d.
William Howlot	8d.
Thomas Touneshend	6d.
Thomas Wiseman	6d.
John Gillyng	6d.
John Walden	8d.
William Bylney	3d.
Thomas Berton	4d.
Roger Clerk	4d.
Thomas Bacon	4d.
Thomas Large	12d.
John Shortrede	3d.
William Holston	3d.
William Tredwey	8d.
Geoffrey Freman	10d.
Roger Walsh	2s.
Ralph Clerk, chaplain	4d.
William Swanton	12d.
John Baker, cook	4d.
Oliver Sherlok	6d.
Walter Wellys	12d.
Terry Robeshert, knight	8d.
Thomas Sekford	8d.
James Hubbart	3s.4d.
Thomas Sendell	8d.
Henry Smyth	5d.
John Wrave	4d.
Thomas Alicok	4d.
[*blank*] Aileward, widow	4d.
John Broun, junior	16d.
Thomas Hook	2s.
Cecily Gante	3d.
Thomas Wisdam	2d.
Richard Hause	4d.
Robert Rose	6d.
Henry Coket	4d.
Geoffrey Tevell	12d.
William Lyncoln	4d.
Phillip Curson	5d.
John Silk	12d.
William Warner	3d.
Thomas Drewe	12d.
John Preston	10d.
William Gyles	12d.
John Harrowe	12d.
Geoffrey Cottyng, chaplain	4d.
Robert Hoo	16d.
John Hirdeler	4d.

[45] A similar entry, often cut down to 'for the tenth part of his there beyond etc', follows each subsequent name.

John Cokks	2d.	Adam Fissh	4d.
William Clough	5d.	Katherine Austyn	12d.
John atte Mere	6d.	Orford [*sic*], widow	2d.
Margaret Stoor	8d.		
Edmund Tasburgh	12d.	Total: £4 3s.5d., half of which is 31s.7½d	
John Lawes	2d.	[*sic*].	
Robert Abel	8d.		
Robert Thorp	6d.	**Trous**	
Isabel Goldbeter	12d.	[*Tenth part of lands and tenements*]	[*Tax*]
John Sweyn junior	20d.	John Clement	2d.
Andrew Pawe	6d.	Simon Gunnore	1d.
Robert Cook	12d.	John Banyard	3d.
Richard Osbern	6d.	John Herman	3d.
Roger Coche	3d.	Ralph Pulvertoft	8d.
Thomas Symondes	3d.	John Nayler	4d.
Ed. Suthwelle, chaplain	6d.	Geoffrey Quyncy	2d.
William Castre	6d.	William Belcungre	2d.
Joan Leuys	8d.	Robert Machon	6d.
William Wayte	6d.	Robert Stoon	3d.
Joan Anyell	6d.	Geoffrey Hamond	2d.
John Clerk	4d.	John Blak	2d.
William Drake	5d.		
William Adams	6d.	Total: 3s.4d. [*sic*][46], half of which is 20d.	
Roger Kirby	5d.		
Robert Beton	5d.	**Berstrete**	
Matilda Godfrey	10d.	[*Tenth part of lands and tenements*]	[*Tax*]
William Heyward	6d.	John Leek, senior,	6d.
[*rot. 3B*] John Sweyn, senior	16d.	Thomas Harald, 'taillour'	2d.
Anne Ovy, widow	12d.	John Thakker	2d.
Thomas Shorde	6d.	Robert Fissher	20d.
John Feld, chaplain	6d.	Robert Thakker	6d.
Thomas Beaufeld	12d.	John Feke	4d.
Edmund Godewyn	2d.	Alice Westerne, widow	4d.
[*blank*] Disse, widow	2d.	Edmund Michell	10d.
Thomas Cowper	8d.	Thomas Hullok	2d.
John Abraham	2d.	Thomas Spirlyng	6d.
Richard Elware	4d.	John Broun, junior	16d.
Nicholas Heyward	5d.	John Leek, junior	8d.
John Gillyng	6d.	Thomas Toly	4d.
Thomas Pert	1d.	Robert Cok	8d.
David Johnson	2d.	Ed. Berton	2d.
Thomas Aldrych & John Randolff	16d.	John Mayn	2d.
William Crosse, chaplain	4s.	John Preste	2d.
William Cristemasse	1d.	Thomas Deye	8d.
John Wylde	2d.	John Gower	4d.

[46] It should be 3s.2d.

Edward Magnus	4d.	Robert Isbell	8d.
John Eston	2d.	Margaret Jamys	6d.
Nicholas Danyell	2d.	William Smyth, 'pynner'	10d.
Nicholas Wright	2d.	John Wode	4d.
Thomas Swayn	6d.	William Tempylman	4d.
Richard Crykemay	4d.	Thomas Marchaunt	4d.
Henry Smyth	8d.	John Brady	2d.
John Syre	4d.	John Geffrey	8d.
Thomas Gardener	8d.	Robert Salter	4d.
Alice Lakenham	2d.	Thomas Briggs, esquire	6d.
Katherine Grene	2d.	William Godes	4d.
John Kechen	1d.	Robert Allele	6d.
Oliva Blake	1d.	Alexander Baxster	4d.
Margaret Kettrych	1d.	John Wylton	12d.
Thomas Beaufeld	2d.	Thomas Pert	4d.
Robert Courle	2d.	William Reder	8d.
Isabel Cowper	6d.	John Swetman	4d.
Gregory Water	2d.	Tenement lately Skerletts	2d.
Robert Thornton, chaplain	1½d.	John Marsshhall	12d.
[rot. 3C] Bartholomew Sergeaunt	2d.	William Barker	3d.
Rose Bowre	1d.	William Swetman, clerk	10d.
John Attilburgh	1d.	John Hogekyns	4d.
Edmund Cullyng	6d.	John Levet	2d.
Thomas Byrde	2d.	Robert Thorne	4d.
Thomas Smert	9d.	Mother Randolff	2d.
John Langes	6d.	Nicholas Brounyng	2d.
Thomas Curveys	6d.	Thomas Bokenham	12d.
Thomas Bisshop	12d.		
Robert Mors	6d.	Total: 45s.5½d., half of which is	
Henry Coket	8d.	22s.13¾d [sic].	
Henry Awbry	2d.	Sum Total: £5 12s.2½d., half of which	
Robert Stibberd	6d.	total is 56s.1¾d [sic].	
John Sixhill	12d.		
John Brigham	4d.	[Goods and chattels worth 10 marks	
Thomas Knyff	4d.	or more]	[Tax]
John Baly	4d.	Item the said jurors certify that	
William Mundes	2s.4d.	Robert Cok has goods and	
Robert Sybald	8d.	chattels according to the form	
John Bisshop	12d.	and effect of the said letters	
John Grys	2s.	patent to the value of 10 marks	20d.
Thomas Alicok	20d.	And that Robert Fissher has in	
Edmund Evet	3d.	a similar way	20d.
Henry Glover	8d.	And that Thomas Large has in	
Roger Ferrour	7d.	a similar way	20d.
Henry Thurton	10d.		
John Michell	4d.	Total: 5s.	
John Davy	2d.		

[*rot. 3D. Ward of*] Mancroft

By virtue of which said letters patent of the lord king we the said commissioners on the day and year aforesaid in the said Guildhall have assigned and deputed Thomas Smerte, William Belward, Robert Carre, Robert Broun, Robert Jolfy, John Styward, Robert Pert, John Furbisshour, John Fen, William Yekesworth, Edmund Silk, John Pethod, Richard Brasier, John Brown, William Blythe, William Arnald, Robert Burgh, Thomas Lykberd, John Carter and John Lawes as jurors for the ward of Mancroft within the said city to inquire, search and take cognizance of the business in the said ward and certify us of it, according to the form and effect of the said letters patent of the lord king.

The which jurors on the twentieth of April in the said year in the said Guildhall certify to the said commissioners both the tenth part of the value of the aforesaid lands and tenements being within the said ward and the persons living within the said ward having goods and chattels to the value of ten marks and more within the said ward or elsewhere, to be levied and collected in the following way and form, namely:

[*Parish of St Peter Mancroft*]			
[*Tenth part of lands and tenements*]	[*Tax*]	William Elys	2s.8d.
John Norman	16d.	John Furbisshour	16d.
Thomas Berwyk	8d.	Beatrice Wymer	6d.
Thomas Dowdy	4d.	William Belward	16d.
Nicholas Nobyll	4s.	John Hendry	12d.
Robert Swyll	4d.	Robert Fissher	6s.
Henry Bowen	16d.	John Denton	2d.
Alexander atte Assh	12d.	Thomas Bokenham	2s.8d.
Lady Elizabeth Brews	20d.	Simon Wiseman & Peter Benet	16d.
Hugh Hastyngs	12d.	Richard Ferrour	2s.8d.
Edmund Erle	2s.	[*blank*] Swayn, widow	20d.
Robert Whynbergh	4d.	Robert Aylmer	4s.
[*blank*] Peper	4d.	Edmund Styward	2s.
Robert Catlyn and Margaret		William London	4s.
his daughter	8d.	John Quynton	2s.
John Setheryngton	20d.	Richard Suthwell, esquire	2s.8d.
John atte Mere	12d.	William Elys & Matilda Elys,	
William Bloker	2s.8d.	by right of her widowhood	2s.8d.
John Josse, clerk	12d.	John Fraunceys	2s.8d.
William Palmer	2d.	Richard Roos, esquire	4s.
Edmund Silk	12d.	William Yekesworth	2s.8d.
William Strynger	8d.	Robert Adams	16d.
Alice Dobbys	6d.	William Styward	2s.
John Holle	10d.	Robert Osbern	4s.
Joan Bukley, widow	8d.	John Pethood	2s.8d.
Henry Wylton	12d.	Bartholomew Northern	16d.
		Robert Cok of London	2s.

Avice Derham	6d.
John Tevell	2s.
Nicholas Pert, clerk	8d.
Robert Pert	16d.
Katherine Feld	12d.
Richard Prywald	6d.
Ed. Bedyngfeld, knight	16d.
Helen Game	8d.
John Burgh	20d.
Margaret Turnour	2s.
Elizabeth Carleton	3s.4d.
Richard Balles	2s.
Walter Wellys	4s.
William Billern	12d.
Henry Goos, clerk	2s.8d.
William Underwode	8d.
[rot.3 ᵈA] William Quyntyn	6d.
John Cokk	12d.
John Fen	2s.
Gregory Stubberd	12d.
Nicholas Lathe, 'parchemyner'	14d.
Simon Wiseman & Peter Benet, for their annuity	21d.

Total: £6 3d., half of which is £3 1½d.
Total: <£5 19s.6d., half of which is 59s.9d.>

[Goods and Chattels]	[Tax]
Nicholas Nobill for his goods and chattels etc.⁴⁷	20d.
William Ferrour	20d.
Thomas Wortes	20d.
William London	10s.
John Crudde	20d.
William Curteys	10s.
William Yekesworth	20d.
Robert Osbern	20d.
Elizabeth Carleton, widow	5s.
Richard Ballys	20d.

Total: 36s.8d.

In the Parish of St Stephen in the Ward of Mancroft

[Tenth part of lands and tenements]	[Tax]
Clemence Howes	4d.
Robert Carre	12d.
John Skyn	4d.
John Saye	4d.
William Skerlet	18d.
Thomas Bokenham	5s.
Thomas Flourdiewe	2s.
William Arnald	12d.
Cecilia Knyght	[blank]d.
Richard Brasier	4s.
John Symond	12d.
Robert Broun	12d.
Geoffrey Lounde	20d.
William Styward	16d.
Thomas Terell	6d.
Katherine Moor	8d.
John Powle	4d.
John Frankessh	10d.
Richard Crykemay	16d.
Edward Rose	12d.
William Moor, clerk	16d.
John Banyerd	20d.
William Capell, clerk	8d.
Agnes Lyster	16d.
Robert Umfrey	12d.
William Sendell	16d.
Robert Broun	8d.
Thomas Wilchon	4d.
William Reder	4d.
John Andrewes	8d.
William Ayleward	16d.
John Erpyngham	8d.
Agnes Scowe	4d.
Robert Machon	4d.
John Partryk	4d.
Edmund Tasburgh	4d.
Thomas Hampton	4d.
John Rede	12d.
William Blythe	20d.
John Stalham	8d.

⁴⁷ All subsequent entries in this section and in the subsequent assessments of goods and chattels contain this same formula.

Robert Hegoner	12d.	Robert Medilton	2d.
Joan Anyell	20d.	Thomas Buk	8d.
Robert Burgh	4d.	Thomas Likberd	5d.
William Norff	16d.	Rose [blank]	3d.
John Galwey	4d.	William Goselyn	3d.
[rot. 3ᵈB] John Dolleale	4d.	Robert Amyson	2d.
Hugh Crowe	4d.	Thomas Forth	2d.
John Broun	20d.	Agnes Norton	2d.
Joan Bowre	4d.	Margaret Millg[a]te	2d.
Clemence Appylton	8d.	Cecilia Davy	2d.
Thomas Motte	8d.	Robert Dalamour	2d.
John Swetman	4d.	Richard Marchaunt	1d.
		Andrew Sneterton	1d.
Total: 51s.2d., half of which is 25s.7d.		Richard Carles	2d.
		John Wode	2d.

[Goods and Chattels in St Stephen]	[Tax]	Etheldred Raveley	1d.
Thomas Bokenham	2s.6d.	John Gilford	2d.
Richard Brasier	20d.	Robert Pecher	2d.
John Stalham	20d.	William Fakke	2d.
Robert Carre	20d.	Peter Mannyng	2d.
John Rightwys	3s.4d.	John Spicer	2d.
John Broun	20d.	Robert Cowper	5d.
Joan Anyell	20d.	Richard Hervy	2d.
Robert Burgh	20d.	Robert Wode	4d.
		Thomas Wottes	4d.
Total: 15s.10d.		John Fygge	2d.
		Nicholas Cory	2d.

In the Parish of St Giles in the Ward of Mancroft

		Nicholas Lenton	2d.
[Tenth part of lands and tenements]	[Tax]	Nicholas Laxham	8d.
Robert Whynbergh	8d.	[rot. 3ᵈC] Robert Gardener	4d.
Thomas Brewer	6d.	Richard Ferrour	8d.
John Tyllye, gentleman	20d.	John Furbisshour	2d.
Richard Bally	6d.	William Nobyll	4d.
John Laws	8d.		
David Multon	6d.	Total: 17s.11d., half of which is 8s.11½d.	
Andrew Quassh	2d.		
[blank] Broun	6d.	Sum total of the tenth part of lands there:	
Robert Jolfy	6d.	£9 9s.4d., half of which is £4 14s.8d.	
John Wilde	6d.	Sum total of goods and chattels there:	
John Norton	8d.	52s.6d.	
John Hornyng	4d.		
John Waryn	8d.		
John Styward	2d.		
Alice Herward	6d.		
[blank] Hurry	6d.		
John Carter	10d.		

The Ward of Wymer in the said City

By virtue of which said letters patent of the lord king we the afore-named commissioners on the day and year aforesaid in the said Guildhall have assigned and deputed Andrew Waleys, William Felippes, Thomas Barly, Simon Bright, Robert Todenham, Robert Courle, John Bowde, Thomas Alberd, John Madys, Thomas Cok, William Ventres, Richard Drake, Thomas Hogon, William Howes, Thomas Caus, Geoffrey Carter, William Wulsy, Nicholas Cowlich, Robert Gilbert, John Tylles, John Withmale, Nicholas Davy, Robert Machon, Thomas Aileward, John Cowper, Stephen Bryan, William Gogeon, John Broun, William Fuller, Thomas Cowper, Nicholas Lathe, Hugh Buxton, William Ferrour, John Wellys and Thomas Shorde as jurors for the said ward of Wymer within the said city to inquire, search and take cognizance of the business in the said ward and certify us of it, according to the form and effect of the said letters patent of the lord king.

The which jurors on the twentieth of April in the said year in the said Guildhall certify to the said commissioners both the tenth part of the value of the aforesaid lands and tenements being within the said ward and the persons living within the said ward having goods and chattels to the value of ten marks and more within the said ward or elsewhere, to be levied and collected in the following way and form, namely:

[Sub-ward of West Wymer]			
		Henry Love	3½d.
		Elizabeth Carleton	7d.
[In the Parish of St Gregory]		John Smyth	6d.
[Tenth part of lands and tenements]	[Tax]	John Deye	8d.
Hamo Claxton	12d.	Roger Waverey	8d.
Thomas Sparrowe	8d.	Nicholas Ovy	8d.
Richard Corpusty	18d.	John Palmer of Costessey	12d.
William Filippes	8d.	Roger Benet	6d.
William Tukke	8d.	Robert Bernard	12d.
John Roo	6d.	John Osberne, clerk	8d.
John Man	8d.	John Wrave	6d.
Katherine Hallys	2s.8d.	Nicholas Casteleyn	12d.
Margery Flourdiewe	4d.	Robert Folsham	4d.
Robert B[ail?]le, clerk	4d.	[rot. 3 ᵈD] Robert Bulle, clerk	8d.
Thomas Maynard	2d.	Peter Barker	8d.
Thomas Berton, 'lister'	6d.	Thomas Barly	4d.
John Chapman	2d.	Thomas Cok	3s.
William Hobbes	6d.	William Ventres	8d.
William Playford	12d.	Thomas Cok	2s.
William Gossellyn	8d.	Elizabeth Carleton	8d.
[blank] Aileward	16d.	John Thorne	4d.
Richard Howard	3s.	John Rede	12d.

Nicholas Cory	2s.8d.
John Peper	6d.
William Foreste	4d.
Nicholas Grene & Robert Farman	8d.
Thomas Alberd	2s.8d.

Total: 40s.11½d., half of which is 20s.5¾d.

[Goods and Chattels]	[Tax]
Thomas Cok	20d.
Thomas Albert	20d.

Total: 3s.4d.

In the Parish of St Lawrence in the same Ward of Wymer

[Tenth part of lands and tenements]	[Tax]
John Wellys	12d.
Robert Longe	18d.
John Bowde	8d.
Thomas Smyth	12d.
John Kyng	12d.
John Wattys	4d.
Robert Wellys	8d.
[blank] Baker	4d.
Richard Freman	8d.
John Madys	4d.
John Symondes	8d.
John Sandryngham	6d.
John Jowell	18d.
John Wellys	8d.
John Bowde	8d.
John Jowell	6d.
Edmund Cowper	2½d.
Robert Lussher	2½d.
Nicholas Gosselyn	4d.
Robert Newman	4½d.
[blank] Wymer	1d.
Nicholas Lakenham	6d.
John Roke	2½d.
John Levott	8d.
[blank] Groos, widow	8d.
John Castre	12d.
Richard Balles	4d.

Total: 16s.7d., half of which is 8s.9½d [sic].

[Goods and chattels]	[Tax]
Robert Longe	2s.6d.
John Jowell	2s.6d.
John Castre	20d.

Total: 6s.8d.

[Sub-ward of Middle Wymer]

In the Parishes of St John [Maddermarket], Holy Cross, St Andrew and St Michael at Pleas within the said City

[Tenth part of lands and tenements]	[Tax]
Thomas Caus	4s.
Hamo Claxton	8d.
Margaret Baxster	8d.
Robert Aylmer	8s.8d.
John Newman	12d.
John Malburgh	2s.
John Rede	6s.
Henry Yemmys	6d.
Geoffrey Carter	8d.
[rot. 2A] William Wulcy	12d.
Henry Falyate	20d.
Robert Gilbert	2s.
William London	20d.
William Cosyn	20d.
John Wylton	10d.
Robert Davy	15d.
Robert Asshton	4s.
Robert Crowche	12d.
Agnes Este	3s.
Thomas Plumpsted	2s.1d.
John Withmale	2s.1d.
John Appilyerd	20d.
Robert Gardener	2s.8d.
Agnes Este	15d.
Nicholas Cowlych	10d.
Walter Goos	8d.
Simon Petyclerk	20d.
William Nobys	15d.
Robert Davy	15d.
John Bloker	15d.
William Gaviard	10d.
Thomas Hood	2s.6d.

Joan Degan	2s.4d.
Robert Kerre	20d.
Robert Aylmer	2s.6d.
William Chaumberleyn	12d.
Anabilla Kyng	14d.
Robert Belton	6s.4d.
William Ferrour	8d.
Philipp Curson	5s.
Robert Dilham	15d.
William Potter, draper	2s.
Thomas Cardmaker	10d.
Richard Peper	20d.
John Tilles, 'smyth'	16d.
John Peterson	4s.
John Julyan, clerk	10d.
The same John Julyan	6d.
Thomas Beawfeld	2s.8d.
Nicholas Davy	2s.8d.
Robert Machon	3s.
John Ayleward	16d.
John Bricham	12d.
William Breton	8d.
Geoffrey Freman	4d.
Thomas Aldrich & John Randolff	4s.
John Bristomer	16d.
Henry Blithe	12d.
William Howes	12d.
John Water	16d.
Thomas Barly	12d.
William Brunham	2s.
Robert Hoo	2s.8d.
Thomas Philippes, baker	2s.8d.
Nicholas Parker	2s.
John Grys	12d.
Margery Thurton	12d.
Thomas Norton	6d.

Total: £6 8s.6d., half of which is
£3 4s.3d.

[Goods and chattels]	[Tax]
John Rede	25s.
Thomas Caus	7s.6d.
John Malburgh	6s.8d.
John Newman	20d.
John Eglyn	2s.6d.
Edmund Davy	20d.

Robert Aylmer	10s.
Robert Gardener	3s.4d.
Nicholas Cowlich	5s.
Robert Gilbert	5s.
John Peterson	5s.
John Orgonmaker	3s.4d.
Agnes Este	20d.
John Withmale	20d.
John Flynte	20d.
William Nobys	20d.
Gerard Johnson	20d.
Robert Elys	20d.
John Peterson	20d.
Robert Crouche	20d.
Richard Partrich	20d.
John Ballys	20d.
William Potter	20d.
[rot. 2B] Robert Belton	20d.
Thomas Beawfeld	13s.4d.
Nicholas Davy	6s.8d.
Robert Machon	20d.
Thomas Aldrych & John Randolff	6s.8d.
William Brunham	20d.
Robert Hoo	20d.
Agnes Parker	20d.
William Doget	20d.
Anabill Kyng	20d.

Total: £6 13s.4d.

[Sub-ward of East Wymer]

In the Parishes of St Peter Hungate, SS. Simon & Jude, St George [Tombland] and St Martin before the Palace Gate of the Lord Bishop of Norwich

[Tenth part of lands and tenements]	[Tax]
John Broun	16d.
Robert Best	22d.
Robert Marbeler	8d.
Geoffrey Styward	16d.
Nicholas Scolehous	8d.
Henry Vyell	4d.
Richard Goldsmyth	6d.
William Barbour, clerk	6d.

John Harrowe	16d.
Mariona Marbeler	6d.
John Riche	4d.
William Hagett	2d.
Agnes Killyngworth	2d.
John Pyke	4d.
Nicholas Ingham	2s.
Stephen Bryan	2s.
Thomas Clyfford	8d.
John Horsley	4d.
William Corne	8d.
Thomas Caps	16d.
John Brasier, clerk	6d.
Thomas Cowper	20d.
William Fuller	2s.
Joan Curteys	16d.
John Walters	16d.
Thomas Dowdy	8d.
Richard Baxster alias Smyth	8d.
Nicholas Lathe	20d.
John Foote	2d.
Robert Gyles	20d.
John Rutter	4d.
Richard Petite	4d.
Hugh Buxton	16d.
Robert Machon	8d.
John Blomvyle	8d.
Thomas Ailward	12d.
William Ferrour	12d.
Richard Ilberd	4d.
[blank] Russell	4d.
William Gogeon	6d.
William Calthorp, knight	12d.
William Jacob	12d.
John Jullys, clerk	8d.
John Antell	8d.
Thomas Baldewyn	6d.
John Wellys	8d.
Henry Cobald	4d.
[blank] Thorp	4d.
Thomas Shorde	12d.
Lyston [sic], widow	6d.
William Wigge	6d.
Nicholas Lathe	6d.
Nicholas Jeve	4d.

Total: 43s.2d., half of which is 21s.7d.

[Goods and chattels]	[Tax]
Geoffrey Styward	2s.6d.
Richard Goldsmyth	20d.
Richard Marbeler	20d.
Robert Best	4s.
John Broun	20d.
William Gogeon	3s.6d.
[rot. 2C] Nicholas Ingham	20d.
John Horsley	20d.
Stephen Bryan	20d.
William Fuller	3s.6d.
Nicholas Lathe	20d.
Thomas Cowper	20d.
Geoffrey Crome	20d.
Joan Curteys	20d.
Robert Gyles	20d.
Hugh Buxton	20d.

Total: 33s.6d.

[Sub-ward of West Wymer continued]

In the Parish of St Margaret [Westwick]

[Tenth part of lands and tenements]	[Tax]
Robert Todenham	12d.
Peter Saye	4d.
Clement Person	8d.
Robert Lussher	6d.
John Baly	8d.
Richard Ante	8d.
Robert Curle	9½d.
Robert Davy	4d.
John Prowet	6d.
The wife of Ed. Ferrour	8d.
Augustine Boys	4d.
William Canon, chaplain	4d.
Thomas Swayn	8d.
The executors of Ed. Clere	2s.8d.
Robert Courle	3d.
Thomas Johnson	3d.
The rector of the church of St Margaret	6d.
John Estaner, clerk & Robert Jolfy	12d.

Total: 12s.1½d., half of which is 6s.¾d.

[Goods and chattels]	[Tax]
Robert Courle	20d.

In the Parish of St Swithin

[Tenth part of lands and tenements]	[Tax]
Thomas Sweyn	2s.
Thomas Barly	12d.
Stephen Stalon	8d.
The same Stephen	8d.
Henry Stalon	12d.
William Barly, clerk	8½d.
The executors of Ed. Clere	16d.
Walter Goos	8½d.
Thomas Avelyn	4d.
Simon Bright	8d.
Thomas Canewald	6d.
John Lawys	12d.
Simon Bright	4d.

Total: 10s.10d., half of which is 5s.5½d [sic].

[Goods and chattels]	[Tax]
Thomas Swayn	2s.6d.

In the Parish of St Benedict

[Tenth part of lands and tenements]	[Tax]
Robert Rose	12d.
John Kyng	4½d.
John Mullyng	6d.

Thomas Goos	4d.
William Smyth	8½d.
Nicholas Rede	6d.
Robert Elys	1½d.
John Parker	4d.
William Stalon	2d.
Robert Longe	12d.
Joan Stalon	4d.
Joan Kyng	2d.
John Kyng	2d.
Richard Drake	8d.
Alice Barly	4d.
Andrew Walissh	4d.
John Kerre	12d.
William Lyntok	8d.
John Smyth	2d.
John Barly, clerk	6d.
John Appilyerd	8d.
William Godewyns	4d.
Simon Bright	4d.

Total: 10s.8½d., half of which is 5s.4¼d.

Sum Total of the tenth part of lands and tenements in Wymer Ward: £13 2s.11½d.

Sum Total of half of the said lands and tenements: £6 11s.5¾d.

Sum Total of goods and chattels there: £9 12d.

[rot. 2D.] The Ward of Ultra Aquam in the said City in Coslany

By virtue of the said letters patent of the lord king to the said commissioners on the said day and year in the said Guildhall we have assigned and deputed John Hermer, John Stalon, Robert Wode, Robert Rose, Gregory Clerk, Thomas Chaunce, Edward Howes, John Brewyn, Thomas Wilkyns, Thomas Richeman, John Reynalds, Richard Tedde, John Butler, Thomas Bevys, Robert Swafham, Richard Hervy, William Stalon, Nicholas Smyth, Nicholas Peyntour, Robert Underwode, John Wighton, John Hadynet, Edmund Yemme, Robert Drury, William Blofeld, Nicholas Corpusty, John Tompson, Peter Payn, John Waryns and John Munke as jurors for the said ward of Beyond the Water within the said city to enquire, scrutinise and take cognizance of the business in the said ward and to certify the aforesaid commissioners of it, according to the form and effect of the said letters patent of the lord king.

The which jurors on the twentieth of April in the said year in the said Guildhall certify to the said commissioners both the tenth part of the value of the aforesaid lands and tenements being within the said ward and the persons living within the said ward having goods and chattels to the value of ten marks and more within the said ward or elsewhere, to be levied and collected in the following way and form, namely:

In [*the Sub-ward of*] Coslany

[*Tenth part of lands and tenements*]	[*Tax*]
Richard Ferrour	10s.
Robert Thorp	6s.8d.
Robert Rose	3s.
John Bisshop	5s.
Thomas Davy	12d.
John Hemmyng	20d.
Robert Wode	12d.
Roger Jekkes	4d.
Thomas Pope	16d.
Gregory Clerk	18d.
John Butler	16d.
Augustine Boys	16d.
William Cheny	4d.
Richard Smyth	8d.
Joan Rose	4d.
Beatrice Lacy	12d.
William Waryn	8d.
Henry Wilton	8d.
Thomas Symondys	2s.
Thomas Drentale, clerk	8d.
Katherine Waryn	4d.
Richard Tedde	12d.
William Smyth	2s.
James Grene	12d.
Robert Porter	6d.
John Fraunceys	2s.
John Brewyn	20d.
John Denton	2s.
Geoffrey Sperlyng	2s.
Robert Hemmyng	6d.
James Gresham	10d.
Joan Swan	6d.
Edward Howys	2s.
John Knowte	20d.
Thomas Chaunce	20d.
Thomas Brouster	4d.

Richard Fawde	6d.
Bartholomew Kyng	3s.
John Slacok	8d.
John Bury	10d.
Thomas Wilkyns	3s.
John Reynaldys	16d.
John Dowse, junior	6d.
Katherine Aleyns, widow	4d.
Thomas Richman	18d.
Geoffrey Garnet	6d.
John Goldston	4d.
Thomas Sweyn	4d.
John Basse	6d.
Sarra Scowe	2d.
Nicholas Heylok	4d.
Brice Scowe	12d.
<Nicholas Heylok	4d.>
Thomas Boustomer	2d.
William Stalon	8d.
Robert Clyfford	8d.
John Bronde	3d.
Robert Scowe	4d.
John Stalon	10d.
William Browett	3d.
Thomas Drye	8d.
William Aleyns	10d.
Margaret Wymer	4d.
Richard Corpusty	4d.
Robert Lounde	6d.

Total: £4 14d., half of which is 40s.6d [*sic*].

<Total: £3 14s.6d., half of which is 37s.4d [*sic*].>

[*Goods and chattels*]	[*Tax*]
Richard Ferrour	25s.
Robert Thorp	16s.8d.
Robert Rose	5s.

John Hemmyng	20d.	Thomas Waryns	6d.
Robert Wode, 'cowper'	20d.	William Swanton	16d.
Thomas Pope	20d.	Master of the Carnary [48]	16d.
Gregory Clerk	2s.6d.	Matilda Govett	4d.
John Butler	20d.	John Frende	10d.
Richard Thorn	20d.	Robert Whetered	6d.
[rot. 2dA] William Ramsey	20d.	Thomas, rector of Carleton	4d.
John Hermer	20d.	Henry Ivys	8d.
John Fraunceys	20d.	Nicholas Bussy	4d.
John Denton	2s.6d.	Matilda Radbot	4d.
Edward Howys	20d.	Geoffrey Carter	4d.
John Knowte	20d.	Nicholas Smyth	8d.
Thomas Chaunce	20d.	John Vyncent	4d.
Bartholomew Kyng	3s.4d.	Clemence Man	6d.
Thomas Wilkyns	5s.	Geoffrey Sperlyng	6d.
Thomas Richeman	2s.	Thomas Heigham	6d.
Brice Skowe	3s.4d.	John Emson	3d.
John Stalon	20d.	John Latered	4d.
John Smyth	20d.	John Cok	4d.
		Edmund Yemmes	4d.
Total: £4 5s.4d. Item 20d.		John Smyth, 'wright'	4d.
		John Elys	3d.
		John Tompson	8d.

In [the Sub-ward of] Colgate

		John Tompson	8d.
		Margaret Coppyng	16d.
		George Launde	6d.
[Tenth part of lands and tenements]	[Tax]	Robert Iryng	10d.
Richard Roos, esquire	2s.	John Wytton	8d.
John Kechen	4d.	John Pyncheamour	2s.
Richard Carter	2d.	Richard Hervy	8d.
Isabel Sterlyng	2d.	Anabilla Brame	8d.
Robert Woderove	5d.	John Garvot	6d.
Alice Crome	16d.	Thomas Brouster	8d.
Alice Pelle	12d.	Thomas Galte	6d.
John Smyth	12d.	John Waryns	2d.
Thomas Surgean	8d.	Thomas Alberd	16d.
Augustine Elsy	12d.	Robert Swafham	6d.
John Hobert	6d.	John Howys	4d.
William Stalon	8d.	Robert Castelteyn, chaplain	14d.
Bartholomew Kyng	2d.	Thomas Holle	6d.
William Birde	16d.	Nicholas Peyntour	5d.
[blank] Foxe	2d.	John Palmer	8d.
Alice Glover	4d.	Katherine Bully	3d.
Ralph Bateman	6d.	John Kewe	4d.
Robert Longe	16d.	Thomas Bevys	8d.
Robert Poyntour	4d.	Robert Gerard	3d.

[48] The Carnary chapel at Norwich cathedral.

John Dannok	3d.
John Sendell	4d.
William Geffreys	10d.
Robert Bloker	5d.
John Launde	5d.
John Alisaundre	6d.
Robert Parnell	5d.
John Julyan, chaplain	4d.
[*rot. 2ᵈB*] Robert Sherman	6d.
Adam Nobys	4d.
Nicholas Corpusty	9½d.
Robert Chapman	4d.
Thomas Sherwyn	6d.
William Bisshop	4½d.
Skrape[*sic*]	8d.
Robert Rose	20d.
Robert Fale	4d.
William Knape	12d.
[*blank*] Stubbe	6d.
John Douse, junior	8d.
Thomas Wilkyns	10d.
Richard Parker	4d.
Bartholomew Kyng	9½d.
Nicholas Rose	3d.
[*blank*] Bene	4d.
Nicholas Lathe, junior	6d.
John Tompson	6d.
William Gale	6d.
William Ferrour	16d.
John Hodge	6d.
Gregory Clerk	4d.
John Russe	6d.
Thomas Hodges	2d.
John Dowse, *senior*	8d.
Edmund Dorman	12d.
Richard Ovy, clerk	2s.

Total: £3 17½d., half of which is
30s.8¾d.

[*Sub-ward of Fyebridge*]

In the Parish of St Clement Fybrigge

[*Tenth part of lands and tenements*]	[*Tax*]
John Baly	6d.
Thomas Hemyng	10d.

Robert Drury	16d.
Richard Peper	8d.
Joan Swan	6d.
Matilda Garnyssh	16d.
[*blank*] Cook	8d.
William Blofeld	12d.
Margaret Wronge	8d.
John Halyday & Alice, by her right	2d.
John Roper	8d.
Richard Corpusty	12d.
Robert Gilman	8d.
Cecilia Wolde	2d.
Ed. Yemme	8d.
Joan Mote	8d.
John Aldewyn	10d.
Edmund Cook	6d.
John Tompson	12d.

Total: 13s.10d., half of which is 6s.11d.

In the Parish of St Saviour

[*Tenth part of lands and tenements*]	[*Tax*]
Richard Pernell	10d.
Margaret Sutton	8d.
John Gilbert	6d.
John Owdolff	6d.
Richard Corpusty, *junior*	8d.
Nicholas Corpusty	12d.
John Pyncheamour	8d.
Joan Brame	6d.

Total: 5s.4d., half of which is 2s.8d.

In the Parish of All Saints [*Fyebridge*]

[*Tenth part of lands and tenements*]	[*Tax*]
Richard Roper	6d.
Thomas Worme	6d.
Robert Machon & Thomas Felippes	6d.
Robert Courle	4d.
John House	2d.
Peter Payn	16d.
John Swayn	16d.
John Wattok	2d.
John Bettys	6d.
Robert Symmes	4d.

John Russe	6d.
John Boxford	6d.
Robert Greve	6d.
John Dewe	2d.
David Martyn	8d.
Walter Baxster	2d.
[rot. 2ᵈC] John Robynson	6d.
John Broun	4d.
Gregory Malenger	4d.
John Renneway	2d.
[blank] Grouby	2d.
Robert Aylmer	3d.
John Seman	4d.
John Wighton	4d.
[blank] Spynke, chaplain	2d.
[blank] Brancastre	4d.
[blank] Holme, widow	2d.
William Knyght	2d.
John Dokkyng	8d.

Total: 12s.1d., half of which is 6s.½d.

In the Parish of St James
[Pockthorpe]

[Tenth part of lands and tenements]	[Tax]
Henry Farman	16d.
Margaret Lyster	2d.
John Skernyng	8d.
Thomas Rowson	4d.
Richard Talvas	4d.
Reginald Lyng	2d.
Adam Everston	2d.
Thomas Love	8d.
John Munke	8d.

Total: 4s.6d., half of which is 2s.3d.
Sum total: [blank]

In the Parish of St Martin before the Palace Gates[49]

[Tenth part of lands and tenements]	[Tax]
John Bordyope	8d.
Thomas Wortes	8d.
Robert Fakes	4d.

Total: 20d., half of which is 10d.

In the Parish of St Edmund

[Tenth part of lands and tenements]	[Tax]
John Waryns	14d.
John Corpusty, chaplain	8d.
John Moor, clerk	8d.
John Walters	6d.
Thomas Godewyn	4d.
Edmund Moor	8d.
Henry Smyth	16d.
Charles [blank]	6d.
Simon Rede	6d.

Total: 6s.4d., half of which is 3s.2d.

[Goods and chattels]	[Tax]
Henry Smyth	10s.
Robert Drury	20d.
Richard Corpusty, junior	20d.
John Waryns	20d.
Thomas Hemmyng	20d.
John Pyncheamour	20d.
John Notell	20d.

Total: 20s.

In the Parish of St Paul

[Tenth part of lands and tenements]	[Tax]
John Hogon, senior	3d.
John Narburgh	14d.
William Webster	8d.
John Newman	10d.
Nicholas Nabbys	7d.
William Wode	3d.
John Bedford	3d.
Thomas Beawfeld	2s.4d.
John Pegeon	5d.
John Wade	5d.
John Russe	12d.
Cristina Godfrey	7d.
John Julyans, clerk	3d.
Mariona Albon	7d.
Denis Hildreston, chaplain	3d.
[rot. 2ᵈD] John Lane	6d.

Total: 10s.4d., half of which is 5s.2d.

[49] The parish of St Martin at Palace extended a short way north of the river.

Sum total of the tenth part of the goods and chattels in the ward of Ultra Aquam: £9 16s.8½d.
Half of which is £4 18s.4¼d.

Sum total of goods and chattels there: £5 7s.

Sum total of the tenth part of lands and tenements in the four wards of the said city with Trous annexed to it: £38 14½d.

Sum total of half of the same: £19 7¼d.

Sum total of goods and chattels there: £17 5s. 6d.

The Cartulary of
St Mary's Hospital, Great Yarmouth

EDITED BY CAROLE RAWCLIFFE

Introduction

The document now known as Bodleian Library, MS Gough Norfolk 20 commands our attention on several counts. It is, first of all, of considerable national as well as local interest, not least because of the light it casts upon the changes in charitable provision which occurred in late fourteenth- and early fifteenth-century England. That the original Latin text, compiled in about 1400, was translated 214 years later for the benefit of the rulers of Yarmouth adds in no small measure to the manuscript's importance. Produced by Henry Manship, one of the borough's earliest and most celebrated historians, this English text provides further information about the way in which the urban authorities of his generation sought to preserve their medieval records. It was copied by him onto the thirty-nine blank parchment folios at the end of the volume, and forms the basis of this edition. Since, unlike other aspects of his colourful career, his work on the cartulary has attracted scant attention, it adds in no small measure to our knowledge of his antiquarian activities.

In contrast to the significant number of monastic cartularies to survive the wholesale destruction of archives that occurred during and after the Dissolution, comparatively few remain to illuminate the history of the pre-Reformation English hospital. In his *Medieval Cartularies of Great Britain* (1958), Godfrey Davis identified only forty-two cartularies compiled for a mere thirty-seven hospitals, together with a further ten rolls of evidence and miscellaneous collections of material. Even if we include a handful of subsequent discoveries, this meagre showing represents a fraction of the grand total of well over one thousand such institutions known to have existed between the Conquest and the 1530s. The loss of records kept by the smaller hospitals that once proliferated throughout the urban landscape was particularly heavy. Some had already incurred censure for neglecting their muniments. Indeed, those of modest size, with correspondingly tight budgets, did not as a general rule go to the trouble and expense of compiling cartularies unless particular circumstances demanded it. Changes in patronage, acrimonious conflicts over jurisdiction or anxiety on the part of lay or ecclesiastical authorities concerning lax administrative standards often provided the necessary catalyst.[1]

The re-foundation of St Mary's hospital by the rulers of Yarmouth in 1386 might not alone have warranted the production of a cartulary, since, even after new endowments had been made upon it by a group of leading residents, it remained far from affluent. But a dispute with the brethren of the neighbouring Benedictine priory, who feared the loss of precious revenues to a potential competitor, along with wider concerns arising from the port's parlous financial situation, stimulated a concern for better record-keeping. Nine important Latin documents, including the initial regulations of 1386 (number 1), the subsequent agreement reached between the burgesses and the monks (number 2), grants of property received before and after the re-foundation (numbers 4, 5, 7 and 8) and a rental of 1398 (number 6) were transcribed in its pages at the turn of the century. Additions were made to the rental in a variety of later hands in an attempt to keep track of changes in ownership, and a new section was added as the hospital acquired further revenues (number 10).

Urban hospitals of all sizes, rich or poor, found it difficult to collect the fixed assize rents that came to them from benefactors of relatively humble status, since the individual sums were often small and derived from widely scattered properties that could change hands with disconcerting frequency.[2] The cartulary of God's House, Southampton, was, for example, compiled in the 1380s as the opening salvo in 'a campaign for recovery of tenements and rents', which, in the event, proved remarkably successful.[3] That commissioned by the master of St Bartholomew's, London, after independence had finally been wrested from the neighbouring priory, in 1420, likewise contains an unusually detailed list of rents and tenancies.[4] Part of the substantial medieval archive of this large and wealthy institution remains intact, but in most cases – including that of St Mary's – we are dependent upon the random survival of a cartulary, without which we would know next to nothing about the house or its patrons.

The final medieval entry in the cartulary of St Mary's comprises an abridged English version of the new Latin rules, written in a clear early

[1] For a wider discussion of these questions, see C. Rawcliffe, 'Passports to Paradise: How English Medieval Hospitals and Almshouses Kept their Archives', *Archives*, xxvii (2002), pp. 2-22; and for the importance of cartularies in general, T. Foulds, 'Medieval Cartularies', *Archives*, xviii (1987-88), pp. 3-33.

[2] C. Rawcliffe, *Medicine for the Soul: The Life, Death and Resurrection of an English Medieval Hospital* (Stroud, 1999), pp. 96-8.

[3] J.M. Kaye, ed., *The Cartulary of God's House, Southampton* (Southampton Records Series, xix-xx, 1976), i, pp. lii-lx, lxix-lxx, xcviii.

[4] It was compiled in 1456 and lists 280 properties: N. Kerling, ed., *The Cartulary of St Bartholomew's Hospital* (1973), pp. 153-74.

fifteenth-century hand by a local scribe (number 11).[5] An accessible translation would have been needed for consultation by the burgesses who
managed the hospital, and for reading aloud at regular intervals to the
sixteen brothers and sisters who now found refuge there. This was a
common practice, being enshrined in the statutes of the almshouse at
Saffron Walden, Essex, which was established in 1400 by the twenty-four
'most worshipful' townsmen 'for the remedy of their own souls'. Here, too,
both Latin and English versions were recorded, the latter for annual recita-
tion before the thirteen almsmen, lest any should be tempted to stray from
the path of righteousness.[6] Of particular value to the historian, such
evidence reflects the local impact of profound demographic and social
changes that were already beginning to alter the shape of institutional
philanthropy throughout England.

The national and local background

Notwithstanding the scale of mortality, the Black Death of 1349–50 caused
fewer long term demographic and economic upheavals than the national
and regional epidemics that followed at regular intervals throughout the
rest of the century and beyond. Since later outbreaks of pestilence, such as
that of 1361, took a particular toll of children and adolescents, it proved
impossible to replace earlier losses and the population continued to fall.
The consequences of this decline were not uniformly bad. Standards of
living rose among the poor, who could now demand higher wages and
afford better housing. Since food became cheaper and more plentiful, all
but the truly destitute benefited from a gradual improvement in health.
Those who did not succumb to disease tended to live longer, with the result
that, by the close of the century, care for the elderly became a far more
pressing issue than the succour of sick and malnourished paupers. Higher
mortality rates among the young (who might otherwise have cared for
elderly dependents) exacerbated the problem. At the same time, a general
mistrust of the feckless or vagrant poor hastened a move away from the
spacious open-ward hospitals of the thirteenth century to a more modest
and select form of endowment that could be effectively managed by the
laity.[7]

[5] The orthography is strongly Norfolk: R. Beadle, 'Prolegomena to a Literary Geography of
Later Medieval Norfolk', in F. Riddy, ed., *Regionalism in Late Medieval Manuscripts and Texts*
(Cambridge, 1991), p. 108.
  [6] F.W. Steer, ed., 'The Statutes of the Saffron Walden Almshouses', *Transactions of the Essex
Archaeological Society*, new series, xxv (1955-60), pp. 161-221, at pp. 172-83.
  [7] For the economic background, see C. Dyer, *Standards of Living in the Later Middle Ages*
(revised edn, Cambridge, 1998), pp. 244-6; and M.K. McIntosh, 'Local Responses to the Poor
in Late Medieval and Tudor England', *Continuity and Change*, iii (1988), pp. 209-45, especially
pp. 213-17. Almshouses are discussed by N. Orme and M. Webster, *The English Hospital 1070-*

The number of new almshouse foundations after 1350 is impossible to determine, especially as so many were small, temporary affairs, established for the care of a few needy individuals known personally to the patron.[8] One such comes fleetingly to light, for example, in 1449, when Thomas Hullys of Yarmouth left six otherwise undocumented dwelling houses near one of the town gates 'for the accommodation of the indigent poor in times of necessity'.[9] In addition, many older hospitals, such as St Mary's, were re-founded, and often rebuilt, as residential homes for reputable men and women who could no longer fend for themselves. Sometimes these larger, more permanent institutions assumed responsibility for the upkeep of neighbouring *maisons Dieu* whose future might otherwise have seemed uncertain.[10] The cartulary of St Mary's furnishes a striking example of this type of arrangement, whereby in 1392 the hospital undertook 'to susteyne and supporte seaven cottages ... called Goddesmenshouse', which had recently been set aside by the wealthy brothers, John and William Stalham, for the accommodation of paupers (number 9).[11]

The landowners and members of the urban elite who tended to support such initiatives were, in many respects, the true victims of demographic change. Falling rents and prices, coupled with a marked rise in the cost of labour, placed them at a serious disadvantage. Along with loss of revenue came challenges to their authority, most notably during the Peasants' Revolt of 1381, but already apparent in the numerous disputes that erupted in English towns and cities over access to trading privileges and markets, the nature of the franchise and other contentious matters. That the rich had a moral obligation to care for their less privileged neighbours in sickness and old age was another potential source of grievance, which undoubtedly served to loosen the purse strings of nervous oligarchs. The endowment of a small almshouse for a few deserving paupers might be dismissed as little more than a gesture of the sort satirised by Robert Burton as the return of a feather after one had purloined an entire goose.[12]

1570 (New Haven and London, 1995), pp. 44, 136-46; and A.D. Brown, *Popular Piety in Late Medieval England* (Oxford, 1995), pp. 180-94; and demands for greater administrative efficiency by Rawcliffe, *Medicine for the Soul*, pp. 191-2.

[8] P.H. Cullum, '"For Pore People Harberles": What Was the Function of the Maisonsdieu?', in D.J. Clayton, R.G. Davies and P. McNiven, eds, *Trade, Devotion and Governance* (Stroud, 1994), pp. 36-54.

[9] NRO, Y/C4/162, rot. 13.

[10] A row of thirty almshouses was, for example, built on the frontage of St Mary Spital, Bishopsgate, London, perhaps with support from the Skinners' Company: C. Thomas and others, *Excavations at the Priory and Hospital of St Mary Spital, London* (Museum of London, Archaeology Service, 1997), p. 79.

[11] John Stalham was bailiff of Yarmouth in 1367-8, 1370-71 and 1373-4: H. Le Strange, *Norfolk Official Lists* (Norwich, 1890), p. 153. For William, see below, nn. 27 and 28.

[12] R. Burton, *The Anatomy of Melancholy*, ed. T.C. Faulkener and others (6 vols, Oxford, 1989-2000), i, p. 87.

Yet, issues of social cohesion and civic pride apart, there were pressing spiritual reasons for the conspicuous exercise of philanthropy. Fear of *mors improvisa*, the sudden death which struck its victims before they had time to prepare their immortal souls, loomed large in the years following the first outbreak of plague. Exercised by the prospect of a long and painful spell in the fires of purgatory, the wealthy turned assiduously to the performance of charitable works. These found perfect expression in the late medieval almshouse. The widespread assumption that intercessionary prayers offered by deserving paupers known personally to their benefactors carried far greater spiritual weight than those of strangers must have provided patrons with a further incentive.[13]

The residents of Yarmouth had particular reason to dread the divine arrows of pestilence. Claims that 7,000 of them died during the Black Death alone may be exaggerated, although it would be unwise to under-play the levels of mortality, which had a devastating effect upon the local economy.[14] Further depopulation followed, in part as a result of the unique combination of circumstances that confronted the survivors during the second half of the fourteenth century. The list makes for gloomy reading. As a leading North Sea port and '*forte ville de guerre*', Yarmouth suffered intermittent loss of shipping and disruption to trade because of the ongoing hostilities with France. The cost of completing and repairing the walls (which took a century to build) proved a serious drain on the local economy, but was far exceeded by the outlay on harbour works, necessi-tated by the effects of silting. Shifting sandbanks rendered the approaches to the port hazardous for foreign ship-owners and fishermen, who were increasingly drawn to Yarmouth's commercial rivals further up the coast and in the Low Countries. Its principal source of revenue, the herring industry, was beset by additional problems. A protracted conflict with Lowestoft over the control of Kirkley Roads, and thus of an effective monopoly over catches, was settled in 1386. The crown's eventual readi-ness to accede to Yarmouth's demands in the face of parliamentary opposi-tion suggests that there was real substance behind the repeated complaints about poverty and desolation. Having ranked fourth among English provincial towns in the tax assessments of 1334, the port had slipped to eighteenth place by 1377, remaining at roughly this position for the next 150 years.

Not surprisingly, Yarmouth experienced more than its share of unrest during this period. Quarrels between the ruling elite and the less affluent

[13] M. Rubin, 'The Poor', in R. Horrox, ed., *Fifteenth-Century Attitudes: Perceptions of Society in Late Medieval England* (Cambridge, 1994), p. 173.

[14] The following account of Yarmouth's economic decline is based upon A. Saul, 'Great Yarmouth in the Fourteenth Century: A Study in Trade, Politics and Society' (Oxford University, DPhil thesis, 1975).

burgesses, who resented their exclusion from trading privileges, came to a head in 1376, when 'the great men of the town' were denounced in a petition to the Good Parliament by 'the poor commoners' for 'various impositions, abuses and oppressions'.[15] Since no fewer than thirty-five prominent residents were subsequently bound over to keep the peace towards their less privileged neighbours, we may assume that matters had by then turned violent.[16] Worse was to follow, however, for during the Peasants' Revolt many of the townsfolk made common cause with the 'bloodthirsty mob' that sacked the houses of the wealthiest individuals. The destruction of the contentious royal charter confirming the monopoly of Yarmouth's leading merchants over the herring industry clearly inspired as much support within the walls as it did in the rival community at Lowestoft.[17] It was against this background of class conflict and economic decline that St Mary's hospital assumed its new form in 1386. Significantly, seven of the men named in the re-foundation charter had been specifically identified as 'oppressors of the poor' a decade before, while a further five belonged to the 'great' families then singled out for attack.

The Hospital of the Blessed Virgin

St Mary's was not the first hospital in Yarmouth, since an earlier one is known to have stood near the river, on the west side of the town, during the second half of the thirteenth century. Described simply as 'the new hospital', it occupied an insalubrious site, next to smokeries and a saltworks, in an area subject to intensive development as the shoreline retreated.[18] A move to less congested and healthier surroundings was clearly desirable by the 1270s, not least because the port was then enjoying a period of unprecedented prosperity. The influx of impoverished and vulnerable people from the surrounding countryside inevitably placed a strain on existing resources, strengthening the case for the provision of at least one other hospital. Although they are not documented before 1349, two adjacent leper houses (one for men and one for women) were probably constructed at the very northern end (*caput*) of the town before the close of the century, being reserved for reputable individuals who were prepared to follow a quasi-religious rule.[19] The main focus of investment and, undoubtedly, of urban pride was, however, the hospital of the Blessed

[15] J. Strachey and others, eds, *Rotuli Parliamentorum* (6 vols, 1767-77), ii, p. 352.

[16] *CCR, 1374-77*, p. 470.

[17] William Worcestre, *Itineraries*, ed. J.H. Harvey (Oxford, 1969), pp. 182-3; B. Dobson, ed., *The Peasants' Revolt* (second edn, 1983), p. 32.

[18] P. Rutledge, 'Before the Walls: The Early Medieval Settlement Pattern of Great Yarmouth', *Yarmouth Archaeology* (1990), pp. 41-8, at p. 45.

[19] H. Manship, *History of Great Yarmouth*, ed. C.J. Palmer (Yarmouth, 1854), pp. 432-4; C. Rawcliffe, *Leprosy in Medieval England* (Woodbridge, 2006), p. 270.

Virgin Mary, which by then stood on Yarmouth's eastern boundary, beside the market place and near St Nicholas' parish church. A precise foundation date cannot now be determined, but it evidently opened its doors to the sick poor not long after the accession of Edward I in 1272. The floods of 1286–7, which caused widespread devastation, may well have destroyed 'the new hospital', since nothing is heard of it from then onwards.

Reputedly founded by Thomas Fastolf, an affluent merchant and leading member of the urban elite, St Mary's initially attracted an impressive amount of support. In his will of 1291, another prominent resident, Oliver Wyth, left property worth an estimated £20 to the hospital, along with his bed, which was presumably equipped with a full set of hangings.[20] It was, even so, not always easy to gain possession of the legacies bequeathed by testators, as we can see from the circumstances surrounding the handsome bequest made by William Gerbrigge, a former bailiff of Yarmouth.[21] His will has not apparently survived, but we know from the evidence of the cartulary (number 8) that he died in about 1278, leaving annual rents worth £6 to the hospital and naming his sons, William and John, as executors.[22] The two brothers were extremely dilatory in implementing their late father's wishes, being finally ordered to do so twenty-six years after his death by Archbishop Winchelsea in his capacity as visiting metropolitan. Negligence of this kind was no doubt common, although it rarely comes to light, and serves as a salutary reminder that testamentary evidence should be interpreted with caution. Conversely, however, the cartulary provides invaluable information about benefactors whose wills have been lost, or are only partially recorded in the borough court rolls. We learn, for example, of a legacy of 6s. annual rent made to the hospital before its re-foundation by the sometime MP and bailiff, Walter atte Sonde, whose testamentary provisions are otherwise now unknown (number 4).[23]

[20] Manship, *Great Yarmouth*, pp. 430-32; P. Rutledge, ed., 'The Will of Oliver Wyth', in *A Miscellany* (NRS, lvi, 1991), pp. 21, 26.

[21] He held office twice between 1270 and 1272: P. Rutledge, 'The Earliest Yarmouth Bailiffs, *NA*, xl (1988), pp. 181-5 at p. 183. Not knowing his death date, Saul ('Great Yarmouth', pp. 244-5) confuses him with William Gerbrigge, *clericus*, who discharged six terms as bailiff between 1275 and 1282 (Rutledge, 'Earliest Yarmouth Bailiffs', pp. 183-4), and became involved in a feud with the Drayton family that ended in his murder, in 1302: *CPR, 1301-7*, pp. 10, 91, 135.

[22] This William, who was not a clerk, apparently acted as bailiff in 1282-3, and again at the end of the decade. John, evidently the younger of the two siblings, served with him in 1282-3, his only experience of the higher reaches of local government: Rutledge, 'Earliest Yarmouth Bailiffs', p. 184.

[23] He was bailiff seven times between 1326 and 1339, and MP on four occasions during his long career, although his return was successfully contested on one of them: Le Strange, *Norfolk Official Lists*, pp. 151, 174, 175.

The striking decline in the value of the rents left by William Gerbrigge, which accounted for less than 13s. a year by 1398 (number 7), suggests that the burgesses who re-founded St Mary's in 1386 were justified in stressing its slide into poverty. It is harder to credit their assertion that the place was by then little more than a ruin, 'fallen downe, prostrated and defaced' (number 1). Yet, like most other English hospitals of the period, it had clearly suffered badly in the decades following the Black Death, and required a hefty injection of capital. Although the onset of plague in Yarmouth prompted a hitherto unprecedented display of largesse on the part of testators, and thus brought some temporary financial relief, the hospital fared badly as recession hit the beleaguered port.[24] Hardship had struck by 1354, when one of the duke of Lancaster's retainers secured a papal indulgence of one year and forty days' remission of enjoined penance for anyone who visited the hospital in order to assist 'the multitude of poor brethren and sisters, for whose sustenance a daily quest has to be made'.[25] Two years later, Richard Fastolf, a kinsman of the founder, bequeathed annual rents of £4 9s. for commemorative masses to be said by his chaplain, specifying that, after the latter's death, the money should be diverted by the bailiffs[26] and commonalty 'towards the support and assistance' of the residents.[27] A trickle of similar donations followed, including a legacy of two fish-houses in Yarmouth made by another former bailiff, William Stalham, who drew up his will in 1379 and died early in 1386.[28] Stalham was almost certainly one of the moving spirits behind the re-foundation of the hospital, having already during his lifetime expended 'good and lardge bounty' upon it (number 9). He had, significantly, been commissioned to raise the hated poll tax of 1377.[29]

The re-foundation of St Mary's was, however, more than a private initiative on the part of a few wealthy merchants. Its new charter of 8 May 1386 was promulgated by the bailiffs and council of twenty-four leading residents, who claimed to be acting on behalf of the entire community (number 1).[30] This important document marked the town's formal assump-

[24] At least eighteen bequests, including land, rents and cash sums, are recorded in 1349 alone: NRO, Y/C4/70, rots 1v-6v; H. Swinden, *The History and Antiquities of the Ancient Burgh of Great Yarmouth* (Norwich, 1772), pp. 816-24.

[25] *Calendar of Papal Registers: Petitions, 1342-1419* (Cambridge, 1896), p. 263.

[26] Great Yarmouth was ruled first by four, and then by two, bailiffs. They were not succeeded by a mayor until the late seventeenth century.

[27] Fastolf was bailiff in 1331-2 and 1334-5: Le Strange, *Norfolk Official Lists*, p. 151. His will was dated 28 May 1356, but was not enrolled until 1371: NRO, Y/C4/85, rots 8v-9; Manship, *History of Great Yarmouth*, pp. 430-31.

[28] NRO, Y/C4/97, rot. 12. He was bailiff in 1378-9 and 1382-3: Le Strange, *Norfolk Official Lists*, p. 153.

[29] *CFR, 1369-1377*, p. 389; Swinden, *Ancient Burgh of Yarmouth*, p. 806.

[30] See Saul, 'Great Yarmouth', pp. 10-11, for an account of the role of the four-and-twenty, who reappear in 1386 after an absence of 114 years, during which they are not mentioned in the town's records. This list of names is consequently of particular value.

tion of responsibility for the oversight and support of the hospital, the earnestness of the venture being signalled by the purchase, in 1392, of a costly royal licence in mortmain. This authorised two prominent burgesses, William Oxney and Robert Howlyn, to acquire a messuage and seventeen cottages, together with rents worth £5 a year, for the relief of 'poore and infirme persons' (number 3). Even if, as has been suggested, the depressed state of the local property market made benefactors unusually responsive to appeals for help, it took some time to achieve this goal.[31] Five years later, in October 1397, the bailiffs and community conveyed the messuage, cottages and Walter atte Sonde's rent of 6*s.* to Oxney and Howlyn, who had presumably raised, or were then still busy raising, the remaining 94*s.* in rental income (number 4). By the following January they were at last in a position to implement the full award, settling both the property and rents upon the bailiffs and community 'to the releivinge of the bretheren and siusters of the hospitall of the Blessed Mary in Yermouth' (number 5).

The move towards corporate ownership was accompanied by radical changes in the house's size and function, as well as in the type of people whom it would now admit (number 1). Sick and vagrant paupers, the utterly destitute or those on the point of death were no longer eligible. Henceforward sixteen reputable bedesmen and women were to be chosen by the warden, bailiffs and burgesses, remaining in the hospital for life unless they committed some serious transgression. All were to live chastely, soberly and peacefully, steering clear of Yarmouth's many taverns and observing a strict curfew. One sister and one brother 'of good fame' were to supervise the behaviour of their fellows, reporting any misdemeanours to the warden, who, in turn, had the right to withhold 'common alms' by way of punishment. None the less, by contemporary standards, the new almsmen and women enjoyed an unusual degree of personal freedom. It was assumed that they would occasionally 'dyne & suppyn & etyn & drynkyn with hyr good frendys in towun' (number 11), and that some would be able to earn extra money by continuing to work. The concept of retirement was virtually unknown in medieval England, and many almshouses required their fitter inmates to undertake light horticultural or domestic duties, not least for therapeutic reasons.[32] Such people might well be expected to contribute towards their own support. A prohibition upon the wearing of silk veils by the sisters, and the insistence that all goods and chattels, as well as uncollected debts, should revert to St Mary's when they died certainly suggests that the residents were far from indigent. They were, in short, the elderly or disabled dependents of those upwardly mobile

---

[31] Saul, 'Great Yarmouth', p. 259.

[32] E.M. Phillips, 'Charitable Institutions in Norfolk and Suffolk *c.* 1350-1600' (University of East Anglia, PhD thesis, 2001), p. 157; C. Rawcliffe, 'Health and Safety at Work in Medieval East Anglia', in C. Harper-Bill, ed. *Medieval East Anglia* (Woodbridge, 2005), pp. 131-2.

tradesmen and artisans who had been most critical of the ruling elite.

Concern about the moral probity of the alms-folk reflected the spiritual as well as the economic and social anxieties of Yarmouth's leading inhabitants. Not content with the purchase of paradise through good works, men such as William Stalham sought to harness the prayers of the grateful poor. In return for their accommodation and support, the residents were not only expected to attend services on a regular basis, but also to offer a total of three hundred *Aves* and *Pater nosters* every day for the salvation of their benefactors. This, in turn, required a liturgical framework centred upon the quotidian celebration of the Mass, the construction of a well-furnished, 'convenyent' chapel and the employment of at least one priest, charged with responsibility for the souls of the patrons as well as those of the residents. All over England, the founders of almshouses demonstrated a similar scale of priorities, in the pious hope of securing their 'parte and porcion of joy and blysse with them that shall be saved'.[33] Not surprisingly, however, such developments occasioned acute anxiety among the parochial clergy and monastic foundations that now faced open competition for diminishing resources. Jurisdictional disputes over the right to celebrate Mass and collect offerings became increasingly common, although few are so well documented as that which arose at Yarmouth. St Mary's close proximity to the port's only parish church and to the Benedictine priory which jealously guarded its rights made a collision of interests between the monks and the burgesses inevitable.

The dispute with the priory

Like those at Aldeby and Bishop's Lynn, the Yarmouth cell of Norwich cathedral priory was intended by the founder, Bishop Herbert Losinga, to support an adjacent parish church and thus remained comparatively small.[34] The church, on the other hand, grew in size to become one of the largest in England. Closely reflecting the fortunes of its congregation, St Nicholas' was initially a relatively modest building dating, along with the Benedictine cell, from the early twelfth century, but, as the port developed, levels of investment in the furnishings and fabric increased. Wide north and south aisles were added, creating 'a most beautiful, large, spacious and lightsome church, not much inferior to many cathedrals in the kingdom'.[35]

[33] J.A.A. Goodall, *God's House at Ewelme* (Aldershot, 2001), p. 224.

[34] C. Harper-Bill, 'The Medieval Church and the Wider World', in A. Atherton and others, eds, *Norwich Cathedral: Church, City and Diocese 1096-1996* (1996), p. 283.

[35] Manship, *Great Yarmouth*, p. 33. A striking late sixteenth-century depiction of the church of St Nicholas and the neighbouring hospital precinct to the south may be found in BL, Cotton MS Augustus I i 74, reproduced in P.D.A. Harvey, *Maps in Tudor England* (1993), pp. 6 (detail), 18-19. See also T. Ashwin and A. Davison, eds, *An Historic Atlas of Norfolk* (third edn, Chichester, 2005), no 40, pp. 82-3.

Ambitious plans for a grand new west front, known as 'the bachelors' aisle', were afoot by 1330, when the foundations were laid. The first outbreak of plague brought them to an abrupt halt, and, as the population continued to fall, the survivors must have been overwhelmed by the scale of the building in which they worshipped.[36]

The modest complement of three or four resident monks in the neighbouring priory contrasts sharply with the sixty or so whom Bishop Losinga regarded as an appropriate number to staff his cathedral.[37] Despite the authority bestowed by his title, the prior of Yarmouth had never ranked among the leading monastic obedientiaries, which explains why the post should have been assigned, just before the re-foundation of St Mary's hospital, to John Hoo, a theologian who had spent most of his career studying at Oxford.[38] Yet even the most naïve and cloistered of monks would readily have appreciated the need for action. Years before, in 1234, the Benedictine cell at Bishop's Lynn had become embroiled in a similar disagreement with the nearby hospital of St John the Baptist over its liturgical provisions. Taking up the cudgels on behalf of his spiritual sons, the prior of Norwich had then forced the master to make numerous concessions.[39] As generally proved the case on such occasions, the real bone of contention was not so much the recognition of a superior ecclesiastical jurisdiction as the right to whatever hard cash went with it. A brief examination of monastic finances reveals why Prior Tottington of Norwich was now even more determined to restrict the religious rites at St Mary's to the bare minimum and to ensure that whatever offerings *were* collected there would immediately revert to his coffers.

At the close of the thirteenth century, when it ranked as the richest landowner in Norfolk after the bishop of Norwich, the cathedral priory (together with its dependent cells) could rely on a net income of about £2,500 a year, roughly half of which came from tithes, offerings and other spiritualities.[40] Despite the heavy loss of life, it seemed at first that the community would weather the crisis of the Black Death relatively unscathed. In 1363–4, the first year for which a full financial record survives, revenues stood at an encouraging £2,260, although running costs, which then exceeded income by £512, were already beginning to reflect

[36] The chequered architectural history of St Nicholas' is described in N. Pevsner and B. Wilson, *The Buildings of England: Norfolk I: Norwich and North-East* (second edn, 1997), pp. 494-8. For plans, see A.W. Ecclestone, *The Rise of Great Yarmouth* (Norwich, 1959), pp. 72-3.

[37] J. Greatrex, *Biographical Register of the English Cathedral Priories of the Province of Canterbury* (Oxford, 1997), p. 466.

[38] Greatrex, *Biographical Register*, p. 525.

[39] NRO, DCN 84/14; D.M. Owen, ed., *The Making of King's Lynn* (Records of Social and Economic History, new series, ix, 1984), pp. 105-6.

[40] R. Virgoe, 'The Estates of Norwich Cathedral Priory, 1101-1538', in Atherton, *Norwich Cathedral*, pp. 352-3.

the rise in wage rates.[41] Caught between the pincers of an unfavourable labour market and falling rents, by 1434–5 the priory could rely on no more than £1,610 a year, while still overspending to the tune of £350, despite stringent economies.[42] Since their income from property was declining so dramatically, the monks became even more reliant upon spiritualities, although these, too, were far from secure, especially at Yarmouth.

Standing at £212 a year in 1355–6, the cell's annual income then derived in part from tithes (£53), although almost half its revenues constituted offerings and oblations made by the residents of Yarmouth at St Nicholas' parish church and its adjacent chapel (£104). Testamentary bequests provided a further £20, but were insufficient to plug the gap between receipts and expenditure, which would have required twice this amount.[43] The annual deficit had barely changed by 1386–7, when the dispute over St Mary's hospital reached its climax. Tithes (£43) had fallen, but, when added together, legacies, oblations and other gifts to the church remained fairly steady (£124).[44] We can see at a glance how difficult it was for the cell to maintain the *status quo* if we turn to the next surviving account, drawn up in 1401. By then annual income had dropped by £65, while the house was overspending at a rate of £70 a year. The most significant shortfalls were in tithes (then no more than £26), testamentary bequests (a mere £7) and offerings to St Nicholas' church (just £55).[45] Viewed with hindsight, Prior Tottington's anxiety was clearly justified, being no doubt compounded by the unambiguous evidence of Yarmouth's continuing economic problems and the success of his ecclesiastical rivals.

As the town's only parish church, St Nicholas' commanded considerable reserves of loyalty and continued to attract generous donations. But there were few grounds for complacency. It is worth noting that, in more prosperous times, Thomas Fastolf, William Gerbrigge and Oliver Wyth had been closely involved in the endowment of Yarmouth's Dominican and Franciscan friaries, as well as the hospital, hoping thereby to augment their reserves of celestial merit.[46] Indeed, Richard Fastolf's above-mentioned bequest of 1356 was conditional upon the perpetual commemoration of him and his wife 'in masses, prayers and other orations' at St Mary's.[47] By then, however, it was the mendicants who posed the greater threat. An analysis of Yarmouth wills drawn up between 1348 and 1380 shows that, whereas the hospital continued to attract around 6 per cent of the monetary value of pious bequests, the town's four friaries were benefiting at the expense of the parish church. Indeed, their share of such bequests rose

[41] NRO, DCN 1/13/1.   [42] NRO, DCN 1/13/2.   [43] NRO, DCN 2/4/1.
[44] NRO, DCN 2/4/2.   [45] NRO, DCN 2/4/3.
[46] W. Page, ed., *Victoria County History of Norfolk II* (1906), pp. 435-6; Rutledge, 'Will of Oliver Wyth', pp. 13-14.
[47] NRO, Y/C4/97, rots 8ᵛ-9; Manship, *Great Yarmouth*, p. 431.

from 37 to 55 per cent, while that of St Nicholas' fell by almost half to an alarming 34 per cent.[48]

The hospital's re-foundation in the 1380s, itself a further manifestation of this ongoing quest for spiritual health, now looked set to outdo the friaries in attracting patronage from the ruling elite. Nervously eyeing the ambitious rebuilding works immediately to the north of their precinct in Norwich, where the hospital of St Giles was emerging as a major liturgical centre, the Benedictines must have made some rapid calculations.[49] The figures were far from reassuring. Although the monks could hardly protest about the provision of support for the deserving poor, they were determined to prevent the creation of a similar institution in Yarmouth. That the burgesses had already been obliged to accept some stringent curbs upon the hospital's liturgical activities – along the lines of those imposed at Lynn – is apparent from the initial regulations of May 1386. The rules then approved by Prior Tottington and Bishop Herbert Despenser precluded the use of music, kept religious observance to a minimum and ensured that parishioners would never be diverted from attendance at St Nicholas', 'which God forbid' (number 1). Significantly, all donations not earmarked for the residents were to be surrendered to the monks within eight days of receipt, thus ensuring that no spiritualities would be lost. For understandable reasons, the towns-people appear to have ignored these restrictions, with the result that, by the following autumn, 'greate matter of question even to the breakinge of all frindshipp' had arisen between them and the priory (number 2). Whereas in Lynn it had proved necessary to resort to the ecclesiastical courts, an accord was reached in Yarmouth by less formal means.

Quite possibly the bishop, who was then in disgrace and thus obliged to reside permanently in his diocese, intervened to broker an acceptable outcome. If so, he handled the affair with uncharacteristic circumspection. The absence overseas of his arch-enemy, John of Gaunt, duke of Lancaster, who had hitherto proved a 'good lord' to members of the Yarmouth elite, removed one potentially disruptive element and may have defused the situation.[50] On balance, Despenser was probably inclined to favour the monks, although the composition achieved on 30 November 1386 and confirmed by him a month later (number 2) did no more than reiterate the salient points made in the earlier regulations.[51] By the time

[48] Saul, 'Great Yarmouth', Appendix VII, O, pp. 385-6.

[49] For the rebuilding of St Giles' hospital, see Rawcliffe, *Medicine for the Soul*, chapter four.

[50] Saul, 'Great Yarmouth', pp. 167-9, 175. Despenser's earlier confrontation with the burgesses of Lynn contrasts sharply with his subsequent restraint: K. Parker, 'A Little Local Difficulty: Lynn and the Lancastrian Usurpation', in Harper-Bill, *Medieval East Anglia*, pp. 120-22.

[51] Despenser's epic struggle with Prior Tottington over monastic liberties in Norwich was then in its infancy, and is thus unlikely to have influenced the outcome: Harper-Bill, 'Medieval Church', pp. 297-8. For an outline of his career, see *DNB*, xv, pp. 910-12.

that Henry Manship came to list the Yarmouth records in 1612–13, the borough's original copy of this new agreement had apparently been lost. It was later purchased by the collector, Sir Thomas Phillipps (d. 1872), having perhaps belonged to one of the eighteenth-century Norfolk antiquaries who acquired the hospital cartulary, and is now in the Norfolk Record Office.[52]

It is easy to see why St Mary's never developed the fund-raising capacity of hospitals such as St Giles', Norwich, or St Thomas Acon, London, which boasted musicianship and ritual of the highest quality. Instead, like so many other poor almshouses, it clung on grimly until the Dissolution, by which time its annual income had slumped to below £5, and only four sisters remained in residence.[53] Such liturgical functions as the house was permitted to perform ceased abruptly after the Second Chantry Act of 1547. The spacious precinct, with its many buildings, offered a prime site for redevelopment, which the borough authorities were eager to exploit. Once an altar stone, part of the sepulchre, two alabaster altars and other ecclesiastical furnishings had been removed, the upper part of the chapel was 'planked' in April 1551 and utilised as a powder store, or 'tresury for the townes ordeynaunces'. The rest was converted into a grammar school at no little expense to the corporation.[54] It was here that Henry Manship received the impressive education that was to serve him so well in later years.[55] In 1598 he was himself one of the burgesses deputed by the Assembly 'to viewe the hospitall and the roomes thereof and to confer togeather' about the creation of a Bridewell designed to implement the draconian Tudor poor laws. Their plans 'for the placing of the poore and setting of idle persons on worke' in another part of the grounds received enthusiastic approval, and the new house of correction began to take shape.[56]

Since land was at a premium because of Yarmouth's cramped geographical position between the river Yare and the sea, the hospital's modest rental income from the rest of the precinct and its other properties assumed unusual importance. But it was first necessary to establish the full extent of these holdings. Even when hospitals and almshouses managed to avoid dismemberment, the survival of their manuscripts remained a lottery, being often dependent upon the efforts of later generations of antiquarians in the face of official indifference.[57] The burgesses of early

[52] NRO, Phi/623.

[53] Page, *Victoria County History of Norfolk II*, p. 453.

[54] *HMC Ninth Report and Appendix: Part 1* (1883), pp. 314-15; Phillips, 'Charitable Institutions', pp. 93-5; Manship, *Great Yarmouth*, p. 431.

[55] Manship, *Great Yarmouth*, p. 45.

[56] NRO, Y/C19/4 (Assembly Book, 1579-1598), ff. 280, 281ᵛ. From 1573 onwards poor children were also accommodated in the precinct: Manship, *Great Yarmouth*, p. 232.

[57] Rawcliffe, 'Passports to Paradise', p. 10.

modern Yarmouth showed a more active interest in their medieval heritage than many urban authorities, although their motives were staunchly pragmatic. Still dogged by the need to pay for costly harbour works, repair the port's defences and wage a constant legal battle in defence of commercial privileges, they were anxious to capitalise upon every potential source of revenue at their disposal. This relentless quest for 'commodite and profight' in turn demanded a well-ordered archive, accompanied, where possible, by English abstracts of the most useful Latin texts.[58]

Aware that many properties owned by St Mary's had fallen into 'gret ruyne, decaye & distruccion' because of mismanagement and the loss of legal records, the Assembly ruled in October 1541 that four of its members should 'advyse aswell the evidences & rentalles perteynyng to the hospitall … and the abuttalles therof, as also the groundes wherof eny rentes be dew'.[59] From this date onwards, the magistrates exercised a far tighter control over the leasing of hospital property, often demanding securities from tenants, whose names were recorded in the Assembly minutes. Once further steps had been taken, in 1542, 'to assesse and qualifie all the rentes', it proved possible to meet unforeseen legal expenses from the surplus, while also paying the three remaining sisters a weekly dole of 3d. in order to keep them from begging.[60] But it was not until the beginning of the seventeenth century that the hospital's medieval muniments - like those of the town itself - became more generally accessible.

Henry Manship and the borough archives

One of the most colourful of British antiquaries, Henry Manship is now chiefly remembered for his *History of Great Yarmouth*, which finally appeared in print in 1854, some 228 years after his death. Such a long delay between completion and publication is no reflection of the work's quality. Recently described as 'an impressively sophisticated intellectual and literary achieve-ment for its time', it bears favourable comparison with any of the more

[58] P. Rutledge, ed., *Great Yarmouth Assembly Minutes 1538-1545* (NRS, xxxix, 1970), pp. 15-17, 43; idem, 'Archive Management at Great Yarmouth since 1540', *Journal of the Society of Archivists*, iii (1965-69), pp. 89-91, at p. 89. For the wider background to such reforms, see R. Tittler, *Architecture and Power: The Town Hall and the English Urban Community c. 1500-1640* (Oxford, 1991), pp. 88-9; and idem, 'Reformation, Civic Culture and Collective Memory in English Provincial Towns', *Urban History*, xxiv (1997), pp. 283-300, at pp. 295-7.

[59] Rutledge, *Great Yarmouth Assembly Minutes*, p. 43. The master of St Mary's had already begun to rent out some chambers and gardens in the precinct by 1530, if not before, and at first the Assembly was content simply to ratify his leases: Rutledge, *Great Yarmouth Assembly Minutes*, pp. 31-2. As a result of these measures income rose steadily after 1543, reaching £22 over the next twenty years: Phillips, 'Charitable Institutions', p. 211.

[60] Rutledge, *Great Yarmouth Assembly Minutes*, pp. 46-7, 49, 53, 55-6.

celebrated urban or county histories produced by his contemporaries.[61] Reflecting on almost every page his knowledge of the borough archives, it was the product of decades spent among the town's remarkable store of medieval records, including those of St Mary's hospital. It also marked a final – and, in the event, unsuccessful – attempt on Manship's part to regain the favour of the exasperated authorities after one escapade too many. Since he had previously managed to ingratiate his way into their good graces by cataloguing the most important of these records and translating the hospital cartulary, a brief account of his chequered career will prove helpful.

Manship was the son and namesake of a Yarmouth merchant whose involvement in local government ceased abruptly as a result of commercial malpractice, and who died a pauper in 1569.[62] Neither rich enough nor sufficiently well-connected to train at one of the prestigious Inns of Court in London, young Henry left the local grammar school to study law, and eventually established himself as a notary public and 'self-styled attorney'.[63] His great intelligence and energy soon attracted attention. Having secured the post of town clerk in 1579, he resigned voluntarily six years later because of the demands placed upon him by his new appointment as controller of customs in the port.[64] At this point his career seemed to be progressing well, for he was by then able to pledge £50 for repairs to the property he rented, on very favourable terms, from the authorities.[65] He was also elected to the eight-and-forty, a council of prominent burgesses which, together with the four-and-twenty, constituted the Yarmouth Assembly. Yet his success was not destined to last. A degree of animosity may already have poisoned his relations with the rich and influential merchant, Thomas Damet, whose *Booke of the Foundacion and Antiquity of the Towne of Greate Yermouthe* appeared in the late 1590s, setting the seal on their rivalry.[66] As his own history of the borough reveals, Manship was a far

---

[61] R. Tittler, *Townspeople and Nation: English Urban Experiences, 1540-1640* (Stanford, California, 2001), p. 122. Chapter five (pp. 121-39) offers an assessment of Manship's *History*.

[62] P. Rutledge, 'Thomas Damet and the Historiography of Great Yarmouth', *NA*, xxxiii (1965), pp. 119-30, at pp. 120-21.

[63] Tittler, *Townspeople and Nation*, p. 128.

[64] NRO, Y/C19/4, ff. 3, 91ᵛ. N.J. Williams, *The Maritime Trade of East Anglian Ports* (Oxford, 1988), p. 42, confuses Henry with his father, and attributes to him the offences demonstrably committed in the 1560s by Manship senior: NRO, Y/C19/2 (Assembly Book, 1559-70), ff. 64ᵛ, 107, 108. Tittler, *Townspeople and Nation*, p. 126, corrects this mistake, but assumes that Henry was removed as controller in 1585 because of similar - undocumented - misdemeanours. The letters patent appointing him were, in fact, cancelled in May of that year on a technicality and reissued later. He was still serving in November 1588: *Draft Calendar of Patent Rolls, 27 Eliz. I, 1584-85* (List and Index Society, ccxli, 1990), p. 192; Williams, *Maritime Trade*, p. 42; *Calendar of State Papers Domestic, 1581-1590*, p. 561.

[65] NRO, Y/C19/4, ff. 88, 99, 114, 143ᵛ.

[66] It was first published in 1847 by the Yarmouth antiquary, J.C. Palmer. Ironically, under

finer scholar, who deployed his archival skills to better and more analytical effect. He also possessed a sharp tongue and a volatile temper. Shortly after Damet's return to the Parliament of 1604, Manship was hauled before the Assembly on a charge of slandering him and his colleague 'in many places and to sundrye persons'. His assertion that the two men had 'behaved them selffes like sheepe in the parliament and were both dunces' was deemed sufficiently inflammatory to warrant his removal from the eight-and-forty 'as not fitt to be of that society', and a long period of disgrace began.[67]

After eight years in the wilderness, Manship finally engineered an opportunity for rehabilitation. Sporadic efforts had already been made to sort and catalogue the innumerable 'charters, recordes & wrytynges' that constituted the borough archives. An *ad hoc* committee had also been established to supervise the loan and return of official documents stored in a 'common hutche' in the vestry.[68] But many had, none the less, gone missing, while others lay in a neglected and 'disorderedly' state in various places, 'to the no little damage of the whole Incorporacion'. The thorny question of who should – and should not – gain access to such sensitive information was, in turn, a matter of growing concern in an age increasingly preoccupied with the issues of secrecy and authority.[69] Seizing the moment, Manship 'profered his paynes' to compile a much-needed survey of the Yarmouth records, and on 16 June 1612 thirteen leading burgesses were authorised to work with him over the next five weeks on a preliminary list.[70] The results, finally submitted in December 1613, were impressive, securing his readmission into the ranks of the eight-and-forty one month later.[71]

Manship's 'summary reporte' still survives among the Yarmouth records, meticulously itemising in his own hand each of the scores of manuscripts examined in the course of twenty-three separate meetings. Among them were five documents relating to St Mary's hospital, including an otherwise unknown 'writing in parchement shewing the indulgences of

the circumstances, he attributed the authorship to Henry Manship senior. Rutledge, 'Thomas Damet', pp. 119-30 (with addendum in *NA*, xxxiv (1969), pp. 332-3), rectifies this common mistake.

[67] NRO, Y/C19/5 (Assembly Book, 1598-1625), f. 41[v]. Williams, *Maritime Trade*, pp. 42-3, suggests that Manship's attack was aimed at the other MP, John Wheeler, a Merchant Adventurer who had condemned fraudulent officials. But his prime target was undoubtedly Damet: Rutledge, 'Thomas Damet', p. 128.

[68] Rutledge, 'Archive Management', p. 89.

[69] P. Griffiths, 'Secrecy and Authority in Late Sixteenth and Early Seventeenth-Century London', *Historical Journal*, xl, 4 (1997), pp. 925-51.

[70] NRO, Y/C1/1, ff. 1-2. Since at least six of the burgesses were to accompany him at all times, the Assembly clearly harboured reservations about his probity: NRO, Y/C19/5, f. 101.

[71] NRO, Y/C19/5, f. 122[v].

the hospitall' dated October 1372, which provides further, tantalising
evidence of financial hardship in the years before its re-foundation.[72] Of
even greater interest is Manship's brief reference to 'an exemplificacion of
the orders of the hospitall under the towne seale' compiled on 12 March
1386 and thus predating the first entry in the cartulary by two months.[73]
Did these regulations differ significantly from the later version preserved in
its pages? Since the manuscript in question has been lost, we shall never
know. The report also lists 'a copye' of Richard II's licence in mortmain of
1392 (number 3 in the cartulary), which is also worthy of comment. It had,
in fact, been purchased from the Tower of London in 1597 because the
original could not be found.[74] As Manship was at pains to stress, the
'greate costs and chardge' involved in procuring authenticated copies of
missing records could easily be avoided by good archival practice.[75]

He found much else to criticise in this respect. Some years later, in his
History of Great Yarmouth, he observed that the Assembly had consistently
failed to exploit its legal title to hospital property because of ignorance
about the extent of the medieval precinct. 'Now', he carefully explained,

> for that it may plainly appear what damage the said town hath sustained for
> not knowing their right and title therein, I have thought good, for the
> avoiding of the like hereafter, to express the abutting and bounding of the said
> ground, as in the ... deed (number 4) passed by the Bailiffs to the said
> [William] Oxney and [Robert] Howlings is expressed, viz. ... that the said
> Hospitall doth lie between the common of Yarmouth south and north, the
> walls of Yarmouth east, and the king's highway west so that it is more than
> manifest that the same Hospitall ground did extend itself from the Pudding
> Gates in the north unto the ... Market Gates to the south; as in and by an old
> parchment book (which, besides the deeds themselves, I have seen) plainly
> appeareth.[76]

The 'old parchment book' was, in fact, the hospital cartulary, the translation of which Manship undertook in 1614 at the behest of the newly
appointed master, Isaac Cowper. Finding the records 'to be by long
continuance of tyme much decayed, defaced and in many places rent and
torne not easylie to be read', Cowper suggested that they, too, should be

[72] NRO, Y/C1/1, f. 7. A manuscript copy of Manship's original report was made in 1763:
BL, Add. MS 2373. The report was privately printed in H. Harrod, *A Repertory of Deeds and
Documents Relating to the Borough of Great Yarmouth* (Yarmouth, 1855), now NRO, Y/C1/2.
[73] NRO, Y/C1/1, f. 10ᵛ.
[74] NRO, Y/C1/1, f. 37ᵛ; Y/C36/8 (the 1597 copy). The other manuscripts noted were the
originals of numbers 1 and 5 in the cartulary: Y/C1/1, ff. 16ᵛ, 22ᵛ. They, too, have since been
lost.
[75] NRO, Y/C1/1, f. 1.
[76] Manship, *Great Yarmouth*, p. 42.

rendered more intelligible.[77] That the bailiffs endorsed his request is hardly surprising, since moves had long been afoot to produce English calendars of the borough's medieval records. Similar activities in other towns and cities throughout England confirm that the approach was utilitarian, being largely determined by the exigencies of national and local government and the growing demand for accurate written information.[78] As early as 1491, the steward, Thomas Banyard, had 'translated oute of Frenssh into Englyssh ... the olde boke of the Lawes and Customes of Yermouth';[79] and almost a century later, in 1580, Manship's *bête noire*, Thomas Damet, produced an English text of royal charters and other important documents for use by his colleagues in the Assembly.[80] It was, no doubt, while engaged upon this exercise that he conceived the more ambitious plan of writing the port's history, which was itself designed 'to the intent that there maye be some good presidentes lefte unto them in the tyme of there necessites to make and frame there sutes and peticions ... and more reedye and speedier dispatche of those busynes'.[81] The prospect of improving upon his rival's efforts would have appealed greatly to Manship, whose translation (like his earlier report) bears his flamboyant notary's mark, ostentatiously decorated with bold black strap-work.[82]

Since his wife, Jane Hall, came from King's Lynn, it seems likely that Manship knew about the legal battles attendant upon the loss of 'sundrie of the deedes, evidences, writinges ... and muniments' belonging to the erstwhile suburban leper house at Gaywood. The recorder, Francis Parlett, was then busy compiling a history of this once affluent hospital for the corporation, and Manship may have been further inspired by his example.[83] At all events, his work on the records of St Mary's helped to accelerate the process of rehabilitation, with the result that, by 1615, he was not only serving on the hutch committee but also as one of the bailiffs' assistants.[84] His archival expertise was, significantly, recognised by his appointment to another body charged with the crucial task of revising and simplifying the borough ordinances.[85] Not content with such marks of

[77] Below, p. 182.

[78] The nearby borough of Ipswich furnishes some striking examples of this process, which began there in the mid-fifteenth century: *HMC Ninth Report: Part 1*, pp. 242-3.

[79] NRO, Y/C18/1, ff. 8ᵛ-16, 26-31, catalogued in *HMC Ninth Report: Part 1*, p. 305.

[80] NRO, Y/C18/4, ff. 1-79, catalogued in *HMC Ninth Report: Part 1*, pp. 321-2. In 1582 the Yarmouth Assembly ruled that the annual audit should henceforward be engrossed in English not Latin (NRO, Y/C19/4, f. 59).

[81] Palmer, *Booke of the Foundacion*, p. 3.

[82] Bodleian Library, MS Gough Norfolk 20, ff. 33, 72ᵛ.

[83] W. Rye, ed., *The Visitation of Norfolk ... 1563, 1613* (Harleian Society, xxxii, 1891), p. 153; NRO, Bradfer Lawrence MS 1C/8.

[84] NRO, Y/C19/5, ff. 139ᵛ, 145, 148, 156, 157, 169ᵛ, 171, 174ᵛ, 177, 178ᵛ, 180, 185ᵛ, 188.

[85] NRO, Y/C19/5, f. 164.

esteem, he attempted to gain further prestige by acting as an unofficial agent for the Assembly on various items of legal business in London.[86]

At first all went well, but, once again, a fatal combination of hubris and impetuosity proved his undoing. By overestimating his own influence at Westminster, while laying claim there to an authority he did not possess, he succeeded only in accumulating unwelcome expenses. An astonishing claim for £60 was rejected out of hand by the borough auditors in May 1617, largely because it had been 'disbursed to small purpose'.[87] Nothing daunted, he compounded the offence by covertly borrowing 'diverse somes of moneys ... not only to his owne discredit but to the discreditt of this Towne'. This flagrant betrayal of public trust could not go unpunished. After a protracted dispute, in March 1619 the Assembly again ejected him 'out of this house & societye', while insisting upon the repayment of loans 'which he pretended to be for the dispatche of the Townes busyness when hee was in nothing imployed'.[88] Manship's response was rash, if predictable, resulting in his appearance before the local bench in the following September, when he was bound over in sureties totalling £60 to keep the peace.[89] He was finally discharged on 6 April 1620, appearing one day later before the Assembly to make an abject apology 'for publishing a pamphlet therbye extolling himselfe & defaming the Towne falselye & for divers other abuses and misdemeanours'.[90] Having done so much to uphold the authority of the ruling elite, Manship once again threatened to undermine its credibility through subversive and reckless speech. His downfall was complete.

In an attempt to restore his tarnished reputation, Manship now completed his *History of Great Yarmouth*. Had this remarkable tribute to his native town appeared a few years earlier, it would undoubtedly have been published at the borough's expense, but it was now too late for redemption. Grown 'old & sicklye', he was instead obliged to petition the Assembly for relief in June 1625, being granted a lump sum of £3, which was augmented four months later by a pension of 4s. a week for what remained of his life.[91] In the following July his widow submitted a similar appeal for assistance, on the ground that 'her husbandes booke, wherein hee made a colleccion & abstracte of this townes chartres, customes, libertyes & other matters concernyng this towne' surely merited reward.[92]

---

[86] NRO, Y/C19/5, ff. 158v, 172v, 174v, 177.

[87] NRO, Y/C19/5, ff. 179v, 192, 194.

[88] NRO, Y/C19/5, ff. 202, 203v.

[89] NRO, Y/C4/311, rot. 19v.

[90] NRO, Y/C4/312, rot. 15; Y/C19/5, f. 218.

[91] NRO, Y/C19/5, ff. 329v; Y/C19/6 (Assembly Book, 1625-1642), f. 3v.

[92] NRO, Y/C19/6, f. 29v.

Conclusion

Manship's achievements were not fully recognised until the nineteenth century. The lawyer and antiquary, Henry Harrod, who was commissioned to examine the borough archives in 1853, discovered that, as a result of negligence and poor security, all but twenty-eight of the 292 'public documents' listed so meticulously in 1612 had since been lost.[93] The hospital cartulary had also by then disappeared. Unlike Thomas Damet, who returned all the manuscripts that he borrowed in order to write his *Booke of the Foundacion*,[94] later generations of scholars proved far less trustworthy. A ruling of 1740 'that no person shall take any of the Town Books from the Town Clerk's Office without Order of Assembly for that purpose' came too late in the day, for by then much of the damage had been done.[95] It would not, in any case, have prevented the removal of a substantial quantity of material by Humphrey Prideaux, dean of Norwich, who was permitted on 14 February 1710 to borrow 'all such books as set forth any of the antiquities of this town, or the County of Norffolk ... for his better making his history of Norffolk'.[96] The loan seems never to have been returned. John Cordy Jeaffreson, who surveyed the Yarmouth records for the Royal Commission on Historical Manuscripts in 1883, felt that Harrod had been unnecessarily hard upon the dean and a myriad other 'pilfering collectors', since the principal culprits, in his view, were the authorities themselves. 'The borough of Yarmouth', he tartly observed, 'has been more fortunate in its historians than in the custodians of its literary evidence'.[97]

Circumstantial evidence suggests that Dean Prideaux may well have appropriated the hospital cartulary. According to a note on the inside cover, it was taken from the Town Clerk's office on 13 February 1710 by Thomas Royall.[98] Although the corporation agreed that the manuscripts earmarked for Prideaux's use were to be delivered to one Captain Fuller, it is quite possible that Royall, too, was acting on his behalf. What happened next? It seems that many of the Yarmouth records retained by the dean eventually found their way into the possession of Francis Blomefield, who intended to use them in his *Essay towards a Topographical*

---

[93] *HMC, Ninth Report: Part 1*, p. 300.
[94] NRO, Y/C19/4, ff. 185ᵛ-6.
[95] NRO, Y/C19/12 (Assembly Book, 1737-1750), f. 32.
[96] NRO, Y/C19/10 (Assembly Book, 1701-1718), f. 171. Prideaux's few surviving notes for the project confirm that he had access to material 'belonging to Yearmouth Towne Hutche', but they do not mention the cartulary: NRO, DCN 115/10, p. 191.
[97] *HMC, Ninth Report: Part 1*, pp. 299-300.
[98] Royall was to serve as town clerk between 1720 and 1739, but did not then hold office: Le Strange, *Norfolk Official Lists*, p. 171.

History of Norfolk.[99] Perhaps the cartulary was among them, but Blomefield died bankrupt in 1752 before starting work on the port, and his papers immediately went on sale. Some were acquired by his friend, 'Honest Tom' Martin, the owner of a magnificent collection of East Anglian manuscripts. In 1775, four years after Martin's death, many of the better items were purchased by the distinguished antiquary and topographer, Richard Gough (d.1809), who bequeathed them, along with all his other papers, to the Bodleian Library.[100] Such, however, was the demand for, and market in, collectable items among Norfolk's thriving antiquarian community that it would be unwise to speculate too closely about the cartulary's peregrinations before its arrival in Oxford as part of Gough's bequest.

Editorial note

Even after six centuries of wear and tear, the cartulary of St Mary's hospital remains a covetable object. Although it is comparatively small (the parchment pages measure 10.5 by 7.8 inches), the finely tooled leather binding, which was embellished with metal bosses and angle pieces delicately worked with a rose design, suggests that considerable care was devoted to its production. It was originally fastened with metal clasps, which have been lost, and was subsequently embossed on the front and back with the words 'Great Yarmouth'. That it was produced at a time when the borough set considerable store upon its written records is apparent from the quality of the script and the fact that spaces were deliberately left in the text for the insertion of decorated, perhaps illuminated initials. These were never added, probably because the hospital did not continue to attract sufficient investment to warrant the expenditure.

This edition of the cartulary of St Mary's hospital comprises Manship's 1614 translation of the original predominantly Latin text (numbers 1 to 9), together with a translation into modern English of the brief supplementary list of rents, also in Latin (number 10), which he omitted. He did not consider it necessary to translate or explain the abridged Medieval English version of the Latin regulations produced for use by the burgesses at the beginning of the fifteenth century (number 11), which is the last entry in the medieval cartulary. It here appears in its entirety.

Manship's translation is workmanlike, if literal, having apparently been

---

[99] Harrod, *Repertory*, p. 76. Other purloined documents were sold by the executors of Henry Swinden, whose *Ancient Burgh of Great Yarmouth* (1772) appeared after his death. But Swinden did not apparently consult the cartulary.

[100] See the relevant *DNB* articles for Blomefield (vi, pp. 249-51), Gough (xxiii, pp. 55-9) and Martin (xxxvi, pp. 983-5).

produced in some haste. Prone to circumlocution in his own writing, he cannot always resist the tendency to embroider the text with legal jargon. Thus, for example, the Latin *elongare* becomes 'to remove, elayn or carry forth'. Although he writes clearly in an excellent attorney's hand, there are occasional slips, redundant interpolations and repetitions, which are recorded in the editor's footnotes. Manship's omissions are indicated in the text through the use of italic in round brackets. Since his primary aim was to produce a legal record that would prove useful to the authorities, he took less trouble with the various addenda to the 1398 rental (number 6), leaving out some of the more illegible details, and generally ignoring changes in tense. Words and phrases emphasised by him through the use of larger, heavier letters are here reproduced in bold print, as are the words underscored by the scribe who produced the English text of the regulations (number 11). Punctuation has been modernised and, where necessary, added, in order to render the text more intelligible for the modern reader.

Manship employs Arabic numerals in his translation. Roman numerals used in document number 10 have been converted to Arabic.

Acknowledgements

The editor is grateful to the staff of the Bodleian Library, Oxford, the British Library, London, and the Norfolk Record Office for their assistance. She would also like to thank Paul Rutledge for placing his expert knowledge of the Yarmouth records so generously at her disposal.

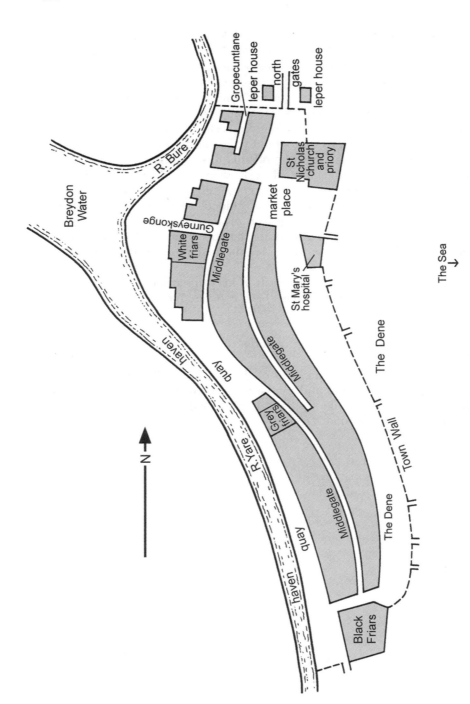

Figure 4. Medieval Great Yarmouth.

THE CARTULARY OF
ST MARY'S HOSPITAL, GREAT YARMOUTH

[*f. 32*] **Hereafter** followeth the true copyes of all the conveyunces of the hospitall of the Blessed Virgyn St Mary as they bee in the originall translated from out of Latyn into English in the yeere 1614, Mr John Gyles & Mr Nicholas Bright balyves & Mr Isaac Cowper custos or gardian of the same, by Henry Manship notary publique & burgis of the incorporacon.

Wheare theare was many hundred yeeres past by the zeale and godly disposition of the good men inhabitauntes of the said towne of Greate Yermouth, our predecessours, at theire owne proper costes and chardges built unto the honour of Almighty God and releife of the poore and miserable distressed persons inhabitinge within the said towne one hospitall, which in processe of tyme utterly decayinge and beinge wholly prostrated was agayne in the yeere of our Lord God one thowsand three hundred eighty six, and in the nynth yeere of the reigne of Kinge Richard the Second, by the balyves, burgesses and cominalty then beinge (who beinge no lesse godly mynded and well devoted) at theire proper costes and chardges allso to the like intent and purpose newly erected and built, with a new chappell in the middest of the same therein to say devyne service, consecratinge the same by the name of the hospitall of the Blessed Virgyn Mary, for rule and governement whereof diverse and sondry good lawes, orders and constitucions were then by them ordeyned and appoynted. Over which was a rectour or custos from tyme to tyme ordeyned to be chosen by the balyves, burgesses and cominalty of the said towne for the tyme beinge. All which were in that yeere by Henry, then bisshopp, and Alexander the deane[1] and (*the*) chapter of the Cathedrall Church of Norwich by theire severall instrumentes [*f. 32ᵛ*] under theire severall seales approved and confirmed, unto whome allso it pleased the said kinge to graunt his lettres patentes of mortmayne bearinge date at Woodstocke the two and twenty day of September in the sixteenth yeere of his reigne, as by the severall instrumentes them selves in that behalfe made more at lardge doth and may appeare. **Which** said office of custos hath been ever sithence the first foundacon thereof, and to this present day is, continewed and observed.

---

[1] Manship is here being anachronistic. Alexander de Tottington was prior of Norwich; the chapter was headed by a dean only after the Dissolution, by royal charter of 2 May 1538: R. Houlbroke, 'Refoundation and Reformation', in Atherton *et al.*, *Norwich Cathedral*, pp. 508-9.

And whereas it hath pleased the balyves, aldermen, burgesses and cominalty now beinge at an assembly holden in the Guildhall theare the fyfteenthe day of November last past to elect and choose Isaac Cowper, one of theire brethren, burgesse and alderman of Yermouth, to be rectour, custos and governour over the said hospitall and other almes howses in Yermouth and of the inhabitantes and fermours of the same and to doo and performe all thinges thereto belonginge,[2] who, fyndinge the old recordes, rentalles and writinges appurteyninge unto them to be by long continuance of tyme much decayed, defaced and in many places rent and torne not easyle to be read, hath with the consent and direccon of Mr John Gyles and Mr Nicholas Bright, now balyves, caused not only the same lettres patentes and sondry other instrumentes appurteyning to the said hospitall, but allso sondry other writinges appurteyninge unto other almes howses now within his chardge, to be truly translated from out of Latyn into [f. 33] English by Henry Manship, notary publique and burgesse of that corporacon, and the old rentalles to them belonginge which were almost worne out of memory to be veiwed and perused by sondry auncient persons and continewed untill this present and every of them to be ingrossed into this parchement booke, by perusall whereof, gentle reader, the posterite to come may easyle fynd out and understand all the forepassed and present estate of the same, as by the contentes followinge more at lardge doo and will manifestly appeare unto you.

Henricus Mansipus Notatorius Publicus

[*1. The refoundation of the hospital of St Mary the Virgin by the bailiffs and burgesses of Great Yarmouth, together with regulations for the staff and inmates, 2 May 1386. Confirmed by Henry Despenser, bishop of Norwich, and prior Alexander de Tottington and the chapter of Norwich Cathedral Priory, 8 May 1386. ff. 1–4 in the original Latin text*]

[*f. 33ᵛ*] **The** copy of the first foundacon of the said hospitall of the Blessed Virgyn Mary and of the orders appoynted to be observed therein with the approbacon of the same by the bisshopp of Norwich and (*the*) priour of that church for the tyme beinge.

In the name of the high and undevidable Trinite of the Father and of the Sonne and of the Holy Ghost and of the Blessed Virgyn Mary, the mother of God and man, Jesus Christ, the Saviour of man kind, **Wee** Raphe of

---

[2] NRO, Y/C19/5, Assembly Book 1598-1625, f. 121. Cowper's tenure of office was brief, for he was removed, on unspecified grounds, on 9 October 1615: f. 157ᵛ. His account, which recorded arrears of over £24, was approved by the Assembly in the previous March: f. 146ᵛ.

Ramsey, Nicholas of Drayton, Warrin Lucas and Adam Haypon,[3] balyves
of the towne of Greate Yermouth, and John of Beverley, John Ellys
(*William atte Gappe, John Beketoun, Richard Elys*), John of Rollisby, Robert at
Gapp, Alexander Fastolff, John Hacon, Edmond Sylke, Hugh at Fenn,
Roger Adam, William of Oxney, Robert Hulm,[4] Thomas March, John of
Hale, Peter Benett, Symon Geryn, Oliver Spycer, Edmond Bee, Lawrence
Stevens, Thomas Bateman, John Rayle, Adam Alot and all and singuler
other the burgesses of the said towne, with one mynd, will and consent of
the cominalty of the same, for the health of our sowles and of our progenitours, one hospitall in honour of the Blessed Virgyn Mary within the
boundes of the parish church of St Nicholas of the same towne, by our
progenitours and predecessours for poore and miserable persons to be
therein received, releived[5] and susteyned first founded and built, but after-
wardes beinge fallen downe, prostrated and defaced, have appoynted to be
renewed, repayred and re-edificed with a convenyent chappell, and have
at our costes and chardges erected and established the [*f. 34*] same.
Which hospitall with the said convenyent chappell wee hope and doe
determyn assoone as convenyently wee may by Godes helpe to indow
accordingly.

In which said hospitall wee will and ordeyne by the consent and
approbacon of the reverend father in Christ, Lord Henry by the grace of
God bisshopp of Norwich, (*and*) the priour and chapter of the Cathedrall
Church of the said city (*of Norwich*) that theare shalbe hereafter one rector
or gardian, eight bretheren and so many systers.[6] Which gardian or custos
shall have the governaunce and rule of the said bretheren and siusters and
of all other theare livinge and the keepinge of the (*afore*)said hospitall, and
by us and our successors balyves (*and*) burgesses and (*the*) comminalty of the
(*afore*)said towne as often as neede shall require shalbe chosen and
appoynted. Neyther will wee that the said custos theare shalbe perpetuall
but for such tyme as wee and our successours for the tyme beinge shall
thinke him meete and profitable.

Yet our will is that aswell those brethren as siusters shall remayne theare
for ever, except theire demerittes shall otherwise worthely require and
procure theire expulsion. **The** (*reception and*) admission of which bretheren
and siusters [*f. 34ᵛ*] so often as he or she shalbe to be receyved shall hereafter perteyne to the gardian or custos of the said hospitall with the consent
of the balyves and burgesses for evermore.

---

[3] *Adam Hayron*: original text, f. 1.   [4] *Robert Hulym*: original text, f. 1.
[5] *lodged*: original text, f. 1.   [6] *and eight sisters*: original text, f. 1.

Allso wee will and ordeyne that every one that is so to be admitted a brother or siuster (*there*) shall before the said custos and others the felow bretheren and siusters of the same hospitall uppon the Holy Evangelist solemply taken sweare fealty to God, the Blessed Virgyn Mary and to the hospitall afore said.

And that all that which they then have, or hereafter shall have, theire sommes of money and the names of theire creditours and debtours to the custos for the tyme beinge ones every yeere (*they*) shall make knowne, discover and reveale with out fraude or coven if thereto they shalbe by the custos reasonable required.

And that the same goodes or any of them, except for theire expences and other honest occacions, out of the said hospitall they shall (*not*) presume to remove, elayn or carry forth; but those theire goodes which they shall happen to have at the tyme of theire death they shall wholly leave and dispose to the said hospitall into two partes to be (*equally*) devyded: that is one parte thereof to the repayringe and sustentacon of the said hospitall and the other parte by the handes of the said custos amongst [*f. 35*] the bretheren and siusters theare faythfully to be imployed and bestowed.

And wee doe moreover ordeyne and appoynt that all and every the said bretheren and siusters within six dayes after theire admission and receipt shall sweare obedyence to the said custos in all lawfull commandementes; and that they shall not thenceforth use in theire upper garmentes or hose any other than darke russett[7] or in parte blacke nor otherwise unlesse it be; vayles of silke they shall not weare.

And wee doe allso will and ordeyne that the custos theare shall take unto him one seculer preist which he shall hyre to serve in the said hospitall and to pray for the balyves and burgesses and all the comminalty of the said towne and for the custos, bretheren, siusters and all benefactours of the said hospitall, and allso devyne rytes theare to celebrate for them in the chappell aforesaid. **Provided** allwayes that the said preist shall not celebrate any those holy exercises uppon the Sonday or on any the festivall dayes which be ordeyned for the worshipp of God or of sayntes, or other dayes wherein the people by any lawes are to absteyne from theire manuall trades whilest High Masse is in celebratinge, nor uppon any other dayes not so festivall whilest the Masse of Requiem which are dulie[8] songe for the dead [*f. 35ᵛ*] within the said parish church of St Nicholas are in celebratinge, but that from the performinge of any such rytes in the said chappell from the tyme

---

[7] *black russet*: original text, f. 1ᵛ.   [8] *daily*: original text, f. 1ᵛ.

of the begyninge of the celebratinge of the said Masses in the foresaid parish church untill the end of the same he shall wholly absteyne, least thereby they doe withdraw the parishoners of the said parish from the said church (which God forbid).

And that the said preist which is to celebrate the rytes in the said chappell[9] shall performe them with a low or modest voice (*that is to say*) with out usinge any note or songe theare.

And that not any other secular or regular preist shall any day say masse theare[10] except he first have and obteyne licence of the priour of the said church of St Nicholas so to doo, except it happen that the preist of the said hospitall by a continuall or present casuall infirmite be letted or (*by other accident be*) hindred, at which tyme any other preist secular or regular, which eyther the said custos or preist of the (*said*) hospitall shall for the tyme of such sicknes or infirmite hyre, may lawfully in manner and forme aforesaid say Masse theare. So allwayes that but one Masse onely be any day theare celebrated except licence first had and obteyned as abovesaid.

[*f. 36*] **And** wee will moreover and ordeyne that in the said chappell theare be a small bell wherewith every morninge they shall ringe to prayers[11] one tyme onely and no more, also to Masse but ones, and after the Ghospell of the Masse before the elevacon of the body of Christ ones, and at eveninge prayer[12] one tyme onely. **Which** eveninge prayers[13] shall not in any wise be sayd whilest other the solempnities[14] be used in the parish church (*of St Nicholas*) of Yermouth aforesaid.

Also that at eveninge prayers in like manner all be done (*so that vespers and prayers are said every day there*) with a low and modest voyce without songe.

And wee doe also ordeyne and appoynt that all such oblacions as shall happen to be offred within the said hospitall or chappell for any cause whatsoever the said custos[15] to the use and profite of the said priour of the said church of St Nicholas shall faythfully and diligently keepe, or elles shall cause them so to be kept, that those wholly and without any diminition or lessinnge within the space of eight dayes after the (*time of the*) receipt of them unto the said priour of the said church of St Nicholas for the tyme beinge, or to his lawfull deputy in that behalfe appointed, he shall deliver. But of the guiftes or rewardes given in pure almes to the said hospitall or to

---

[9] *in the said hospital*: original text, f. 2.   [10] *in the said chapel*: original text, f. 2.
[11] *ring to matins*: original text, f. 2.   [12] *and to vespers*: original text, f. 2.
[13] *which vespers*: original text, f. 2.   [14] *solemn vespers*: original text, f. 2.
[15] *the custos of the said hospital*: original text, f. 2.

the sustentacon of the said brothers or siusters, especially uppon Good Frydayes or the feast of th'Anunciacion of the Blessed Virgyn Mary,[16] the said priour shall not receyve or have any thinge.

[*f. 36ᵛ*] **And** wee will and ordeyne that the said brothers and siusters dayle and at all canounicall howres, and especially at the tyme of celebrating of Masse theare,[17] shalbe altogether present untill the end thereof; and that every one of them shall say one hundred and fifty tymes the Lordes Prayer with so many tymes Salutacions of the Blessed Virgyn Mary most humbly and devoutly, except by a very reasonable cause to the contrary they be lett and hindred, for the wellfare of all the benefactours of the said hospitall. **Also** that they all doe live continently and chastly, and that if any of them of any incontinency be lawfully convicted he (*or she*) shall loose the fowrth parte of his or theire porcion which that yeere shall of the common almes or otherwise of the alowance of the said hospitall happen to him or her. Which wee will, in manner aforesaid expressed, into two partes to be equally devyded and bestowed; and if any of the bretheren or siusters shall restore to any such offender any parte of that which shalbe so geven unto him or her, and thereof shalbe duly convicted, the same parte and so much more of his own porcion he shall loose, which wee will to be observed uppon the buildinge of the said hospitall.

And wee will and ordeyne that no maryed man or maryed woman shall from henceforth be admitted to be brother or siuster of that hospitall.

[*f. 37*] **And** moreover wee will and graunt that every one of the said bretheren and siusters, after the canonicall howres and that they have heard the Masse aforeseid and shall have said theire prayers beforemencioned, they shall or may use and exercise every day which is not a holy day theire art or gaynfull occupacon in the hospitall afore said or withoute (*in the town*), so allwayes that they doe not any thinge in preiudice, damage or scandale of the said hospitall. Neyther shall they lay owte (*of the said hospital*) in the night or otherwise absent them selves after the bell of cover fyer hath doone ringinge (*in the said parish church*).

And wee will also that they may dyne with theire freindes in the towne and may travayle also to visite theire freindes in the country,[18] havinge first had and obteyned leave of the said custos so to doo.

---

[16] 25 March.   [17] *in the aforesaid chapel*: original text, f. 2ᵛ.

[18] *and they may go on pilgrimage (peregrinare) outside the town and visit their friends who are outsiders (amicos suos forinsecos visitare)*: original text, f. 2ᵛ.

And that none shalbe receyved to bee a brother or siuster theare except he or shee have accomplished the thirteth yeere of theire age, without an evident and reasonable cause shall in that behalfe be apparant.

And we (*also*) will and ordeyne that the said brothers and siusters shall live peaceably and modestly together without usinge any contumelious or unbeseeminge or scoldinge wordes whatsoever. **And** also shall absteyne from accustomable hauntinge of [*f. 37ᵛ*] taverns, and shall not discover any of the counselles of theire bretheren or siusters, nor make any complaynt against any of theire bretheren and siusters of any offence doon by one to another but only to the said custos of the said hospitall, unlesse the offence be of such qualitie as by the said custos it may not justly be corrected or lawfully amended.

Wee will allso that the brothers and siusters of the said hospitall which be able to worke or digg in theire gardens or to dresse them or doo other light workes shalbe there unto compelled by the said custos, and he to rewarde them accordinge to his discretion.

And wee will also and decree that the custos for the tyme beinge shall ordeyne and appoynt one of the brothers and one of the siusters which he shall thinke to be of an honest life and good conversacon,[19] and shall cause them to sweare that they shall day and night take an earnest care over the bretheren and siusters (*aforesaid*), and the offendours shall reprove and rebuke; and that if any of them after such reprofe or correccion shall not reforme and amend them selves then they the name of the offender with the qualitie of the offence unto the (*afore*)said custos without delay shall reveale and make knowne, to th'end that the custos him selfe (as by (*the obligations of*) his office he is bound) may them ponish, keepe under and restreyne accordinge as shall be [*f. 38*] most pleasinge to Almighty God, so allwayes that the offence be such that the (*aforesaid*) custos may lawfully doe[20] it without prejudicinge the right of any other.

And wee will (*also*) that by the same custos theare shalbe assigned one of the felow brethren aforesaid which every night shall shut the gate with a lock and key, which doth inclose the places within which the said bretheren and siusters doe lodge[21], and the same key shall he diligently keepe so that neyther any brother or siuster unto or from the said hospitall after the ringinge of the cover fyer at the parish church aforesaid be finished be

---

[19] *honest conversation and good life*: original text, f. 3.
[20] *may lawfully correct and punish*: original text, f. 3.
[21] *sleep*: original text, f. 3.

permitted to goe owt or in, the parish preist which shall heere confession or shall administer the sacramentes theare if neede require onely except.

And wee doe allso ordeyne and establish that if any of the brothers or siusters aforesaid against theise statutes or ordinances (*beforesaid*) or any article in them conteyned by any collorable meanes shall be mischievous, litigious or contentious he or she by the said custos, by with holdinge such porcion as shall happen to fall to him or her so offendinge due, or by any other lawfull meanes, shall duly (*be*) chastice(*d*); and if he or she will not amend they shall be wholy expelled from the said hospitall, neyther shall they be at any tyme admitted thither agayne without the speciall assent and admission of the comminalty of the towne aforesaid.

[*f. 38ᵛ*] **And** wee allso will (*and ordain*) that the (*afore*)said custos (*of the aforesaid hospital*) shall within three dayes after admission present the (*aforesaid*) preist whome he will hyre to performe devyne service in that place unto the priour of the church of St Nicholas of Greate Yermouth for the tyme beinge, before whome, in the presence of the balyves of the said towne, if theare they will (*beinge required*) be present, (*we will that*) the said preist, layinge his hand uppon the Holy Evangelist, shall take a corporall oath that he all the articles aforesaid so many as concerne himselfe or his office (*and*) especially the savinge of the rightes of the church of the (*afore*)said St Nicholas, shall withoute all fraud and subtilty faithfully and wholly preserve and keepe, and that to the said parish church of St Nicholas in any thinge he shall not harme, nor asmuch as in him is suffer any damage to be doone there unto by any other.

Unto the true performance of all which abovesaid, aswell concerninge the foresaid church as the ordinances and statutes above written, every custos (*there*) for the tyme beinge in his first creacion or admission shall take his corporall oth before he doth any thinge in the busynes before the said priour of Greate Yermouth and the balyves of the said towne which for the tyme shalbe withoute all fraud or covin.

And because wee will that all and singuler the premisses may have firme and stable perpetuite and continuaunce wee have in more (*fidelity and*) testimony there- [*f. 39*] of caused the seale of our cominalty aforesaid, with the consent of all the said cominaltye, to these (*our*) presentes (*letters*) to be affixed. **And** wee doe requyre[22] and most instantly requyre the foresaid reverend father, Lord Henry, by the grace of God bisshopp of Norwich our diocesian, and the worshippfull and religious men, the priour and

---

[22] *request*: original text, f. 3ᵛ.

chapter of the Cathedrall Church of Norwich, that in expresse approbacon of all and singuler the premisses abovesaid they wold be pleased theire seales to these presentes to command and cause to be sett, that so by the puttinge of the seales thereunto this our present intent may be cleerely defended and strengthened forevermore. Dated at Yermouth the second day of the moneth of May in the yeere of Our Lord one thowsand three hundred fower score and six (*etc*).

And wee Henry, by the devyne permission bishhopp of Norwich, consideringe all and singuler the premisses (*above written*) to be pleasinge and acceptable to Almighty God, the same asmuch as to us belongeth and the law doth permit, at the instance and request of the balyves and burgesses aforesaid, by aucthorite episcopall doe approve and confirme by these presentes, which by the fixing of our seale to the perpetuall memory of future tymes we have caused to be published, savinge to us and to our successours in all[23] thinges all manner ordinary power and episcopall customes and usages and to our church of Norwich by right and dignite belonginge. Dated at Norwich the eight day of the moneth of May in the yeere of [*f. 39ᵛ*] Our Lord God one thowsand three hundred fower score and six, and of our consecration the seaven(*teen*)th.

And wee brother Alexander, (*the*) priour, and (*the*) chapter of the Cathedrall Church of Norwich doe acknowledge and confesse that wee upon all and singuler the premisses have had oversight and provident deliberacon and fyndinge the same to agree well together, whereby wee doe approve, ratifie and asmuch as in us is doo confirme, savinge in all thinges to the church of Norwich and to the church of St Nicholas of Greate Yermouth to which wee doo canonically reteyne to the propre use all rightes, and allso to the church of Norwich the dignite thereof. **In more** testimony whereof the comon seale of our chapter to these presentes is appendant. Geven in our chapiter howse at Norwich the eight day of May in the yeere of Our Lord God one thowsand three hundred fower score and six abovewritten.

[*2. Agreement between Prior Alexander de Tottington and the chapter of Norwich Cathedral Priory, on the one part, and the bailiffs and burgesses of Yarmouth, together with the warden and residents of the hospital of St Mary the Virgin, on the other, for the settlement of disputes arising over religious observance in the hospital, 25 November 1386. Confirmed by Henry Despenser, bishop of Norwich, 20 December 1386. ff. 4ᵛ-6 in the original Latin text*]

---

[23] Manship interpolates a redundant 'and all' here.

[*f. 40*] **All the** children of the blessed mother the Church shall knowe, (*and*)
more especiall those whome the busynes underwrittwen doth or may in
any wise hereafter touch or concerne, **That** wheare lately betweene the
religious men brother Alexander, priour of the Cathedrall Church of
Norwich, and the covent of the same place, havinge and inioyinge to there
owne use the parish church of St Nicholas of Greate Yermouth within the
diocesse of Norwich, on the one partye, and the balyves and burgesses of
the said towne of Greate Yermouth and the custos, bretheren and siusters
of the hospitall of the Blessed Virgyn St Mary of the same towne, which
hospitall the same balyves and burgesses have of late founded and builded
and repayred for the receipt and sustentation of poore and miserable
persons, with a decent chappell therein, on the other partye, (*of and*)
Uppon the foundinge and buildinge of which hospitall and chappell and
of the celebratinge of the devine rightes theare, and allso uppon the
indempnifyinge in that behalfe of the (*afore*)said priour and covent and of
the (*afore*)said church of St Nicholas, greate matter of question even to the
breakinge of all frindshipp hath arysen. Which the partyes afore said
beinge willinge to avoyd, and desyrous to have peace and amytie uppon
the premisses to the honour of God (*and*) of the Glorious Virgyn Mary and
of Christian zeale to the effectinge [*f. 40ᵛ*] of a worke of such charitie,[24]
many treatyes beinge had and the lawfull rytes, allegacions and reasons
seen and heard[25] that this question or contention may be wholy quyeted
and that tranquilite may flourish, desyre of charite and the unitie of
concord may be strengthened, the learned counsell of eyther side medi-
atinge the cause for them and theire cause,[26] least the said busynes may
eftsoones hereafter fall agayne into question they have with one mynd
ordered, agreed and freindly compounded, oredeyned and a perpetuall
gladsome end have made in manner followinge (that is to say): That the
custos, brothers and suisters of the said hospitall which forthe tyme shalbe
may have one seculer preist, who for the balyves (*and*) burgesses (*of Great
Yarmouth aforesaid*)[27] and the custos, bretheren and siusters and all benefactours of the same hospitall and allso for the whole comminalty of the said
towne and for the sowles of all deceased faythfull beleevers devoutly to
pray, and other devyne rytes every day in the (*afore*)said chappell to celebrate, observinge the moderations underwritten:

First that the preist which theare shall celebrate shall with a modest and
low voice, that is without note, the devyne rytes shall celebrate, and that he

---

[24] *out of zeal for the honour of God and of the Glorious Virgin Mary, the mother of Christ, that a work of
such charity may be effected*: original text, f. 4ᵛ.
[25] *the rights (iuribus) examined and the allegations and reasons in respect thereof heard*: original text, f. 4ᵛ.
[26] *for them and their successors*: original text, f. 4v.
[27] Manship here adds a redundant 'and cominalty'.

shall not administer them uppon the Lordes day or of any festivall dayes appoynted for the reverence of God or his saintes to absteyne from (*manual*) workinge [*f. 41*] whilest High Masse, nor uppon any other dayes not so holy whylest the Masse of Requiem for the dead, usually made (*each day*) with note, in the said parish church of St Nicholas are celebrating. But from the celebratinge of the same devyne rites in the said chappell from the tyme of the (*beginning of the*) celebratinge of the said Masses in the fore-said parish church untill the end of them he wholy shall absteyne, least the parisshioners from the said theire parish church by any meanes they be withdrawne, which God forbid.

Also it is further covenaunted and agreed betwene the partyes abovesaid that not any other preist whatsoever − secular (*or*) regular or exempt or not exempt - then the aforesaid preist of the hospitall shall at any tyme be suffered to say Masse in the said chappell, except by the licence desyred and (*also*) obteyned of the said priour of the foresaid church of St Nicholas for the tyme beinge he be permitted, except onely if it shall happen the preist of the hospitall aforesaid by infirmite not perpetuall, but for that present accidental, or other cause lawfull to be lett or hindred, that then any other preist regular or secular which the custos or preist of the (*said*) hospitall shall hyre for that purpose duringe this impedyment devyne rytes theare in manner abovesaid lawfully may cele-brate (*so that each day one Mass only is celebrated, unless licence is sought and obtained*). **And** if it shall happen any oblations hereafter to be made in the (*afore*)said hospitall or chappell that then all [*f. 41ᵛ*] and singuler the said oblacions, whensoever or for what cause soever (*made*), the said custos (*of the said hospital for the time being*) shall (*faithfully and diligently*) keepe or (*thus*) cause to bee kept, and the same within the terme of eight dayes then next followinge after the (*day of the*) receipt of them to the foresaid priour of the said church of St Nicholas of Greate Yermouth, or in his absence to his deputy leiuetenaunt, without any diminution shall fully and wholy deliver; but of the guiftes or colleccions which shalbe geven to the said hospitall or bretheren and siusters (*of the same*) in pure almes unto theire releife, (*and*) especially uppon that day on which our Saviour Christ Jesus suffered death uppon the crosse and (*also*) uppon the day of the Anunciacon by the Aungell unto the Blessed Virgyn that Christ shold of her be borne, the foresaid priour of the church of St Nicholas shall not chalendge any thinge.

And it is moreover agreed and ordeyned betweene the said partyes that the foresaid chappell shall have onely one litle bell, with the which they shall every day ringe to morninge mattens onely one tyme, and to Masse but ones, and after the Ghospell of the Masse before the elevacon of the body of Christ ones, and at evensonge[28] ones and but onely one tyme at the sayinge of eveninge prayer, which (*vespers and prayers*) daylie shall be theare performed with a submisse or low voyce without note. Which eveninge prayer[29] shall not in any wise at any tyme be sayd at [*f. 42*] such tyme as the solemne prayers[30] in the parish church of St Nicholas of the said towne of Yermouth are celebrated.

Also that the brothers and siusters of the said hospitall shall daylie in (*each of*) the canonicall howers and in celebratinge of the Masse theare be present together from the begyninge to th'end, and every one of them shall every day duly and devoutly say one hundred and fifty tymes the Lordes Prayer with so many tymes the Salutacon of the Blessed Virgyn for the benefactours of the said place, except there shalbe lawfull cause to hinder the same.

It is allso by the partyes aforesaid agreed, covenaunted and ordeyned that every custos in the said hospitall takinge uppon him the chardge thereof, in the begyninge before any his administracon theare, he shall execute before the priour of the (*afore*)said church of St Nicholas and the balyves of the said towne which for the tyme beinge shalbe, if uppon notice they will be theare present,[31] an oth uppon the Holy Evangelist that he without deceipt or fraud the fore said (*premises,*) covenauntes and ordinances asmuch as in him is inviolable shall keepe and performe and shall doe his best to have them faythfull observed and kept.

And it is moreover agreed and ordeyned that in every admission of the preist to serve the said hospitall (*in spiritual matters*) the foresaid custos which for the tyme shalbe within three dayes after such admission [*f. 42ᵛ*] (*the same priest*) to the said priour of the church of St Nicholas shall present. Which preist, before the tyme he shall take uppon him to administer any thinge in the busynes, shall take the like oth before him, that is to say that the foresaid covenauntes and ordinances so many as doe concerne him or his office shall observe and keepe, and that the said church or the rightes of the said church of St Nicholas in any thinge he shall not in any wise preiudice or hinder, nor by any other asmuch as in him is shall permitt to be preiudiced or hindred.

In Witnesse and fayth whereof the partyes aforesaid, that is the foresaid priour and covent of the Cathedrall Church of Norwich theire common

---

[28] *vespers*: original text, f. 5ᵛ.

[29] *which same vespers*: original text, f. 5ᵛ.

[30] *solemn vespers*: original text,, f. 5ᵛ.

[31] Manship interpolates a redundant 'shall take' here.

seale, and the foresaid balyves and burgesses and the custos, bretheren and siusters of the said hospitall the common seale of the said towne of Greate Yermouth to this present writinge in the manner of a *(chirograph)* made and indented have[32] putt, whereof one parte doth remayne with the priour and covent and the other with the balyves and burgesses *(and the)* custos, bretheren and siusters aforesaid. **And** that this present writinge and all thinges in them conteyned may be firmely kept forevermore, the fore said partyes the seale of the reverend father in Christ, *(Lord)* Henry, by the grace of God busshop of Norwich, who willingly *(proffers his consent to them,)* in approbacon and confirmacon of all and every the premisses aforesaid[33] have caused to be sett. Dated at Norwich the fyve and twenty day of the moneth of November in the yeere of Our Lord God one thowsand three hundred fowerscore and six.

[*f. 43*] **And wee** Henry, by the devyne permission bisshop of Norwich, desyringe with such affeccon as is meete the peace and tranquilite of our subiectes, perusinge all and singuler the premisses abovesaid and the same beinge diligently examined and discussed, the same asmuch as to us appurteyneth and by law is permitted doe approve and ratifye and by our bishoplike *authoritie* doe confirme. **And** because wee doe consider and fynd the foresaid hospitall to have been and is godly and meritoriously built and made, and to a laudible use founded and ordeyned, therefore at the instant request and devoute desyre of the partyes aforesaid, to the liftynge up of the honour of God and of the Glorious Virgyn Mary, the mother of Christ, that a worke of such charite that the devyne rytes in the chappell of the *(afore)*said hospitall may in manner aforesaid be lawfully celebrated, and *(that)* the foresaid custos, bretheren and siusters and theire successours heere and the preist in forme aforesaid theare celebrate, by the tenour hereof doo give leave and licence and most gratiously faviour the same forever hereafter to indure, savinge unto us allwayes all busshoplike customes aswell to our church of Norwich as to our dignite by law appurteyninge. Given under our signet in the chappell of our pallace of Norwich the twenty day of the moneth of December in the yeere of Our Lord one thowsand three hundred fower score and six and of our conse-cration the seaventeenth.

[*3. Licence in mortmain granted by letters patent of Richard II to William Oxney and Robert Howlyn, burgesses of Yarmouth, permitting them to settle a messuage, seventeen cottages and 100s. annual rent in the town upon the bailiffs and comminalty for the*

---

[32] Manship here repeats 'have'.
[33] Manship here interpolates a redundant 'his seale'.

support of the hospital of St Mary the Virgin, 22 September 1392.[34]
f. 6ᵛ in the original Latin text]

Heere followeth the licence of mortmayne graunted by King Richard the Second touchinge the hospitall aforesaid.

Richard, by the grace of God Kinge of England [*f. 43ᵛ*] and of Fraunce and Lord of Ireland, to all that these presentes shall see or heare greetinge. Although by the common counsayle of our realme of England it is enacted and ordeyned that it shall not be lawfull to religious men or others to enter into the fee symple of any other, so that the same to mortmayne shall comme, without the licence of us and of the capitall lordes of whome the same be (*directly*) holden,[35] wee not withstandinge of our especiall grace and for the somme of forty markes,[36] which our welbeloved the balyves and comminalty of the towne of Greate Yermouth to us have paid, have graunted and given licence for us and our heires asmuch as in us lyeth unto William Oxney, burgesse of the towne of Greate Yermouth, and to Robert Howlyn, burgesse of the towne of Greate Yermouth, that they one messuage, seaven*ten* cottages and one hundred shillinges of rent, with theire appurtenaunces in the towne of Greate Yermouth, which of us is holden in burgage, may give and assigne to the foresaid balyves and comminalty, **to have** and to hold to the said balyves and cominalty and to theire successours to the use and sustentacon of certeyne poore and infirme persons within the (*afore*)said towne and for certeyn other workes of pyete and devotion, accordinge to the ordinaunce of the said William and Robert in this behalfe to be made, supported and susteyned forevermore, and unto the said balyves and cominalty that they the said messuage, cottages and rentes aforesaid with theire appurtenaunces of the foresaid William and Robert [*f. 44*] may receive and hold to them and to theire successours aforesaid in forme aforesaid forever as is aforesaid. And by the tenour hereof likewise wee have given speciall licence, the said Statute or for that the foresaid messuage, cottages and rentes of us be holden in burgage as is aforesaid not withstandinge. Not beinge willinge that the foresaid William and Robert or theire heires, or the foresaid balyves and cominalty or theire successours by reason of the premisses by us or our heires, our iustices, escheatours, sheriffes or other the balyves or ministers of us or our heires whosoever by that occacon be burthened, molested or in any thinge shold be chardged, savinge not withstandinge to us and to our heires the services thereof due and accustomed. **In Witnesse** whereof

---

[34] *CPR, 1391-1396*, p. 170.

[35] See S. Raban, *Mortmain Legislation and the English Church 1279-1500* (Cambridge, 1982), chapters one and two, for the background to this legislation.

[36] £26 13s. 4d.

these our lettres wee have caused to be made patentes. Witnesse my selfe at Woodstock the two & twenty day of September in the yeere of our reigne the sixteen.

[*4. Grant by the bailiffs and comminalty of Yarmouth to William Oxney and Robert Howlyn, burgesses, of one messuage, seventeen cottages and 6s. annual rent, 1 October 1397.*
ff. 7–8 in the original Latin text]

A Copy of the graunt of the said premisses from the balyves of Yermouth unto William Oxney and Robert Howlyn.

Know all men present and to come that wee, the balyves and cominaltye of the towne of Greate Yermouth, have graunted and given and by this our present writinge doe confirme unto William of Oxney and Robert Howlyn, burgesses of the said towne of Yermouth, one messuage with (*its*) buildinges and appurtenaunces scituate [*f. 44ᵛ*] in the said towne of Greate Yermouth between the comon ground of the said towne of Yermouth on the south and north, and abutteth uppon the common wall of the said towne of Yermouth towardes the east and uppon the kinges high way towardes the west.

And wee have also graunted and given to the foresaid William and Robert seaventeen cottages with theire buildinges and appurtenaunces lyinge in the said towne of Greate Yermouth, whereof the first cottage lyeth in the said towne of Greate Yermouth between two comon lanes on the south and north, and abutteth uppon Middlegate towardes the west and uppon the land (*formerly*) of one Thomas of Drayton towardes the east.

The second cottage lyeth between the common lane on the north and the land (*formerly*) of one John of Ocle and John of Wickampton on the south, and abutteth uppon the land (*formerly*) of one Hanon[37] of Berton towardes the west and uppon the land (*formerly*) of one John Heldey[38] towardes the east.

The third cottage lyeth betweene the common lane on the south and the land of the chapleynes of the Charnell on the north, and abutteth uppon the Deane towardes the east and uppon the land of the said chapleynes of the Charnell and the land (*formerly*) of one Hugh Pamflot[39] towardes the west.

[37] *Hamon of Bertoun*: original text, f. 7.   [38] *John Holdeye*: original text, f. 7.
[39] *Hugh Panflot*: original text, f. 7.

The fowrth cottage lyeth between the comon lane on the south and the land of Thomas Bateman on the north, and abutteth upon the land of the said Thomas towardes the east and the land (*formerly*) of one Thomas[40] Beere towardes the west.

[*f. 45*] **The** fyveth cottage lyeth betweene two comon lanes on the south and north, and abbuteth uppon the Denn towardes the east and uppon the land of William (*of*) Oxney towardes the west.

The sixt cottage lyeth betweene two (*common*) lanes on the south and north, and abutteth uppon the land of Andrewe Bowyer towardes the east and uppon the land sometyme Clement Beere towardes the west.

The seaventh cottage lyeth betweene the comon lane on the south and the land (*formerly*) of John Reapes[41] on the north, and abutteth uppon the land of John Wrangill towardes the east and uppon the land (*formerly*) of the said John Reppis towardes the west.

The eight cottage lyeth betweene two comon lanes on the south and north, and abutteth uppon the Denn towardes the east and uppon the land of Thomas Westgate, taylour, towardes the west.

The nynth cottage lyeth betweene the comon lane on the north and the land (*formerly*) of John of Hall on the south, and abutteth uppon the Deane towardes the east and uppon the land (*formerly*) of William of Ludham, skinner, towardes the west.

The tenth cottage lyeth betweene the comon lane on the north and a certeyne entry perteyninge to the said cottage & the land of Peter Baxter on the south, and abutteth uppon the Deane towardes the east and the land (*formerly*) of John of Stalham, which be called Godsmen howses,[42] towardes the west.

The aleventh cottage lyeth betweene the comon lane on the north & the land (*formerly*) of [*f. 45ᵛ*] one Edmond Bee on the south, and abutteth on the land once of the said Edmond towardes the west and uppon the land of John of Byrlingham towardes the east.

The twelfe cottage lyeth betweene the common lane on the north and the

---

[40] *Clement Beere*: original text, f. 7.

[41] *John Reppis*: original text, f. 7.

[42] *Goddesmenshous*: original text, f. 7ᵛ. See number 9, below, for the hospital's acquisition of these almshouses.

land of Symon Catt, baxter,[43] & the land once of Robert of Marton on the south, and abutteth on the land of William Buskyn towardes the west and on the land once of John of Hunyngham towardes the east.

The thirteenth cottage lyeth betweene the land of John Wither, William Potter & William of Eccles on the south and the common lane on the north, and abutteth on the Deane towardes the east and on the land of Robert att Crosse towardes the west.

The fowerteenth cottage lyeth betweene the common way on the north and the land of John Dodge, bocher, on the south, and abutteth on the common way towardes the east and on the land of the said John Dodge towardes the west.

The fifteenth cottage lyeth betweene the common lane on the south and the land of Nicholas of Fordele on the north, and abutteth on Middlegate towardes the west and on the land of John of Hall towardes the east.

The sixteenth cottage lyeth betweene two common lanes on the south and north, and abutteth on the land once of Edmond of Burghe towardes the [*f. 46*] west and on Middlegate towardes the east.

And the seaventeenth cottage lyeth betweene the common lane on the north and the land of William of Worsted on the south, and abutteth on the land of Robert Bell towardes the west and on Middlegate towardes the east.

Wee have graunted allso and given and by this our present writinge confirmed to the foresaid William and Robert six shillinges of yearely rent to be given every yeere at the feast of St Edmond the Kinge and Martir[44] of the capitall messuage which once was Thomas Cobbals,[45] the which said messuage Robert Cobbals, nephew to the said Thomas, late heald in Yermouth aforesaid, and which six shillinges wee late had of the guift and legacy of Walter att Sonde towardes the keepinge of the bretheren & siusters of the hospitall of Blessed Mary in Yermouth aforesaid, as in the testament of the said Walter att Sonde appeareth. To have and to hold the said messauge and seaventeen cottages aforesaid, together with the foresaid six shillings (*rent*) yeerely to be given, with all theire appurtenaunces to the foresaid William & Robert, theire heires and assignes for ever of the capitall lordes of the fee by services from thence due & (*legally*) accustomed.

---

[43] A baxter is a baker.
[44] 20 November.
[45] *Thomas Cobbald*: original text, f. 8.

And wee the balyves and cominalty of the towne of Yermouth abovesaid the foresaid messuage (*and*) seaventeene cottages aforesaid, together with the foresaid rent of six shillinges yeerely to be given, with all theire appurtenaunces, to the [*f. 46*] foresaid William & Robert theires [*sic*] heires and assignes against all nacions will warrant forever. In more testimony whereof to this our present writinge our seale of cominalty of the towne of Yermouth aforesaid to these presentes is hanged, these beinge witnesses: John Elys, Raphe Ramsey, John att Cappe,[46] Edmond With, William Savage, Alexander att Capp,[47] Thomas Redberd & others. Dated at (*Great*) Yermouth aforesaid the Monday next after the feast of St Michaell th'archaungell[48] in the yeere of the reigne of Kinge Richard the Second after the Conquest the one and twenty, in the tyme of William Oxeney, John Beketoun, Thomas March and Thomas of Halle, then balyves of Yermouth aforesaid, &c.

[*5. Grant by William Oxney and Robert Howlyn, burgesses of Yarmouth, to the bailiffs and comminalty of a messuage, seventeen cottages and 100s. annual rent for the support of the inmates of the hospital of St Mary the Virgin, 5 January 1398.*
ff. 8ᵛ-14 in the original Latin text]

[*f. 47*] In the honour of our Lord Jesus Christ, the Blessed Virgyn Mary and of all the saintes Richard, by the grace of God Kinge of England and Fraunce and Lord of Ireland, to all to whome (*these*) present lettres shall comme greetinge.[49] Seeinge that of late our said Lord Richard, Kinge of England, of his especiall grace & for forty markes which the balyves and comminalty of the towne of Greate Yermouth to the said Lord Kinge paid, by vertue of the writinge of the said Lord Kinge dated at Woodstocke the two and twenty day of September in the yeere of the reigne of the said Kinge the sixteenth, graunted & gave liberty to William of Oxney and Robert Howlyn, burgesses of the said towne of Greate Yermouth, that they hold one messuage and seaventeene cottages & a hundred shillinges of yeerely rent with theire appurtenaunces in the said towne of Yermouth of the said Lord Kinge, which holden in burgage (*they*) may give and assigne to the foresaid balyves and cominalty. Wee the foresaid William and Robert, by vertue of the writinge of the lord Kinge aforesaid,[50] have graunted & by this our present writinge confirmed to the foresaid balyves

---

[46] *John atte Gappe*: original text, f. 8.

[47] *Alexander atte Gappe*: original text, f. 8.

[48] 29 September.

[49] The scribe begins this entry with the invocatory address of Richard II's licence in mortmain of 1392 (number 3 above), but perhaps realising that he had already transcribed it breaks off abruptly: original text, f. 8ᵛ.

[50] Manship here interpolates a redundant 'wee'.

and cominalty of the towne of Yermouth aforesaid towardes the keepinge of some poore men & of infirmities[51] within the towne aforesaid, and to certeyne other workes of piety & devotion, ny unto the ordinacon of those William and Robert in this parte to be done, supported and susteyned forever, all the [f. 47ᵛ] foresaid messuage, seaventeene cottages and one hundred shillinges of yeerely rent with all theire appurtenaunces in the towne of Greate Yermouth aforesaid under the forme which followeth ... [with minimal variations, the text of the previous charter is repeated, the messuage and seventeen cottages being described exactly as in number 4, above]

[f. 49] Wee have graunted allso and by this our present writinge confirmed to the foresaid balives and cominalty of the towne of Yermouth aforesaid one hundred shillinges of yeerely rent /And rent 5 li. in partes following/ to begyn every yeere at the feast of St Edmond the Kinge and Martir of diverse tenementes in the said towne of Greate Yermouth (that is to say):

Of the capitall messuage which once was Thomas Cobball,[52] which said messauge Robert Cobball, the nephew of the said Thomas, late held in Yermouth aforesaid, six shillinges of yeerely rent /6s. rent/, which six shillinges Walter atte Sonde gave and bequeathed in his testament to the keepinge of the brethren and sisters of the hospitall of the Blessed Mary in Yermouth aforesaid, as it [f. 49ᵛ] appeareth in the said testament of the said Walter atte Sonde.

Likewise of a tenement which John, the sonne of John Elys, late heald two shillinges and six pence /2s. 6d. rent/, which tenement lyeth in Yermouth aforesaid between two common lanes on the south and north, and abutteth on Middlegate towardes the east and on the land of the said John Elys towardes the west.

Likewise of a tenement which John of Beketon lately heald two shillings /2s. rent/, and lyeth betweene the land of Nicholas Kirkowe on the north and the land of William of Runham on the south, and abutteth on Middlegate towardes the east and on the land once of Bartholmew Nogan towardes the west.

Likewise of a tenement which William of Runham late heald two shillings /2s. rent/, and lyeth between the comon lane on the south and the land of John of Beketon on the north, and abutteth on the land of the said John of Beketon towardes the west and on Middlegate towardes the east.

---

[51] of the infirm (infirmorum): original text, f. 8ᵛ.
[52] Thomas Cobbald: original text, f. 9ᵛ.

Likewise of a tenement which John, the sonne of William att Cappe,[53] late heald twelve pence of yeerely rent */12d. rent/*, and lyeth between the comon lane on the north and the land of Bartholmew Elys on the south, and abutteth on Middlegate towardes the east and on the land of Symon Aunsell towardes the west.

Likewise of a tenement which Symon Thurkell[54] late heald two shillinges and six pence[55] of yeerely rent */2s. 6d. rent/*, and lyeth between the common lane on the north and the land of Thomas atte Chirche [*f. 50*] on the south, and abutteth on the Deane towardes the east and on the land of the said Symon towardes the west.

Likewise of a tenement which Thomas att Chirch late heald three pence of yeerely rent */3d. rent/*, and lyeth between the common lane on the south and the land of Symon Thurkild on the north, and abutteth on the land of the said Symon (*towardes the west*) and on the Deane towardes the East.

Likewise of a tenement which Roger of Drayton late heald, which once was Lawrence of Drayton, two shillinges of yeerely rent */2s. rent/*, and lyeth between two common lanes on the south and north, and abutteth on the Deane towardes the east and on the land of the said Roger towardes the west.

Likewise of one tenement which Alice of Drayton late heald twelve pence of yeerely rent */12d. rent/*, and lyeth between the common lane on the south and the land of Roger Kithode and the land of John of Ocle on the north, and abutteth on the land of John of Wykampton towardes the west and on the Deane towardes the east.

Likewise of a tenement which Peter of Selby late heald twelve pence of yeerely rent */12d. rent/*, and lyeth between the common lane on the north and the land once of Joffry of Drayton on the south, and abutteth on the land once of Simon Ta(*i*)lliard towardes the east and on the haven of Yermouth towardes the west.

Likewise of a tenement which John of Beverle late heald twelve pence of yeerely rent */12d. rent/*, [*f. 50ᵛ*] and lyeth betweene the common lane on the south and the land of John, the sonne of William Elys, on the north, and abutteth on the land of William Goddefeild[56] towardes the west and the land of the said John Elys towardes the east.

53 *William atte Gappe*: original text, f. 10.
54 *Symon Thurkeld*: original text, f. 10.
55 *two shillings and ten pence*: original text, f. 10.
56 *William Goddesfeld*: original text, f. 10ᵛ.

Likewise of a tenement which Thomas Martyn late heald two shillinges and six pence of yeerely rent /2s. 6d. rent/, and lyeth between the common lane on the north and the land once of Symon Hastinge on the south, and abutteth on Middlegate towardes the east and on the land of John Hacun towardes the west.

Likewise of one fishouse called Gavell Fishouse which John Houghesson late heald twelve pence of yeerely rente /12d. rent/, and lyeth between the comon lane on the south and the land of Henry Colman on the north, and abutteth on the land of Thomas White towardes the east and on the land of the said John Hughesson towardes the west.

Likewise of one tenement which Symon Aunsell late heald twelve pence of yeerely rent /12d. rent/, and lyeth between the common lane on the north and the land of Bartholmew Elys on the south, and abutteth on the land of John atte Cappe[57] towardes the east and on the land once of Richard att Cappe[58] towardes the west.

Likewise of one tenement which Robert Gare late heald twelve pence of yeerely rent /12d. rent/, and lyeth between the comon lane on the north and the land of Richard Midward on the south, and abutteth on the land of [f. 51] the prior and covent of Siltoun[59] and the land once of Peter Bennett towardes the east and on Middlegate towardes the west.

Likewise of one tenement which Nicholas Frere late heald twelve pence of yeerely rent /12d. rent/, and lyeth betweene the comon lane on the south and the land of Margery Bange on the north, and abutteth on the Deane towardes the east and on the land of Thomas Stace towardes the west.

Likewise of one tenement which Bartholmew Protolfe[60] late heald fower shillinges of yeerely rent /4s. rent/, and lyeth betweene two common lanes on the south and north, and abutteth on the Deane towardes the east and on the land once of Hughe of Norwich towardes the west.

Likewise of one tenement which Roger Fuller late heald fyve shillinges of yeerely rent /5s. rent/, and lyeth betweene the comon lane on the north and the land of the said Roger on the south, and abutteth on the Deane towardes the east and on the land once of Hugh Pannflott towardes the west.

[57] *John atte Gappe*: original text, f. 11.

[58] *Richard atte Gappe*: original text, f. 11.

[59] Sibton, the only Cistercian monastery in Suffolk, lay down the coast, a short distance inland from Dunwich: W. Page, ed., *Victoria County History of Suffolk*, *II* (1907), pp. 89-91.

[60] *Bartholmew Sprottolf*: original text, f. 11.

Likewise of a tenement which Beatrix of Blofeild late held twelve pence of yeerely rent */12d. rent/*, and lyeth between two common lanes on the south and north, and abutteth on the land once of Robert Cany[61] towardes the west and on the land once of Thomas White towardes the east.

Likewise of one tenement which Robert of Cantele, barbour, late heald twelve pence of yeerely rent */12d. rent/*, and lyeth between the common lane on the north and the land of the said [*f. 51ᵛ*] Robert and Thomas Bateman on the south, and abutteth on the land of John Lawes, maryner, towardes the west and on the land of the said Thomas Bateman towardes the east.

Likewise of a tenement which Alice, once the wife of John of Filby, late heald three shillinges of yeerely rent */3s. rent/*, and lyeth between two common lanes on the south and north, and abutteth on the Deane towardes the east and on the land once of Clement Bere towardes the west.

Likewise of one tenement which Richard Yuy late heald six shillinges[62] of yeerely rent */6s. rent/*, and lyeth betweene two common lanes on the south and north, and abutteth on the land of John of Hall and the land once of William of Ludham towardes the east and (*on*) the land once of the said Willliam of Ludham towardes the west.

Likewise of one tenement which Adam Hayron, spicer, late heald fyve shillinges of yeerely rent */5s. rent/*, and lyeth between the comon lane on the north and the land once of Jeaffry of Fornell[63] on the south, and abutteth on the Deane towardes the east and (*on*) the land once of Hughe of Baggele towardes the west.

Likewise of one tenement which William Stallon late heald twenty pence of yeerely rent */20d. rent/*, and lyeth betweene the common lane on the north and the land once of Jeoffry of [*f. 52*] Fordele on the south, and abutteth on Middlegate towardes the east and on the haven of Yermouth towardes the west.

Likewise of a tenement which William of Brissele late heald twelve pence of yeerely rent */12d. rent/*, and lyeth betweene the comon lane on the south and the land of Robert Bell on the north, and abutteth on the land of Jeoffry Wymark towardes the east and on the haven of Yermouth towardes the west.

[61] *Robert Davy*: original text, f. 11.
[62] *six pence*: original text, f. 11ᵛ.
[63] *Jeaffry de Fordele*: original text, f. 11v.

Likewise of a tenement which William of Worsted late heald eighteen pence of yeerely rent / 18d. rent/, and lyeth between the land once of Bennett of Rockhawe on the south and the comon lane and the land once of John of Ocle on the north, and abutteth on the have(n) of Yermouth towardes the west and the land once of the said John of Ocle and Middlegate towardes the east.

Likewise of a tenement which John Halman late heald six shillinges and eight pence of yeerely rent / 6s. 8d. rent/, and lyeth between the comon lane on the north and the land of Thomas of Aylesham on the south, and abutteth on the land of the said Thomas towardes the east and on the haven of Yermouth towardes the west.

Likewise of a tenement which Thomas of Hall, the sonne of John of Hall, late heald six shillinges and eight pence of yeerely rent / 6s. 8d. rent/, and lyeth between the comon lane called Cameanelynsrowe[64] on the south and [f. 52ᵛ] the land once of Adam of Claxton on the north, and abutteth on the Deane towardes the east and on the land of the said Thomas of Hall towardes the west, and which tenement conteyneth in length three score feete of men.

Likewise of a tenement which Leticia Pette, wortwoman,[65] late heald seaven pence of yeerely rent / 7d. rent/, and lyeth betweene the common lane on the south and the land of William of Barsham on the north, and abutteth on the land of the said William towardes the west and on Middlegate towardes the east.

Likewise of a tenement which William of Barsham, wright, late heald tenn pence of yeerely rent / 10d. rent/, and lyeth betweene the land of John of Halis, shipwright, on the north and the land of Letice Pette, wortwoman, and the common lane on the south, and abutteth on the land once of Richard Tyler towardes the west and on Middlegate towardes the east.

Likewise of a tenement which John Hales, shipwright, late held twelve pence of yeerely rent / 12d. rent/, and lyeth betweene the land of William of Barsham, wright, and the comon lane on the north and the land of the said William of Barsham, the land once of Richard Tyler and the land of John Bylewe on the south, and abutteth on the land of Henry[66] Cooke towardes the west and on Middlegate towardes the east.

[64] Probably Dame Avelinesrowe. See K.I. Sandred, ed., *The Place-names of Norfolk, Part Two* (English Place-Name Society, 1996), p. 34.
[65] A wortwoman sells herbs and green vegetables.
[66] *Hervey Cook*: original text, f. 12.

[*f. 53*] Likewise of a tenement with a shopp to the same belonginge and adioyninge which Thomas Bateman late heald fyve shillinges of yeerely rent */5s. rent/*, and lyeth betweene the capitall messuage of the said Thomas, which once was of Raphe Marshale, on the north and west and the common lane on the south, and abutteth on the Deane towardes the east.

Likewise of one tenement which Raphe of Gunton late heald three shillinges and fower pence of yeerely rent */3s. 4d. rent/*, and lyeth betweene the land of Thomas Wright, baxter, on the north and east and the common lane and land of the said Thomas towardes the south, and abutteth on Middlegate towardes the west.

Likewise of one tenement which Thomas of Barsham late heald twelve pence of yeerely rent */12d. rent/*, and lyeth betweene the land once of John Latoner on the south and the land of William Waryner,[67] fletcher, on the north, and abutteth on the land of the said William towardes the west and on the Dane [*sic*] towardes the east.

Likewise of one tenement which William Waryn, fletcher, late heald two shillinges of yeerely rent */2s. rent/*, and lyeth betweene the comon lane on the north and the land once of John Latiner and Thomas of Barsham on the south, and abutteth on the land of the said John Latoner towardes the west and on the Deane towardes the east.

Likewise of a tenement which John att Church of Ornesby[68] late heald six pence */6d. rent/* of [*f. 53ᵛ*] yeerely rent, and lyeth betweene the common lane on the south and the comon lane and the land of Thomas Erfeld on the north, and abutteth on the land of the said Thomas and on the land of John Vou[69] towardes the west and on the land of Thomas Hunt and the wast land, which once was Thomas Baa, towardes the east, which said place of ground conteyneth in length on the north from the land of the said Thomas Erfell towardes the east twenty fyve feete of men.

Likewise of one tenement which John of Riston, smith, late heald nyne pence of yeerely rent */9d. rent/*, and lyeth betweene the common lane on the south and the land once of Richard Broun, barker, on the north, and abutteth on the land of the said Richard towardes the east and on Gropecunt lane towardes the west.

[67] *William Waryn*: original text, f. 12ᵛ.
[68] *Ornesby*: original text, f. 12ᵛ.
[69] *John You*: original text, f. 12ᵛ.

Likewise of one tenement which Margarett of Kilham late heald fyve shillinges of yeerely rent /5s. rent/, and lyeth betweene the common lane on the south and the land of John of Lesingham, pelter, on the north, and abutteth on the Deane towardes the east and on the land once of Bartholmew of Holdernes towardes the west.

Likewise of two tenementes which Henry Crane, chandler, late heald three shillinges & six pence of yeerely rent /3s. 6d. rent/: that is to say of one tenement lyinge betweene the land of Richard [f. 54] Bellman on the north and the land of Oliver Spicer on the south, and abutteth on the common lane towardes the west and on the land of John of Buttele towardes the east, three shillinges of yeerely rent /3s. rent/; and of another tenement lyinge betweene the common lane on the north and the land of Jeoffry Twynne on the south, and abutteth on the land of John of Lesingham towardes the east and on the land once of Richard Trynman towardes the west, six pence of yeerely rent /6d. rent/.

Likewise of one tenement which William Benale late heald twelve pence of yeerely rent /12d. rent/, and lyeth betweene the comon lane on the south and the land once of Robert Barker on the north, and abutteth on the land of the said Robert towardes the west and on Middlegate towardes the east.

Likewise of one tenement which John[70] White, tailour, late heald eighteen pence of yeerely rent /1s. 6d. rent/, and lyeth betweene the common lane on the south and the land of Robert Robelle and John of Hall on the north, and abutteth on the land of William of Hedynham, smyth, towardes the east and on the land of the said John of Hall towardes the west.

Likewise of one tenement which John Lawes, bocher, late heald six pence of yeerely rent /6d. rent/, and lyeth betweene the comon lane on the north and the land of John Harpour on the south, and abutteth on the land of the said John Harpour towardes the east and on [f. 54ᵛ] the land of the said John and the land of John Clerke, bocher, towardes the west.

Likewise of one tenement which Nicholas Kates and Beatrice his wife, late the wife of Peter Bennett, late held six pence of yeerely rent /6d. rent/, and lyeth betweene the common lane on the south and the land once of Edward Ambrose on the north, and abutteth on the land of Henry Barsham, wright, towardes the east and on Middlegate towardes the west.

Likewise of one tenement which William Perer[71] late heald eighteen pence

[70] Manship here repeats 'which John'.
[71] *William Peper:* original text, f. 13ᵛ.

of yeerely rent /1s. 6d. rent/, and lyeth betweene the common lane on the north and the land of Thomas of Hall, draper, and the land of Thomas Grigges, wright, on the south, and abutteth on Middlegate towardes the west and on the land of John of Ingham, fishbwyer, towardes the east.

Likewise of one tenement which Robert Godfry late heald twelve pence of yeerely rent /12d. rent/, and lyeth betweene the land of William att Dam on the north and the comon lane called Gurnardkonge on the south, and abutteth on Middlegate towardes the east and on the land of Nicholas Kates towardes the west.

Likewise of one tenement which Thomas Hunte late heald fower pence of yeerely rent /4d. rent/, and lyeth betweene the common lane on the north and the land of the said Thomas, which once was of Stephen Davy, on the south, and abutteth on the land once of Jeoffry Wymark [f. 55] towardes the west and on the land of William Warryn, fletcher, towardes the east.

Likewise of one gardyn which William of Oxeneye late heald six pence of yeerely rent /6d. rent/, and lyeth betweene two common lanes on the south and north, and abutteth on the land of Hue att Fenn and on the land of the said William towardes the east and on Middlegate towardes the west.

Likewise of one tenement which William Ive late heald seaven pence of yeerely rent /7d. rent/, and lyeth betweene the common lane on the north and the land of Walter Davy and the land once of Walter[72] Skynner on the south, and abutteth on the land of John of Hanworth of the chapell towardes the east and on Middlegate towardes the west.

Likewise of the capitall messuage of the said William Ive eighteene pence of yeerely rent /1s. 6d. rent/, and lyeth betweene the comon lane on the north and the land of William Oxeneye on the south, and abutteth on the land of the said William Ive towardes the west and on the Deane towardes the east.

Likewise of one tenement which John Hacon late held two shillinges and six pence of yeerely rent /2s. 6d. rent/, and lyeth betweene the common lane on the north and the land of the said John, which once was Rose Thurkell,[73] on the south, and abutteth on the land of Thomas Martyn towardes the east and on the haven of Yermouth towardes the west.

---

[72] *Robert Skynner*: original text, f. 14.
[73] *Rose Thurkeld*: original text f. 14.

To have and to hold and take the foresaid messuage and seaventeen cottages [*f. 55ᵛ*] and the hundred shillinges of yeerely rent aforesaid, which wee late had of the graunt of the said Lord Kinge (*by charter*) graunted unto us, (*to*) the foresaid balyves and comminalty of the towne of Greate Yermouth and to theire successours, balyves and cominalty of the said towne of Yermouth, to the releivinge of the bretheren and siusters of the hospitall of the Blessed Mary in Yermouth aforesaid forever. In witnesse whereof to this our present writinge wee have sett our seale, these beinge witnesses: John Elys, Raphe Ramesey, Huge att Fenne, John att Cappe,[74] Roger of Drayton, Bartholmew Elys, Bartholmew of Drayton, Edmond With, Alexander att Capp,[75] Thomas Bateman and others. Dated at Greate Yermouth the first[76] day of the moneth of January in the yeere of the reigne of Kinge Richard the Second after the Conquest the one & twenty, in the tyme of William Oxeney, John of Beketon, Thomas March and Thomas of Hall then balyves of the towne of Yermouth aforesaid &c.

[*6. Rental of the hospital of St Mary the Virgin, Yarmouth, 23 April 1398, with subsequent addenda in a variety of rough later hands recording the names of fifteenth- and sixteenth-century tenants.*
ff. 14ᵛ-22ᵛ in the original Latin text]

[*f. 56*] **The** rentall of the hospitall of Blessed Mary made in the feast of St George in the yeere of the reigne of Kinge Richard the Second after the Conquest the one and twenty.

[*1*] **Of** one tenement with the appurtenaunces lyinge in Yermouth aforesaid betweene two common lanes on the south and north, and abutteth on Middlegate towardes the east and on the land of John Elys towardes the west: two shillinges six pence. Late held by John Elys, as it appeareth by the writinge of the said John, &c; after that (*held Dominus*) John Fastolff, then (*held*) John Paston, then William Paston & now of [*blank*].

[*2*] **Of** one tenement with th'appurtenaunces lyinge in Yermouth aforesaid betweene the common lane on the south and the land of John of Beketon on the north, and abutteth on the land of the said John of Beketon towardes the west and on Middlegate towardes the east: two shillinges. By William of Runham late heald, as it appeareth by the writinge of the said William; after that Margarett Streate, then John Neal, (*brother of the hospital,*) then Edmond Jorden, (*smith,*) then Edmond Hopper; after that John Grosse, then Thomas Grosse.

---

[74] *John atte Gappe*: original text, f. 14.
[75] *Alexander atte Gappe*: original text, f. 14.
[76] *fifth*: original text, f. 14.

[*3*] **Of** one tenement with the appurtenaunces lyinge in Yermouth aforesaid betweene the land of Nicholas Kirkhawe on the north and the land of
John of Beketon on the south, and abutteth on Middlegate towardes the
east [*f. 56ᵛ*] and on the land once of Bartholmew Nogon towardes the west:
two shillinges. Late heald by John of Beketon, as it appeareth by the
writinge of the said John; after that John Cokerem, then Edmond Jorden,
(*smith*,) then Edmond Hopper.

[*4*] **Of** one tenement with th'appurtenaunces lyinge in Yermouth aforesaid
betweene the common lane on the north and the land of Bartholmew Elys
on the south, and abutteth on Middlegate towardes the east and on the
land of Symon Aunsell towardes the west: twelve pence. Late heald by
John att Cappe,⁷⁷ as it appeareth by the writinge of the said John; after
that William att Cap⁷⁸ (*held*), then (*held*) Robert Gedge,⁷⁹ then Edmond
Cowper; after that Robert Alexander, then Raphe Wullhowse and now of
[*blank*].

[*5*] **Of** one tenement with the appurtenaunces in Yermouth aforesaid
betweene the common lane on the north and the land of Bartholmew Elys
on the south, and abutteth on the land of John ate Cappe⁸⁰ towardes the
east and on the land once of Richard atte Cappe towardes the west: twelve
pence. Late heald by Symon Aunsell, as it appeareth by the writinge of the
said Symon; late belonginge to every of the persons abovenamed succes-
sively⁸¹ and now of [*blank*].

[*6*] **Of** one tenement with the appurtenaunces lyinge in Yermouth afore-
said betweene the common lane [*f. 57*] on the south and the land of John,
the sonne of William Elys, on the north and abutteth on the land of
William Goddiffeld⁸² towardes the west and on the land of the said John
Elys towardes the east: twelve pence. John of Beverle before heald, as it
appeareth by the writinge of the said John; late heald by Alexander atte
Cappe;⁸³ after that Roger Hoddis (*held*), then (*held*) Nicholas Ludham, then
Robert Clerke, then Stephen Watson, then Peter Helton, then John Levile,
then William Bisshop th'elder and now of [*blank*].

[*7*] **Of** one tenement with the appurtenaunces lyinge in Yermouth aforesaid betweene the comon lane on the south and the land of Margery Bange

---

⁷⁷ *John atte Gappe*: original text, f. 15.
⁷⁸ *William atte Gappe*: original text, f. 15.
⁷⁹ *Robert Gegch*: original text, f. 15.
⁸⁰ *John atte Gappe*: original text, f. 15.
⁸¹ That is the persons listed in the previous entry: original text, f. 15.
⁸² *William Godisfeld*: original text, f. 15.
⁸³ *Alexander atte Gappe*: original text, f. 15.

on the north, and abutteth on the Deane towardes the east and on the land
of Thomas Stase towardes the west: twelve pence. Before heald Nicholas
Frere, as it appeareth by the writing of the said Nicholas, and before him
Thomas Tyler; late heald by Robert of Plumsted; after that John
Ministurch (*held*), then (*held*) Walter Aldrig, then John Pilt, &c, (*Spryngwell,
Herre Bemond,*) then John Salley; after that Hugh Salley, then John Salley;
after that (*John*) Bartholmew, then [*blank*] Say.

[*8*] **Of** one tenement with the appurtenaunces lyinge in Yermouth aforesaid betweene the common lane on the south and the land of Symon
Thurkyld on the north, and abutteth on the Deane towardes the east and
on the land of the said Symon towardes the west: three pence, as it
appeareth by the writing of the said Thomas Smyth. Late heald by the
said Thomas atte Church, smyth, then John Turnour (*held,*) &c, (*then* [*blank*]
Byllet, schypwryte, Robert Craske;) after that John [*f. 57ᵛ*] Levile, then Margaret
Chamberlyn, then Henry Naperson, now of [*blank*].

[*9*] **Of** one tenement with the appurtenaunces lyinge in Yermouth aforesaid betweene the common lane on the north and the land of Thomas att
Church, smyth, towardes the south, and abutteth on the Deane towardes
the east and on the land of Symon Thurkel(*d*) towardes the west: two
shillinges tenn pence. Late heald by Symon Thurkels,[84] as it appeareth by
the writing of the said Symon, then Richard Elys (*held*), then Thomas
Bucket, then Thomas Newes, then Robert Drawer & now of [*blank*].

[*10*] **Of** one tenement with the appurtenaunces lyinge in Yermouth aforesaid betweene the common lane on the north and the land of Roger Fuller
on the south, and abutteth on the Deane towardes the east and on the land
of Hughe Pamflot towardes the west: fyve shillinges six pence.[85] Late heald
by the said Roger Fuller, as it appeareth by the writing of the said Roger;
after that John Goodwin, then John Pigin, then William Ilberd, then Joane
Bebnes, then Robert Drawer & now of [*blank*].

[*11*] **Of** one fisshouse with the appurtenaunces lyinge in Yermouth aforesaid called Gavelleshouse betweene the common lane on the south and the
land of Henry Colman on the north, and abutteth on the land of Thomas
White towardes the east [*f. 58*] and on the land of John Hughesson
towardes the west: twelve pence. Late heald the said John Hughesson, as it
appeareth by the writing of the said John; after that William Hemsted
(*held, then Christopher Hunyn,*) now Edward Couper, then Richard Bishop,
then Rose Bisshop, widdow, now of [*blank*].

---

[84] *Symon Thurkeld*: original text, f. 15ᵛ.
[85] *fyve shillings* only; Manship interpolates 'six pence': original text, f. 15ᵛ.

[*12*] **Of** one tenement with the appurtenaunces lyinge in Yermouth afore-said betweene the common lane on the south and the land of John of Ocle and the land of Roger Kirthold[86] on the north, and abutteth on the Deane towardes the east and on the land of John of Wykanton towardes the west: twelve pence. Late Alice of Drayton held, as it appeareth by the writinge of the said Alice, (*then held William Sechenys,* [*blank*] *London, Thomas Rant & other, then*) long after that John Midleton, (*marener,*) then Edward Hungate, late Henry Lowes and now of [*blank*].

[*13*] **Of** one tenement with the appurtenaunces lyinge in Yermouth which once was Laurence of Drayton betweene two common lanes on the south and north, and abutteth on the Deane towardes the east and on the land of Roger of Drayton towardes the west: two shillinges. Late heald by Roger of Drayton, as it appeareth by (*the writing*) of the said Roger; (*memorandum: this tenement ys a gardyn and ys fullyn in to the haven;*)[87] after that (*held*) William Richman, (*then John Pynne, then John Schave, then*) long after that William Haws,[88] then Edward Musgrave, then Richard Bright & now of [*blank*].

[*14*] **Of** one tenement with the appurtenaunces lyinge in Yermouth afore-said betweene the common lane on the north and the [*f. 58ᵛ*] land once of Jeoffry of Drayton on the south, and abutteth on the land once of Symon Talyard towardes the east and on the haven of Yermouth towardes the west: twelve pence. Late heald Peter of Selby, as it appeareth by the writinge of the said Peter; after that Thomas Chapman, late John (*Bencelyn,*) then Robert Mann, then John Smyth, carpenter, then ([*blank*] *Foxe, then*) John Howse; after that Walter Cotes, late Robert Browne, then John Gyles.

[*15*] **Of** one tenement with the appurtenaunces lyinge in the towne of Yermouth aforesaid betweene the common lane on the north and the land once of Symon Hastinge on the south, and abutteth on Middlegate towardes the east and on the land of John Hacon towardes the west: two shillinges six pence. Thomas Martyne late heald, as it appeareth by the writinge of the said Thomas; after that Robert Pyn (*held*) and once of John Crane,[89] late Robert Tasburgh (*held*), then John Alman, then Robert Tasborough & now of [*blank*].

[*16*] **Of** one tenement with the appurtenaunces lyinge in Yermouth afore-said betweene the common lane on the north and the land of John Hacon,

86 *Roger Kythod*: original text, f. 16.
87 This memorandum should appear in the following item (number 14).
88 *William Shave*: original text, f. 16.
89 *John Cromere*: original text, f. 16ᵛ.

which once was of Rose Thurkell,⁹⁰ on the south, and abutteth on the land of Thomas Martyn towardes the east and on the haven of Yermouth towardes the west: two shillinges six pence. Late heald John Hacon, as it appeareth by the writing [*f. 59*] of the said John; after that William Richman, (*then William Arhyton,*) late Robert (*Canyard,*) and then Roger Bassett, then John James (*held, then Richard James,*) then of (*William*) Bisshopp th'elder; after that (*Symond Moore, then William Welles,*) Nicholas Firmage (*the younger, then John Ussherwode,*) then Richard Firmage, then Raphe Ebbott, then Thomas Cotty & now of [*blank*].

[*17*] **Of** one tenement with the appurtenaunces lyinge in Yermouth aforesaid betweene the (*two*) common lanes on the south and north, and abutteth on the Deane towardes the east and on the land once of Hughe of Norwich on the west: fower shillinges six pence.⁹¹ Late heald Bartholmew Sprotholf, as it appeareth by the writing of the said Bartholmew; after that Richard Grome, (*spycer, Robert Ylberd,*) then Robert Edmundes, then of the wife of the said Robert (*Edmundes*), then John Lovell, then John Yonge & now of [*blank*].

[*18*] **Of** one tenement with the appurtenaunces lyinge in Yermouth aforesaid betweene two common lanes on the south and north, and abutteth on the land once of Robert Davy towardes the west and on the land once of Thomas White, clerk, on the east: twelve pence. Which Beatrix of Blofeld before held, as it appeareth by the writing of the said Beatrix; late heald Nicholas of Blofeld, his sonne;⁹² after that Letyce Smyth (*held*), then Robert Ylberd, then Robert Edmundes, then the wife of the said Robert (*Edmundes*), then John Lovell & now of [*blank*].

[*19*] **Of** one cottage with a shopp to the same adioyninge and belonginge lyinge in Yermouthe aforesaid betweene the capitall tenement of Thomas Bateman, in which [*f. 59ᵛ*] the said Thomas once dwelt, and the capitall tenement of Raphe Marchall on the north and west and the common lane on the south, and abutteth on the Deane towardes the east: fyve shillinges six pence.⁹³ Late heald Thomas Bateman, as it appeareth by the writing of the said Thomas; after that John Seccly (*the elder*), then Robert Mar (*held*), then Henry Komer,⁹⁴ draper, then (*William Swolle, then*) John Ylberd, (*ropere,*) then (*John Bussh,*) William Benchelyn & now of [*blank*].

---

⁹⁰ *Rose Thurkeld*: original text, f. 16ᵛ.
⁹¹ *four shillings* only; Manship interpolates 'six pence': original text, f. 17.
⁹² *her son*: original text, f. 17.
⁹³ *five shillings* only; Manship interpolates 'six pence': original text, f. 17.
⁹⁴ *Henry Kemp*: original text, f. 17.

[*20*] **Of** one tenement with the appurtenaunces lyinge in Yermouth aforesaid between the land of Thomas Wright, baxter, on the north and east
and the common lane and the land of the said Thomas towardes the south,
and abutteth on Middlegate towardes the west: three shillinges fower
pence. Late heald Raphe of Gunton, as it appeareth by the writing of the
said Raphe; after that (*held*) Alexander Brygitte, (*John Berel,*) then John
Dubbylday, then John Yvess,[95] then Anthony Loveday & now of [*blank*].

[*21*] **Of** one tenement with the appurtenaunces lyinge in Yermouth aforesaid between the common lane on the north and the land of Robert of
Cantele and Margarett his wife and Thomas Bateman on the south, and
abutteth on the land of John Lawys, maryner, towardes the west and on
the land of the said Thomas towardes the east: twelve pence. [*f. 60*] Before
heald Robert of Cantele and Margarett his wife together, as it appeareth
by the writing of them, and late heald by the said Margarett; after that
Roger Redhyd (*held*) & now of [*blank*].

[*22*] **Of** one garden lyinge in Yermouth aforesaid betweene two common
lanes on the south and north, and abutteth on the land of Hughe att Fenne
and the land of William of Oxeney towardes the east and Middlegate
towardes the west: six pence. Late heald William Oxeney, as it appeareth
in the greate writing made and sealed by the said William and Robert
Howlyn,[96] (*then Cristian Felysson held, then*) long after that Robert Barrett,
then William Dorant, then Thomas Elys; long after that (*Richard Rudraham
ijd. and*) William Tomson (*iiijd.*), then William Tanfold, (*Nycolas the elder;*)
long after that William Bisshop & now of [*blank*].

[*23*] **Of** one tenement with the appurtenaunces lyinge in Yermouth aforesaid betweene two common lanes on the south and north, and abutteth on
the Deane towardes the east and on the land once of Clement Bere
towardes the west: (*three shillings.*) Before heald by Alice of Filby, as it
appeareth by the writing of the said Alice; late held William of Oxeney;
after that Hewe Ofen (*held*), then William Dorant, then John Jamys (*then
Edward Jamys, then Symond Yoor;*) long after that William Sylyard,[97] then
William Collen; after that John Gyles, then William Cubit & now of
[*blank*].

[*24*] [*f. 60ᵛ*] **Of** one tenement with the appurtenaunces lyinge in Yermouth
aforesaid betweene the common lane on the north and the land of William
of Oxeney on the south, and abutteth on the land of William Ive towardes

---

95 *John Yvell*: original text, f. 17ᵛ.
96 The conveyance of 5 January 1398, number 5 above.
97 *William Stylyarde*: original text, f. 18.

the west and on the Deane towardes the east: eighteen pence. Late heald William Ive, as it appeareth by the writinge of the said William; after that Robert Chandeler, (*then John Jonson;*) long after that Richard Buck; after that Bennett Cubit, then John Bennet & now of [*blank*].

(*The tenement of Thomas Elwyn, then Symon Oldryng; memorandum: newe dede*)

[*25*] **Of** one tenement with the appurtenaunces lyinge in Yermouth afore-said betweene the common lane called Comanelynsrowe[98] on the south and on the land once of Andrew of Claxton on the north, and abutteth on the Deane towardes the east and on the land of Thomas Hall towardes the west, which tenement conteyneth in length three score feete of men: six shillinges eight pence. Late heald Thomas Hall, as it appeareth by the writinge of the said Thomas; after that John Ydon, (*then Nicholas Yden;*) long after that Robert Claunfeld, then Abraham Elys & now of [*blank*].

[*26*] **Of** one tenement with the appurtenaunces lyinge in Yermouth afore-said between two comon lanes on the south and north, and abutteth on the land of Thomas of Hall and the land once of William of [*f. 61*] Ludham towardes the east and on the land once of the said William towardes the west: six pence. Late held Richard Ivy, baxter, as it appeareth by the writinge of the said Richard; after that (*held*) Symond Baxter, then John Yngram, then Robert Barret, carpenter, then William Denne & now of [*blank*].

[*27*] **Of** one tenement with the appurtenaunces lyinge in Yermouth afore-said betweene the comon lane on the north and the land once of Jeoffry of Fordele on the south, and abutteth on Middlegate towardes the east and on the haven of Yermouth towardes the west: twenty pence. Late held William Stallon and William Hedman, smyth, together, as it appeareth by the writinge of them; (*then held Jefferey Hemmyng, John Bresle, then*) long after that Henry Bemond, then John Palmer, then Edmond Wood, (*aldyrman*) of Norwich,[99] John Est eight pence, William Mayhow eight pence, Thomas Bayly fower pence.

[*28*] **Of** one tenement with the appurtenaunces lyinge in Yermouth afore-said betweene the common lane on the north and the land of Thomas of Alysham on the south, and abutteth on the land of the said Thomas towardes the east and on the haven of Yermouth towardes the west: six shillinges eight pence. Beforee heald John Halman, as it appeareth by the

[98] Probably Dame Avelinesrowe. See n. 64.
[99] Edmund Wood was alderman of North Conisford ward between 1535 and 1537: T. Hawes, *An Index to Norwich City Officers 1453-1835* (NRS, lii, 1986), p. 168.

writinge of the said John; late held Thomas Belle, meysmaker;[100] after that Thomas Belle, [*f. 61ᵛ*] meysmaker, then Christofer Watson,[101] then Henry Payce, then his wife, then Thomas King, then William Durrant & now of [*blank*].

[*29*] **Of** one tenement with the appurtenaunces lyinge in Yermouth afore-said betweene the common lane on the south and the land of Robert Belle on the north, and abutteth on the land of Geoffry Wymark towardes the east and on the haven of Yermouth towardes the west: twelve pence. Late held William of Brisle, as it appeareth by the writinge of the said William; after that (*held*) John Mullynge, then John But, (*steynour,*) then Henry Smyth, then his wife, then William Dorant, then (*John Perfecte,*) Edward Watson & now of [*blank*].

[*30*] **Of** the capitall messuage once of Thomas Cobbald, which said messuage Robert Cobbald, the nephew of the said Thomas, late heald and remaynes in it, in Yermouth aforesaid: six shillinges of yeerely rent, which six shillinges Walter att Sond gave and bequeathed in his testament to the balyves, cominalty, brethren and siusters of the hospitall of the Blessed Virgyn Mary towardes the releivinge of the said brethren and siusters, as it appearerth in the testament of the said Walter. Late heald Robert Cobbald, as it appeareth by the greate writinge; after that John Cobbald, now William Alban, (*then John Pydgon;*) long after that William Ilberd, then Raphe Wood, then Thomas Bylbow & now of [*blank*].

[*31*] [*f. 62*] **Of** one tenement with the appurtenaunces lyinge in Yermouth aforesaid betweene the land once of Bennett of Rockhawe on the south and the common lane and the land once of John of Ocle on the north, and abutteth on the haven of Yermouth towardes the west and on the land once of John of Ocle and Middlegate towardes the east: eighteen pence. Late held William of Worsted, as it appeareth by the writinge of the said William, (*then held Jamys Brond;*) long after that Robert Glover (*att Lamb*), then William Felaws,[102] then his wife, then John Doke, (*Hemysby*) & now of [*blank*].

[*32*] **Of** one tenement with the appurtenaunces in Yermouth aforesaid betweene the common lane on the south and the land once of Robert Barker on the north, and abutteth on the land of the said Robert towardes the west and on Middlegate towardes the east: twelve pence. Late heald William Benale, mason, as it appeareth by the writinge of the said William;

---

[100] A meysmaker is a cooper, specifically making barrels for the storage of herring.
[101] *Stephen (Sthephanus) Watson*: original text, f. 18ᵛ.
[102] *William Felawe*: original text, f. 19.

after that John Bulle, (*schypman,*) then John Dyxon, then William Ilberd, then Henry Mauson[103] (*per annum vjd.*), then Gregory Goose, then Clement Nixon & now of [*blank*].

[*33*] **Of** one tenement with the appurtenaunces lyinge in Yermouth afore-said betweene the common lane on the north and on the land of Walter Davy and the land once of Robert S(*k*)ynner on the south, and abutteth [*f. 62ᵛ*] on the land of John of Hanworth of the chappell towardes the east and on Middlegate towardes the west: seaven pence. Late heald William Ive, as it appeareth by the writinge of the said William: after that Nicholas at Mere, then Thomas (*Deynston held,* [*blank*] *Batman held, then Nicholas Kynge;*) long after that Richard Dyxson, then Edmond Sawar & now of [*blank*].

[*34*] **Of** one tenement with the appurtenaunces in Yermouth aforesaid betweene the land of William atte Dam on the north and the comon lane called Gurneyskonge on the south, and abutteth on Middlegate towardes the east and on the land of Nicholas Kates towardes the west: twelve pence. Before heald Robert Godfrey, as it appeareth by the writinge of the said Robert; after him held Stephen Turnur; late held Richard Dokelyng of Runham; late held John Hanworth of the chappell, (*then held Necolas [?]Bruederin, mason;*) long after that Robert Kent, then Robert Watson, then Peter Gomer;[104] after that Adrian Mellow & now of [*blank*].

[*35*] **Of** one tenement with the appurtenaunces lyinge in Yermouth afore-said betweene the comon lane on the south and the land once of Edward Ambrose on the north and abutteth on the land of Henry of Barsham, wright, towardes the east and on Middlegate towardes the west: six pence. Late held Nicholas Cates and Beatrix his wife together, as [*f. 63*] it appeareth by theire writinge; after that (*held*) Nicholas Bere, then John Cooke (*reder*), then John Bonnde of the chappell; after that William Ylberd, then John Pratt, then Christofer Sylle; after that Paule Peterson, then Richard Hearne & now of [*blank*].

[*36*] **Of** one tenement with the appurtenaunces lyinge in Yermouth afore-said between the common lane on the north and the land of Richard Midward on the south, and abutteth on the land of the priour and covent of Silton[105] and the land once of Peter Benet towardes the east and on Middlegate towardes the west: twelve pence. Late heald Robert Gare, as it appeareth by the writinge of the said Robert, (*&c;*) after that (*held*) Symon Pecock, (*meysmaker,*) then Thomas Pecocke & William Buck, then William

---

[103] *Henry Watson*: original text, f. 19ᵛ.

[104] *Peter Cromer*: original text, f. 19ᵛ.

[105] Sibton, Suffolk.

Aldryche, then John Clerk, then John Browne, (*mason;*) Symon Barker payeth vjd. & John Browne vjd., then Edmond Sawar, (*then William Sewill, then*) long after that Richard Frost & now of [*blank*].

[*37*] **Of** one tenement with the appurtenaunces lyinge in Yermouth aforesaid between the comon lane on the north and the land of Thomas of Hall and Thomas Grigges, wright, on the south, and abutteth on Middlegate towardes the west and on the land of John Ingham, fisbyer, towardes the east: eighteen pence. Before heald William Peper, as it appeareth by the writinge of the said William; late held Margarett his wife; after that (*held*) William Yngram, then John Baydon, then Henry Bemond, then John Pratt, then John Stase; after that William Woodruff & then Elizabeth Holmes & now of [*blank*].

[*38*] [*f. 63ᵛ*] **Of** one tenement with the appurtenaunces lyinge in Yermouth aforesaid between the common lane on the south and the land of William of Barsham on the north, and abutteth on the land of the said William towardes the west and on Middlegate towardes the east: six pence.¹⁰⁶ Late heald Letice Pette, wo(*r*)twoman, as it appeareth by the writinge of the said Letice (*then held Alice Talyour;*) long after that William Seman (*at the Red Heethe*), then John Ylberd, (*ropere,*) then Thomas Dabny, then Robert Godfrey, then (*Thomas*) Dabney, then Webstar & now of [*blank*].

[*39*] **Of** one tenement with the appurtenaunces lyinge in Yermouth aforesaid between the land of John of Halys, shipwright, on the north and the land of Letice Pette, wortwoman, and the common lane on the south, and abutteth on the land once of Richard Tyler towardes the west and on Middlegate towardes the east: tenne pence. Late held William Barsham, wright, as it appeareth by the writinge of the said William; after that (*held*) William¹⁰⁷ Danyel, (*talyour, Schyfeld, then [blank] Kyppyng, then*) long after that John Dorell, then Jamys Smyth, then Thomas Dabney, then Robert Godfrey, then William Godfrey & now of [*blank*].

[*40*] **Of** one tenement with the appurtenaunces lyinge in Yermouth aforesaid between the land of William of Barsham, wright, [*f. 64*] and the common lane on the north and the land of the said William and the land once of Richard Tyler and the land of John Below, lyster, on the south, and abutteth on the land of Henry Cook of Southgate towardes the west and on Middlegate towardes the east: twelve pence. Late heald John of Halys, shipwright, as it appeareth by the writinge of the said John; after that (*held*) Thomas Danyell, (*talyour, William Schefeld, then*) long after that

---

¹⁰⁶ *Seven pence (vijd.)*: original text, f. 20ᵛ.
¹⁰⁷ *Thomas Danyell*: original text, f. 20ᵛ.

John Dorell, then Edmond Saber, then Robert Lessey, then ([*blank*] *Malham, then*) William Gybberd & now of [*blank*].

[*41*] **Of** one tenement with the appurtenaunces lyinge in Yermouth aforesaid betweene the comon lane on the north and the land once of Geoffrey of Fordele on the south, and abutteth on the Deane towardes the east and on the land once of Hughe of Baghele towardes the west: fyve shillinges six pence.[108] Adam Hayron before heald, as it appeareth by the writing of the said Adam; late heald Sibilla, his wife; after that (*held*) John Chapman, then Edmond Peers (*held*), then John Peers, then Thomas Gladon, then William Dem & now of [*blank*].

[*42*] **Of** one tenement with the appurtenaunces lyinge in Yermouth aforesaid betweene the comon lane on the south and the land of Robert Robel and the land once of John of Hall on the north, and abutteth on the [*f. 64ᵛ*] land of William of Hedenam, smyth, towardes the east and on the land once of the said John of Hall towardes the west: eighteene pence. Before held John White, tailour, as it appeareth by the writing of the said John; late heald Robert Banchon, fissher; after that John Coddelyng, then Thomas Jely,[109] then his wife, then William Deene & now of [*blank*].

[*43*] **Of** one tenement with the appurtenaunces lyinge in Yermouth aforesaid between the common lane on the south and the land of John of Lesyngham, pelter, on the north and abutteth on the Deane towardes the east and on the land once of Bartholmew of Holdernes towardes the west: six shillinges six pence.[110] Before held Margarett of Kylham, as it appeareth by the writing of the said Margarett; late held by Henry Crane; after that (*held*) Thomas Ellyngham, then John Yngram, then John Godfrey, (*then John Har[?]lon*) and now of [*blank*].

[*44*] **Of** one tenement with the appurtenaunces lyinge in Yermouth aforesaid betweene the common lane on the north and the land of Thomas Hunte, which once was Stephen Davy, on the south, and abutteth on the land once of Geoffry Wymark towardes the west and on the land of William [*f. 65*] Waryn, fletcher, towardes the east: fower pence. Late held Thomas Hunte, as it appeareth by the writing of the said Thomas; after that (*held*) John Goodknape, then Alexander Manthorp (*meller*),[111] then (*held*) Walter Ingram, then Walter Atkyns,[112] then William Gegeball, then William Wellys, then John More & now of [*blank*].

---

[108] *five shillings* only; Manship interpolates 'six pence': original text, f. 21.

[109] *Thomas Joly*: original text, f. 21.

[110] *five shillings (vs.)*: original text, f. 21.

[111] That is a miller.

[112] *Geoffrey Atkyns*: original text, f. 21ᵛ.

[45] **Of** one tenement with the appurtenaunces lyinge in Yermouth aforesaid between the comon lane on the north and the land of Geoffry Twyn
on the south, and abutteth on the land of John of Lesyngham towardes the
east and on the land once of Richard Trymman towardes the west: six
pence. Before held Henry Crane, chandeler, as it appeareth by the
writinge of the said Henry; late held Geoffry Twyn; after that (*held*)
Thomas Yngham, then John Pydgan, then Jacob Scerlyng, (*then* [*blank*]
Blome;) long after that William Longback, (*now*) Thomas (*the*) yonger, (*ech
ijd., then Dey of Ocle*) & now of [*blank*].

[46] **Of** one tenement with the appurtenaunces lyinge in Yermouth aforesaid between the land once of John Latoner on the south and the land of
William Waryn, fletcher, on the north, and abutteth on the land of the said
William towardes the west and on the Deane towardes the east: twelve
pence. Late heald Thomas of Barsham, mason, as it appeareth by the
writinge of the said Thomas; after that (*held*) John Yngram, then William
Byllyng, then John Ylberd,[113] then his wife, then Robert Sponer & now of
[*blank*].

[47] [*f. 65ᵛ*] **Of** one tenement with the appurtenaunces lyinge in Yermouth
aforesaid between the common lane on the north and the land once of
John Latoner and the land of Thomas of Barsham on the south, and abut-
teth on the land of the said John Latoner towardes the west and on the
Deane towardes the east: two shillinges six pence.[114] Late held William
W(*h*)aryn, fletcher, as it appeareth by the writinge of the said William; after
that (*held*) Nicholas Cave, barbour, ([*blank*] *Sporle;*) long after that Mr
Garrad, (*rector of Stokisby;*)[115] long after that John Rogerson viijd., then
Arnold (*Nesche*) & now of [*blank*].

[48] **Of** one tenement with the appurtenaunces lyinge in Yermouth aforesaid betweene the land of Richard Belman on the north and the land of
Oliver Spicer on the south, and abutteth on the comon way towardes the
west and on the land of John of Buttele towardes the east: three shillinges.
Before held Henry Crane, candeler, as it appeareth by the writinge of the
said Henry; late held Oliver Spicer, (*then John Schurloc held, then*) long after
that (*held*) John Davy, then Thomas Greene, then William Byddynge (*then
William Jollys*); long after that William Grese, (*baxter, and*) then (*Dominus*)
John Bound, (*chaplain, then Thomas Whyghtyng;*) long after that Robert
Coppyng & John Wesse, (*prest,*) then John Cowper, (*goldsmith,*) & now of
[*blank*].

---

[113] *Henry Ilberd:* original text, f. 21ᵛ.

[114] *two shillings* only; Manship interpolates 'six pence': original text, f. 22.

[115] The parish of Stokesby lies to the north east of Yarmouth.

[*49*] [*f. 66*] **Of** one place of ground with the edifices and appurtenaunces lyinge in Yermouth aforesaid betweene the common lane on the north and the land of John Harpour on the south, and abutteth on the land of the said John towardes the east and on the land of the said John Harpour and the land of John Clerk towardes the west: six pence. Before held John Lawes and Joane his wife together, as it appeareth by the writinge of them; late held John Harpour; after that (*held*) Walter Holycome, then Alice Hed,[116] then Robert Tylberd,[117] then Robert Edmundes, then Jeoffry Buxton, (*Nicolas Catour, Nycholas Catour;*) long after that Christofer Selle & now of [*blank*].

[*50*] **Of** one tenement with the appurtenaunces lyinge in Yermouth aforesaid betweene the comon lane on the south and the comon lane and the land of Thomas Erfeld (*fflesheuer*) on the north, and abutteth on the land of the said Thomas and the land of John [*blank*] towardes the west and on the land of Thomas Honte and the wast land, which once was Thomas Baa, which place of ground conteyneth in length on the north from the land of the said Thomas Elfeld[118] towardes the east fyve & twenty feete of men: six pence. Before held John att Chirch of Ormesby, as it appeareth by the writinge of the said John; late held Robert Clerk, wryght: after that (*held*) John Torald, (*Vincent Bowre, then*) long after that John Chamber, then Robert Parker [*f. 66ᵛ*] & now of [*blank*].

[*51*] **Of** one tenement with the appurtenaunces lyinge in Yermouth aforesaid betweene the common lane on the south and the land once of Richard Brom on the north, and abutteth on the land once of the said Richard towardes the east and on Gropekontlane towardes the the west: nyne pence. Late held John of Riston, smyth, as it appeareth by the writinge of the said John; after that (*held*) John Davy, (*barker,*) then Robert Man, then Vincent Bowre, then John Williams (*the younger*) & now of [*blank*].

[*52*] **Of** one garden lyinge in Yermouth aforesaid betweene the land once of Walter Roke on the south and the land of John Dannard of Norwich on the north, and abutteth on the land of the said Walter[119] towardes the east and on the haven of Yermouth towardes the west: fower pence. Late held John Hestynge;[120] after that John Tolke & now of [*blank*].

(*Memorandum: that Symon Oldryng hath govyn to the ospytale of Owr Lady jd. a yere of yerly rent of ij closys lynygt with owt the north gatys, the qweche closys he bowt of Rychard Bongey, to paye it the fest of Seynt Edmund.*)

---

[116] *Alice Heche*: original text, f. 22.   [117] *Robert Ylberd*: original text, f. 22.
[118] *Thomas Erfeld*: original text, f. 22ᵛ.
[119] Manship here corrects an error in the original, which has *Matthew*: original text, f. 22ᵛ.
[120] *John Herlyng*: original text, f. 22ᵛ.

[7. List of rents previously settled by William Gerbrigge of Yarmouth (d. c. 1278) upon the hospital of St Mary the Virgin for the support of religious services there, probably compiled c. 1398.
f. 23 in the original Latin text]

[*f. 67*] **Those** are the rentes of mortmayne of the guift of William Gerbrigge purteyninge to the service of preisthood: that is to say, of the tenement of Thomas Martyn and John Hacon with the appurtenaunces, which once was the tenement of Micha*e*ll Hardman, and lyeth between the common lane on the north and the land of Rose Thurkyld on the south, and abutteth on Middlegate towardes the east and on the key towardes the west: fyve shillinges six pence[121] /*5s. 6d. rent*/, as it appeareth by the writinge of the said William.

Allso of Thomas Bateman for one place of ground joine*t*lye[122] of John Smyth, and lyeth betweene the land of Geoffry of Somerton, smyth, towardes the north and the common lane towardes the south, and abutteth on the land of Thomas Bellard towardes the west and on the Dene towardes the east: fyve shillinges six pence[123] /*5s. 6d. rent*/, which once paid aleven shillinges six pence, as it appeareth by the writinge of the said William.

Allso of Robert Bauchon, fishbyer, of one tenement sometyme of Henry of Stoke, which lyeth betweene the land which once was of Nicholas Rake towardes the north and the common lane towardes the south, and abutteth on the land of John Austyn towardes the east and on the land of Geoffry Silke towardes the west: [*f. 67ᵛ*] eighteen pence /*1s. 6d. rent*/, which once paid three shillinges and six pence as it appeareth by the writinge of the said William.

Allso of William of Worsted of one place of ground which was Henry Bassett, which lyeth betweene the land of William Stannard towardes the south and the land of the said Henry towardes the north, and abutteth on the land of Henry, the sonne of the said William, clerke, towardes the west and on Middlegate towardes the east: nyne pence /*9d. rent*/, which paid twelve pence as it appeareth by the writinge of the said William.

[8. Conveyance by William and John Gerbrigge to the hospital of St Mary the Virgin of rents originally bequeathed by their father, William Gerbrigge of Yarmouth, to the

---

[121] *fyve shillinges* only; Manship interpolates 'six pence': original text, f. 23.

[122] *formerly*: original text, f. 23.

[123] *fyve shillinges* only; Manship interpolates 'six pence': original text, f. 23.

hospital for the support of two chantry priests there, 5 September 1304. Sealed by the
archdeacon of Norwich's Official, 8 October 1304.
ff. 24–25ᵛ in the original Latin text]

[*f. 68*] **In the name** of God Amen. Unto the perpetuall memory of all
men, especially unto all the sonnes of our holy mother the Church that
this present instrument shall see or heare, William and John the sonnes of
William Gerbregg th'elder, sometyme burgesse of the towne of Greate
Yermouth lately deceased, and executours of his testament, send greetinge
in our Lord God everlastinge. **Wee** will it by the tenour of these presentes
unto the knowledge of you all in generall to come that, whereas the said
William, our deceased father, lyvinge[124] in his extreame sicknes now six
and twenty yeeres and more past, made his testament, which (*he*) so willed
and firmely commanded to be holden for his last will,[125] in which testament the said testatour the rentes underwritten, amountinge by estemacon
to the somme of nyne markes[126] of the tenementes undermencioned
yeerely in tyme to comme (*to be raised from*) whosoever shall hold or inioy
the same tenement(*s*), for the mayntenance of two preistes in the hospitall
of the Blessed Virgyn Mary in the foresaid towne of Yermouth, there to
celebrate devyne rytes for the sowle of him and Isabell his wife and of
theire children and for the sowles of all faithfull people deceased forevermore, did will and assigne [*f. 68ᵛ*] to be received and had.

That is to say, at the feast of St Martyn in wynter[127] of a tenement with the
buildinges and appurtenaunces sometyme Hughe of Waxtenesham
sixteene pence /*1s. 4d. rent*/, as it lyeth between the common lane towardes
the south and the land sometyme Richard Fastolf towardes the north, and
abutteth on the land which once was of the foresaid Richard towardes the
east and on the key towardes the west.

Of one tenement with the buildinges and appurtenaunces once of Michaell
Hardman fyve shillings /*5s. rent*/, as it lyeth between the land of Rose
Thurkyld towardes the south and the common lane towardes the north, and
abutteth on Middlegate towardes the east and on the key towardes the west.

Of Oliver de la Mawe and Nicholas Cook and theire heires sixteen
shillinges /*16s. rent*/ of that ringe[128] or small parcell of ground with the

---

[124] *labouring*: original text, f. 24.
[125] Manship here interpolates a superfluous 'in which he lawfully graunted'.
[126] £6.
[127] 11 November.
[128] The Latin term *rengiata* is peculiar to the region and means a strip of land: original text,
f. 24.

buildinges and appurtenaunces, as it lyeth between the land of Richard of Lincolne towardes the north and the common lane towardes the south, and abutteth on Middlegate towardes the east and west.[129]

Allso of the said Oliver de la Mawe and his heires and assignes fower shillinges */4s. rent/* of that rindge or peece of ground with the buildinges and appurtenaunces, which once was of William de la Crane, and lyeth betweene the land of Geoffry[130] Pelerym [*f. 69*] towardes the north and the common lane towardes the south, and abutteth on Middlegate towardes the east and on the haven of Yermouth towardes the west.

Of the heires and assignes sometyme of John of Fishelee, fyve shillinges */5s. rent/* of that place of ground with the buildinges and appurtenaunces which lyeth between the land which once was of the said John of Fishelee towardes the south and the common lane towardes the north, and abutteth on the land of John Gerberge towardes the west and on the Deane towardes the east.

Of John Smyth and his heires and assignes aleven shillinges and six pence */11s. 6d. rent/* of that place of ground with the buildinges and appurtenaunces which lyeth between the land of Geoffrey of Somerton, smyth, towardes the north and the comon lane towardes the south, and abutteth on the land of Thomas Bellard towardes the west and on the Deane towardes the east.

Of Margarett of Scrouteby and her heires and assignes twenty three shillinges */23s. rent/* of that place of ground with the buildinges and appurtenaunces which lyeth between the common lanes on the south and north, and abutteth on the land of William of Antingham towardes the west and on the Deane towardes the east.

Of Adam of Stratton and his heires and assignes thirty eight shillinges and fower pence */38s. 4d. rent/* of that place of ground with the buildinges [*f. 69*ᵛ*] and appurtenaunces which lyeth betweene the land of Clement of Trunch and Robert le Corder towardes the south and the comon lane towardes the north, and abutteth on the land of Thomas Ayssheman towardes the west and on the Deane towardes the east.

Of Henry of Stoke, his heires and assignes three shillinges six pence */3s. 6d. rent/* of that place of ground with the buildinges and appurtenaunces

---

[129] All three north-south streets in Great Yarmouth were referred to as Middlegate.
[130] *Godfrey*: original text, f. 24.

which lyeth betweene the land which once was of Nicholas Rake towardes the north and the common lane towardes the south, and abutteth on the land of John Austyn towardes the east and on the land of Geoffry Silk towardes the west.

Of Raphe le Tanner and his heires and assignes eight shillinges /*8s. rent*/ of that place[131] of ground with the buildinges and appurtenaunces which lyeth betweene the land of Agnes Gobot towardes the south and the common lane towardes the north, and abutteth on the land of Henry Rose towardes the west and on the kinges high way towardes the east.

Of Henry Basset and his heires and assignes twelve pence /*12d. rent*/ of that place of ground with the buildinges and appurtenaunces which lyeth between the land of William Stannard towardes the south and the land of the said Henry towardes [*f. 70*] the north, and abutteth on the land of Henry, the sonne of the said William, clerke, towardes the west and on Middlegate towardes the east.

Of Geoffry of Knapeton and his heires and assignes sixteen pence /*1s. 4d. rent*/ of all that rindge of ground with the buildinges and appurtenaunces which lyeth betweene the land which once was of William of Moneslee the yonger towardes the north and the Deane towardes the south, and abutteth on the Deane towardes the east and on the Kinges [*high*] way towardes the west.

Of Elvered Potekyn and his heires and assignes two shillinges /*2s. rent*/ of that place of ground with the buildinges and appurtenaunces which lyeth betweene the land of the foresaid Elvered towardes the north and the common lane towardes the south, and abutteth on the land of the said Elvered towardes the east and (*towards the*) west.

And whereas the said rent was[132] hitherto by us with holden and to the said hospitall not paid, although the same elswhere for the soules of them accordinge to our will and pleasures wee have caused to be done, wee now beinge mynded that th'aforesaid last will of the said testament in all thinge heretofor bee observed, aswell by the consent and assent of the whole cominaltye of the towne of Yermouth abovesaid [*f. 70ᵛ*] as allso the aucthoritye and comandment of the reverend father, the Lord Robert of Winchester,[133] by the grace of God Archebisshopp of Canterbury,

---

[131] Manship here repeats 'of that place'.

[132] *rents were*: original text, f. 25.

[133] *Wynchelsea* (Robert of Winchelsea, archbishop of Canterbury, 1294-1313): original text, f. 25.

prymate of all England, and of the dioces of Norwich by right of metro-
politanship then visiting, in his visitacon findinge us in the tyme of the
withholdinge the said rentes, for us, our heyres and executours (*by force and
virtue of the aforesaid testament, by tenor of the present letter do grant, from now
onwards surrender and in executorship*) doe deliver into the handes of the
balyves, which at the tyme of the makinge of this present instrument bee in
(*the town of*) Yermouth aforesaid and hereafter shalbe, and allso to the
burgesses and cominaltye of the said towne, which now are or hereafter
shalbe, all and singuler the rentes aforesaid of the foresaid tenements and
(*of*) every of them whosoever shall inhabite therein, peaceably and without
any lett to receive, with full power to distreine for the same whensoever
and as often they shall need, to the sustentacon aforesaid in the said hospitall, to be done accordinge to the will of the said deceased (*and declaration by
the same testator*) unto us in the same his testament made. **Butt** if[134] it shall
happen that the said preistes to be found negligent in the celebratinge
aforesaid it shalbe lawfull to the master of the said hospitall then to remove
(*them*) and appoynt others conformable in theire places. **And** the said
preistes ones in the yeere, that is to say the Monday next after the sinode
[*f. 71*] of St Michaell,[135] to appeare before the said balyves and (*said*)
cominaltye so that the said balyves and (*said*) cominaltye may have knowledge of the persons of the said preistes. **In more** testimony whereof unto
this oure present instrument between the said burgesses and us in the
manner of a publique writinge indented[136] the seale of the cominaltye
aforesaid and our seale interchangeably are putt, whereof one parte
remayneth with the cominaltye and the other parte with us is free to
remayne (*in perpetuity*). Dated at Greate Yermouth aforesaid the Satterday
next after the (*feast of the*) translacon of St Cuthbert the bisshopp and
confessour[137] in the yeere of grace one thowsand three hundred and
fowre, and in the yeere of the reigne of Edward, the sonne of Kinge
Henry, the two and thirty.

And wee the Officiall of the lord (*archdeacon of*) Norwich, the eight of the
Ides of October in the yeere (*of Our Lord*) one thowsand three hundred * &
4*, sittinge in the parish church of Filby in the full courte for causes
iudiceall, at the instance of the said partyes, for that the seales of the said
William and John to many are unknowne, for more certayntie of the
premisses the seale of our office to these presentes have affixed.

---

[134] Manship here repeats 'if'.
[135] That is Michaelmas, on 29 September.
[136] *in the manner of a chirograph (cyrographi)*: original text, f. 25ᵛ.
[137] 4 September.

[9. Indenture between three of the executors of William Stalham of Yarmouth, on the one part, and the master (also an executor), brothers and sisters of the hospital of St Mary the Virgin, on the other, for the support of an almshouse, comprising a row of seven cottages for seven poor people, 10 August 1392.
ff. 26–26ᵛ in the original Latin text]

[f. 71ᵛ] **This Indenture** witnesseth that thus it is agreed betweene Joffry of Somerton, Robert Howlin and John Seford, executours of the testament of William Stalham of Greate Yermouth, on th'one partye, and William Ive, executour of the testament of the said William and gardian of the hospitall of the Blessed Virgyn Mary in the said towne of Yermouth, the brothers and siusters of the said hospital, on th'other partye, that is to say, in consideracon of the good and lardge bounty which the said William of Stalham in his[138] life tyme to the foresaid hospitall hath doone and allso the said executours of the testament of the said William after his decease have doone to the foresaid hospitall, the said gardian, brothers and siusters of the (afore)said hospitall with one assent have graunted to and with the (afore)said executours that they shall susteyne and suppourte seaven cottages, which sometyme were John of Stalham of Yermouth aforesaid and be now called Goddesmenhouse, and lyeth in Yermouth aforesaid betweene the comon lane on the north and the land of Peter Baxter and the land sometyme Thomas Cobbald on the south, and abutteth uppon the land sometyme of (the said) John of Stalham towardes the east and the land sometyme of the said Thomas Cobbald towardes the west, unto the sustentacon and releife of seaven poore and indigent persons, which for evermore day and night shall pray for the *[f. 72]* soules of John of Stalham, William his brother and for such as they bee bound <for> to pray for.

And whensoever it shall happen that any of the said poore people shall decease this life that by and by within tenn dayes another shalbe received by the said custos or gardian of the said hospitall.

Moreover the said executours doe agree for themselves for ever that the said gardian or custos, brethren and suisters of the said hospitall shall receive yeerely of every person dwellinge in the said cottages fower pence at fower termes of the yeere to be paid: that is at the feast of St Michaell th'archaungell[139] of every person a penny, at the feast of the Circumsicion of Our Lord[140] one penny, at the feast of th'Anunciacon of the Blessed Mary[141] one penny, at the feast of the Nativity of St John Baptist[142] one penny, to the repayringe of the said cottages. And that the said money so

---

[138] Manship here repeats 'his'.   [139] 29 September.   [140] 1 January.
[141] 25 March.   [142] 24 June.

received shall ever more be put into one box by the oversight of the said gardian and one of the brethren of the said hospitall. And that one of them shall keepe with him the key and the other the box untill the said cottages[143] shall want reparacons and mendinge. **And** to the releife and mayntenance of the brethren an(*d*) siusters of the hospitall aforesaid the foresaid executours graunt of the goodes of the said William into mortmayne of the said hospitall one hundred shillinges. In witnesse whereof unto one parte of this indenture remayninge with the said executours the seale of the said hospitall to these presentes is [*f. 72ᵛ*] hanged, and to th'other parte of the said indenture remayninge with the said custos, brethren and siusters of the said hospitall the seales of the said executours to these presentes are hanged. Dated at Greate Yermouth the tenth day of the moneth of August in the yeere of the reigne of Kinge Richard the Second after the Conquest the sixteenth.

Henricus Mansipus Notatorius Publicus

[*10. Untitled and supplementary list of rents added in a variety of fifteenth-century hands and not translated by Manship.*]

[*f. 27*] Of one tenement lying between the common lane on the north and the land of William Bettys on the south, and abbuts on the land of John Medylton towards the west and on the Dene towards the east; sometime of Thomas Rant; afterwards of John Medylton, now Edward Hungate & renders by year 12*d.*

Of one tenement with its appurtenances, which once was of Laurence Drayton, lying in Yarmouth aforesaid between two common lanes on the south and north, and abbuts on the Dene towards the east and on the land late of Roger Drayton [*to the west*], then of [*blank*] as appears by charter; afterwards of John Pynne, lately John Shaue, then William Shaue; renders by year 2*s.*

Of one tenement with appurtenances lying in Yarmouth aforesaid between the common lane on the north and the land late of Geoffrey Drayton, then of John Lande, on the south, and abbuts on the land sometime of Simon Talyard, then of [*blank*] towards the east and upon the haven of Yarmouth towards the west; renders by year 12*d.* as Peter Selby lately held by charter, then held John Fox.

---

[143] *houses (domus)*: original text, f. 26.

Of one tenement with appurtenances lying in Yarmouth aforesaid between the common lane on the north and the land of Robert Osteler, lately of William Parant, on the south, and abbuts on the land lately of John Jamis, then of William Bishoppe, towards the west and upon Middlegate towards the east. Thomas Martyne lately held by charter; renders by year 2s. 6d.; after that Robert Pynne, then Robert Tasburgh.

[f. 27ᵛ] Of a tenement with appurtenances lying in Yarmouth aforesaid between the common lane on the north and the land sometime of Rose Thyrkill, then of William Bisshope, parcel of the said messuage, on the south, and abbuts on the land of Robert Tasburgh towards the east and upon the haven of Yarmouth towards the west, sometime held by John Hakon by charter; lately John Jamis held, then William Bisshoppe held; by year 2s. 6d.

[11. Ordinances for the inmates of the hospital of St Mary the Virgin, Yarmouth, written in English in a neat early fifteenth-century hand, based upon the refoundation charter of 2 May 1386.]

[f. 28ᵛ] These arn the constitucionys & ordinaunces mad & ordined to be kept in the hospitall of Seynt Mary of Gret Yermuth a mong the brederyn & systeryn of the same place.

Fyrst constitucion & ordinauns is that ther be a gouernour the qwech is clepyd hir custos & viij broderyn & [viij][144] systeryn, of the qwech brederyn & systeryn the forsayd custos xal haue rewle & gouernauns wyth in the sayd hospitall. **The** qwhiche custos xal be chosyn be the balyes & odyr burgeyses of the sayd town of Gret Yermuth not to be custos there perpetuell but quan nede is to remeue hym & nede is to chese a newe for more profyte of the hows & at the wille of the balyes that be balyes for that tyme.

Also is ordeyned that quat so euyr persone be it man or be it woman that xal be schosyn to be ther brodyr or sustyr that he or she be chosyn be the custos & be the balyes & odyr burgeyses of the same town. **The** qwyche brodyr or systyr so lawfully amyttyd xal a byde in the sayd place on to hyre lyues ende, lasse than hyr trespas or hyr offens be the gretter.

Also it is ordeynyd that euery persone thus lawfully chosyn un to brodyr or systyr xal sweryn a for the custos on the Holy Dom to be trewe to the

---

[144] A figure has been scratched out, presumably at a time when the number of inmates was reduced.

sayd hospitall, & all here goodys & catall the qwheche that thei han, or arn lykely to han aftyr ward, and also the names of hyre detowres, eyf ony haue ther, & also the summe of the dette to shewe & tellyn with outtyn ony fraude to the sayd custos *and* euery yeer onys quan the sayd Custos wil aske hem ther after for to shewe. **And** that noon of here goodys lytell ne mekyl be put [*f. 29*] owith of the said hospitall, but if it be for hyr expences or ellys odyr cawsys honeste, but only for to by leue in [*i.e. but they must leave them to*] the sayd hospitall, trewly to be diuyerced by the handis of the custos aftyr her dethe in too euyn partes, oon part to the reparacioun of the hospitall, the odyr part [*to*] the brederyn & systren by equal porcyoun.

Also it is ordeyned that euery brodyr & syster with in vj dayes aftyr that he or sche be amyttyd to be brodyr or syster xal swere obeyshauns to the custos in thingis that be leffull & leffull commaundementes. **Also** that nodyr syster ne brodyr were noon ouyr clothe but if it be of russet or ellys blekkyd. Also the sisteryn xal not weryn no veylys of silke vp on hir heedys.

Also it is ordeyned that the custos xal hyryn a *[in a later hand] secular* prest, the qwhich prest xal say all dyuyne seruyse, that is to say mateynes, prime & owrys, euesong & Messe in the hospitall, and for to praye for the balyes & burgeyses & all the comounte of the sayd town, for the custos & all the brederyn & systeryn & all the benefactoures of of [*sic*] the sayd hospitall. Neuyr the lesse, the sayd prest xal not kast hym to say Messe on holy dayes in tyme of Messe of the day is in saying att the parysh chyrche, ne no werke day in tyme of Requiem Messe is in saying att the parysh chirche. Ne he xal not sayn his euesong in tyme that euesong is in saying att the parysh schyrche, so that the paryshones be the more withdrawyn fro hir parish chyrche, the qweche God forbade. And that all the seruyse that is sayd in this hospitall xal [*f. 29ᵛ*] be sayd with outth note. **Also** that non odyr prest syng ther with outth lycens of the priour, lasse than the prest that is hyred be seek or ellys outth of town. And that ther be sayd but oo[n] Masse on the day with outt lycens of the priour as it is forsayd.

Also it is ordeyned that ther xuld be a lytel belle with the qwheche it xal be rungen onys to mateynes, onys to Messe, onys aftyr the gospell, onys to euesong, & onys aftyr euesong att euyn quan thei xal say here prayer.

Also it is ordeyned that the custos xal kepe trewly & delyueryn vp trewly on to the priour wyth in viij dayes all maner of oblacyon that is offeryd in the sayd hospytall for quat cawse at euyr it be offeryd with outt any lessyng. Except that is gouyn to the brederyn & systren in pure elmesse to there sustentacyon, & namely quat som euyr be offred on good Fryday or ellys in the feste of the Annuncyacyoun of our Lady, ther of the priour xal not reseyue.

Also it is ordeyned that euery brodyr & systyr be present in the sayd hospitall att all seruyse & namely at Messe, and that eche of them say euery day thryes L[145] Pater Noster and as many Aue Maria, lowly & deuowtly lasse than thei be lettyd be any cawse resonable.

Also it is ordeyned that euery brodyr & syster in the [f. 30] sayd hospitall xal leuyn chaste & if it may be knowe that ony of them to odyr wyse it is ordeyned [word scratched out] that same persone xal lesyn the iiij part of the comowun elmesse that xuld comyn to hys persone that yeer. The qwheche xal be deuyded in to euyn partes, oo[n] part to be deuyded among the brederyn & the sisteryn & the odyr to reparacyoun of the place. **And** if *it* may be knowen that eydyr brodyr or syster geue a gayn the part thus receyued to hym thus conuycte & chastyzed for to be seruyd on the same wyse. Also that ther be non weddyd man nor woman receyued to be brodyr nor systyr in the sayd hospitall.

Also euery brodyr and syster may don & vsyn hyr craftys that thei han lernyd, so that thei ben honeste, to getyn with all here lyuyng as wel in towun as in the hospitall, so it be no slaundyr nodyr to the personys ne hurt to the hospytall, so that thei be present at all dyuyne seruyse sayd in the hospitall. **And** also thei mown dyne & suppyn & etyn & drynkyn with hyr good frendys in towun, but thei xul not ben outth on nytes, ne be outth of the hospitall aftyr couyr fyer belle [curfew] rongen at the parysh chyrche. **Also** that the sayd brederyn & systeryn with lycens of the custos may goon on pylgrimage & to vysyten hyr frendys as well in the cuntre as in the same towun.

Also it is ordeyned that no persone xal be receyued to be brodyr or syster in the sayd hospitall but he or sche be xxx wynter [f. 30v] of age, lasse than it be for a cawse resonable. **Also** that thei leuyn to gedyr in pes & reste with outtyn chydyng or flytyng & that thei haunten not of custom comoun tauernes, and noon of them by wreye odyr councel ne make no playnt for no trespas but to hyre custos, but if it be swech a trespas or offens the qwyche may not lawfully ne dewly be amendyd by the sayd custos.

Also it is ordeyned that the custos may compellyn the brederyn & systeryn tho that mow laboryn for to deluyn & wedyn in the gardeyn & to do odyr lyth werkys, so that he rewardyn hem att his owyn wyll for there labour.

---

[145] One hundred and fifty.

Also it is ordeyned that the custos xal chesyn on of the brederyn & a nodyr of the systeryn that be of good name & of good fame & make them for to sweryn that thei tak heed of hyre odyr brederyn & systeryn yf thei do any trespas or ony offens, and that *thei* vndyrnemyn hem ther of & if thei wil not be rewlyd aftyr them that thei *to* telle the persones names and also the trespas on to the custos that he may chasteyse that persone as he seeth it is worthy. So that it be swyche a defaute that the sayd custos may corretten it with outten any preiudize of odyr iurisdictyoun. **Also** it is ordeyned that the custos xule chesyn oon of the brederyn, the qwhech xuld haue charge of the keyes of the dorys of the cloyster wyth in the qwheche the brederyn and the systeryn slepyn, that thei ben speryd & shett that noon of [*f. 31*] the broderyn ne systeryn goo owtth of the sayd hospitall aftyr couer ffyer belle be rongen at the parysh cherche, ne no persone to be latyn in to hem, except the parisch preste quan he comyth to geuyn hem hire sacramentis in tyme of neede.

Also it is ordeyned that if any syster or brodyr of the sayd hospitall be rebelle a geyns these ordinauns & constitucyones or any [*word scratched out*] artykle of them that thei be chastyzed by the custos by wyth drawyng of here elmesse that xuld come to hem of rygth yf thei wer wel gouernyd. **And** if thei wyl not be pesyd & styllyd with this chastyzement all holy to be put outth of the sayd hospitall, and neuyr to be reseyued a geyn with outth a specyall assent of all the comounte of the sayd town of Yermuthe.

Also it is ordeyned that the preste, the qwheche is hyred by the custos to serue & say diuine seruyse in the sayd hospitall, xal be brouth be the custos on to the priour with in iij dayes that he be comyn for to serue in the sayd hospitall & he xal swere a forn the priour & the balyes, yf thay wyl be there present, that he xal kepe the artykles a forn seyd that longyn on to his part and se that the parysh chyrche be not hurt ne harmyd for his defaute for sayeng of his seruyse as it is forsayd.

(*31v*) **Also** it is ordeynyd that euery custos that is amyttyd & chosyn for to haue the gouernauns of the hospitall & of the brederyn & systeryn dwellyng in the same hospitall, a forn any admynystracyon that he xal make in the sayd place, xal make a othe a forn the pryour & the balyes that trewly & dewly he xal obserue & kepe all the constituciones & ordynauns wretyn here by forn on to his power, un to the qwhech god send hym grace. Amen.

[*Inside the back cover*] This Book was delivered out of the town Clerks office in Great Yarmouth in Norfolk the 13th of February 1709 to Mr Henry Borrett by me Thomas Royall.

Index

Places are in Norfolk unless otherwise specified.

Carleton, Thomas rector of 153
Carman, John 37
Carre, Robert 144–6
Carrowe, John 124–5
Carter, Geoffrey 147–8, 153; John 144, 146; Richard 153; Thomas 64
Castelyn, Nicholas 147; Robert 153
Castile, Spain, merchants 107
Castre, John 148; William 142
Cates see Kates
Catlyn, Margaret 144; Robert 144
Catour, Nicholas 219
Catt, Simon, baxter, 197
Catton 13, 21, 28, 30, 38, 45, 58; accounts of, 29–31, 41, 64–5, 96; gild of St John, 58; manors receiving sheep from, 34, 36, 38–40, 70; manors sending sheep to, 34–5, 37; prior's sheep at, 41, 69–70; shepherds of, 68–9; total sheep at, 68–9
Catton, Robert 46, 57, 59, 74, 77, 82–3, 85, 87–8
Caus (Cawes), Robert 26; Thomas 147–9
Cave, Nicholas, barber, 218
Cawston 29; accounts of, 36, 38, 96; manors receiving sheep from, 38; manors sending sheep to, 32, 36; shepherds of, 69; total sheep at, 69
Chamber, John 219
Cha(u)mberl(e)yn, Margaret 209; Robert 55, 75–6; William 149
Chandeler, Robert 213
Chapman, John 138, 147, 217; Richard 32; Robert 154; Thomas 210
Chaunce, Thomas 151–3
Cheny, William 152
Childe, Simon 126; Stephen 124
Church (Chirch), John at, of Ormesby, 204, 219; Thomas at, smith, 200, 209
Claunfeld, Robert 213
Clavering hundred, 1489 income tax 109
Claxton, Adam of 203; Andrew 213; Hamo 147–8
Clement, John 121, 123, 142
Clere, Ed. 150–1; Robert 28, 58
Cleres, William 76–8
Clerk(e), Gregory 136–8, 151–4; Joan 137–8; John 33, 42, 55–7, 59, 79, 142, 216; John, butcher, 205, 219; Robert, wright, 208, 219; Roger 122
Clifforth (Clyfford), Robert 138, 152; Thomas 150

Clough, William 142
Cobbald (Cobald, Coball, Cobbals), Henry 133, 150; John 214; Robert 197, 199, 214; Thomas 197, 199, 214, 225
Cob(be), John 39–40, 122
Cod(de)lyng, John 122, 217
Cok (Cocke, Coke), Henry 123; John 134, 143, 145; Robert 122–3, 125, 139–40, 142–4; Thomas 125, 147–8; William 137
Cokerem, John 208
Coket, Henry 126–7, 141, 143; William 125
Cokks, John 142
Cole, John 127
Collen, William 212
Colles, Edward 31, 40; Matilda 25; Robert 25, 31; Walter 25, 32
Colman, Ed. 126; Henry 201, 209; John 135–6
Colough, Catherine 128
Cook(e), ―― 154; Edmund 154; Henry 203, 216; Hervey 203; John, reeder, 215; Nicholas 221; Robert 28, 142; Thomas 24, 28
Coppyng, John 137; Margaret 153; Robert 218
Corbowe, John 85
Corder, Robert le 222
Corne, William 150
Corpusty, John 155; Nicholas 151, 154; Richard 138, 147, 152, 154–5
Cory, Nicholas 146–8
Cosyn, William 148
Cotes, Walter 210
Cotty, Thomas 211
Cottyng, Geoffrey 141
Couper (Cowper), Edmund 148, 208–9; Isaac 174–5, 181–2; Isabel 143; John 122–3, 147; John, goldsmith, 218; Richard 121; Robert 146; Thomas 142, 147, 150
Couperwrythe, Andrew 127
Courle (Curle), Robert 143, 147, 150–1, 154
Cowlich, Nicholas 147–9
Crabbe, Robert 23; Thomas 23
Crane, Henry, chandler, 205, 217–18; John 210; William de la 222
Craske, Robert 209
Cringleford 67
Crisp, Richard 36–9, 42–3, 51–2, 56
Cristemesse, William 142
Crome, Alice 153; Geoffrey 150
Cromer(e), John 210; Peter 215
Crosse, Robert 130; Robert at 197; William 142

Yngham *see* Ingham
Yngram (Ingram), John 213, 217–18; Walter
    217; William 216
Yonge, John 211
Yoor, Simon 212

Yorkshire rebellion 108
You (Vou), John 204
Yuy (Ivy), Richard, baxter, 202, 213
Yvell (Yvess), John 212